OLUSEGUN OBASANJO

NIGERIA'S MOST SUCCESSFUL RULER

OLUSEGUN OBASANJO
NIGERIA'S MOST SUCCESSFUL RULER

by

ADEBAYO ADEOLU

Safari Books Ltd
Ibadan

Published by
Safari Books Ltd
Ile Ori Detu
1, Shell Close
Onireke
Ibadan.
Email: info@safaribooks.com.ng
Website: http://safaribooks.com.ng

© 2017, Adebayo Adeolu

First Published 2017

All rights reserved. This book is copyright and so no part of it may be reproduced, stored in a retrieval system, or transmitted, in any form or by any means, electrical, mechanical, electrostatic, magnetic tape, photocopying, recording or otherwise, without the prior written permission of the author.

ISBN: 978-978-54785-2-5

Dedication

Bruce Mayrock: He was a Columbia University student, twenty years of age from old Westbury, New York. He died for Biafrans who he never knew but the pictures of Biafra genocide he had seen drove him to sacrifice his life to attract humanitarian attention to Biafra. He actually poured petrol all over his body and set himself on fire at the United Nation's building headquarters to protest against the genocide.

Table of Contents

Dedication .... *v*
Preface .... *ix*
Acknowledgments .... *xi*

Chapter 1:	Early Beginnings....................................	1
Chapter 2:	The BBHS Years.....................................	7
Chapter 3:	Nigerian Army.......................................	15
Chapter 4:	Marriage In London..............................	29
Chapter 5:	Coups In Nigeria...................................	35
Chapter 6:	Genocide on the Igbos and the Aburi Report...	51
Chapter 7:	Civil War Years......................................	61
Chapter 8:	Humanitarian And International Organisations...	75
Chapter 9:	Taking Command..................................	89
Chapter 10:	Military Rule 1970-1975........................	101
Chapter 11:	Stella Obasanjo......................................	113
Chapter 12:	Military Rule 1975-1979: Obasanjo Emerges Emperor.................	123
Chapter 13:	Obasanjo Becomes Head of State 1976-1979...	135

Chapter 14:	Retirement from the Army..................	145
Chapter 15:	Obasanjo and the Press.........................	165
Chapter 16:	The June 12 Saga: Abiola offered Premier	169
Chapter 17:	Obasanjo Goes to Prison.....................	187
Chapter 18:	Obasanjo Anointed by the Kingmakers...	201
Chapter 19:	Obasanjo as Civilian President (1999-2007)..	209
Chapter 20:	Obasanjo's Hot Romance with America...	243
Chapter 21:	Iyabo Obasanjo and Her Letter.........	255
Chapter 22:	Nigerians Most Successful Ruler......	273
	Index	**281**

Preface

The name Olusegun Obasanjo is not strange to anybody around the world. In Nigeria, Obasanjo is a household name, a civil war hero, an administrator, a successful farmer, the first military head of State to have organized an election and handed over successfully to a civilian government, a nation-builder who initiated most of Nigeria's national heritage and a builder of men who introduced many Nigerian technocrats to governance and their indelible marks in governance are still very visible, the only Nigerian to have been nominated as United Nation's Secretary General, the first former head of State to be imprisoned, though on a wrong accusation, and the first person to have ruled Nigeria twice (between 1976-1979 and 1999-2007). Obasanjo is known to be a detribalised and selfless Nigerian.

Apart from many books that have been written about this great Nigerian, he himself had published so many controversial books on his adventure on earth. The controversial nature of Obasanjo in Nigeria and beyond and his giant strides in governance and humanity in general informed my desire to write about him. There may be no major thing that is new about Obasanjo, but this book is to acknowledge him as the most successful Nigerian ruler.

At this time that the new generation of Nigerians are losing faith in the peaceful co-existence of the different tribes of Nigeria due to the effects of bad leadership, it is important to use the life and story of a man who stand out to defend a united Nigeria, as a case study, that if we can follow his philosophy about nation-building, Nigeria can be great again.

I believe this book will achieve the patriotic objectives that made me to put together the history of this great Nigerian and I hereby recommend it to all Africans who have lost faith in good leadership in Africa that even here in Nigeria, a good thing can still come out of our Jerusalem.

Acknowledgements

I like to acknowledge all the people who have written books on Chief Olusegun Obasanjo which were indeed very helpful when writing this book. Mrs. Oluremi Obasanjo's *Bitter Sweet* and Dr. R. B. Alade's *Broken Bridge*, written on the Nigerian civil war were very helpful. I got a balanced understanding of the crisis and humanitarian activities of foreign countries and organisations in Dr. Alade's book. What impressed me about Dr. R. B. Alade was that I had gone to him asking to rent one of his houses for a car dealership. Despite the fact that the house had been given to somebody else he was so pleasant and he gave his usual words of encouragement. He invited me over as he was curious to meet me, it was then he autographed his books to me and it became a major reference for this book.

I thank my brother, Adekunle Adeolu, who encouraged me to write the book. He persisted in motivating me even when I was not well disposed to writing. I appreciate Chief Olusegun Osoba who had engineered my meeting Olusegun Obasanjo. When I met Aremo, he asked if I had earlier met Olusegun Obasanjo. I said no and he gave a look that said: "You are Lost and have not started! I also remember when I went to see Donald Duke to present my book on Bakassi, he told me Obasanjo is his best friend so I got more encouragement to know this unique personality which led to the writing of this book.

I cannot forget the professional inputs of staff members of Safari books Limited, Ibadan. George Berkhout and Olalekan Odetola contributed a lot to the successful publication of this book. Chief Joop Berkhout, chairman of Safari Books gave good approval rating for the book.

Mr. Vitalis Ortese who was the first person to read the manuscript gave his approval rating also. He is a very calm personality to who God has bestowed wisdom and humility. I sincerely acknowledge your efforts.

SPECIAL THANKS FOR THE CARTOONS

- Mr. Adeniyi Odeleye
- Mr. Segun Awosiyan
- Mr. Kenny Adamson
- Mr. Boye Gbenro
- Mr. Kola Joseph
- Mr. Aliu Eroje

CHAPTER ONE

Early Beginnings

Obasanjo Bankole, the father of Olusegun Obasanjo, was among the early settlers who founded the rural village of Igbogun Olaogun in the early 1920s. It was a remote village surrounded by thick rain forest and was a farm settlement of Abeokuta. He was a peasant farmer who planted cassava, yam, rice, maize, cocoyam and cocoa and he also climbed palm trees to harvest kernels for red oil and to tap wine. He also set traps to catch fowls, grass cutters, bush rats etc. Obasanjo Bankole was hard-working but was considered poor by the standard of living they had at the time as he did not belong to the elite group who had western education.

It was at Igbogun that he met his wife, Bernice Ashabi, where they got married. Ashabi was a petty trader who sold kola nuts, tobacco leaves, cigarettes, pain killers, soap and beverages. Obasanjo Bankole and Bernice Ashabi had gone through difficult times together. They had six children but only two survived. The first was Mathew Fajinmi Aremu Olusegun Obasanjo and the second was Adunni Oluwola, Olusegun's only sister and sibling. They both were brought up in the traditional Yoruba way wherein discipline, hard work, and the fear of God were the norm.[1]

Mathew Fajinmi Aremu Olusegun Obasanjo was born on March 5, 1937 in the obscure Yoruba village of Igbogun Olaogun near Ota and north of Ifo town in Ogun State southwestern Nigeria which is half way between Lagos and Abeokuta.[2] This rural area was often referred to by Europeans and Americans as the Bush country.

Olusegun Obasanjo manifested early in his life the traits and character of a serious-minded person with an independent strong-willed personality who knew what he wanted. For example, as a young man whenever he wanted to do anything he felt was right for him, if his parents disagreed with him, he rejected his food and went on hunger strike. He was much focused. However, as the son of a peasant farmer he became a farm hand as soon as he was old enough. It was the trend at the time that when children (especially boys) turned five or six years old they would start accompanying their parents to the farm. They were not doing any hard work as to warrant calling it what is deemed child abuse today, but maybe helping in little ways to carry a hoe or cutlass and observe how things were done. The kids carried the hoe or cutlass and they let it rest on their shoulder as they walk to the farm, in some cases with their mothers who sometimes also farm. It is still the same in many rural communities today.

Obasanjo's father, despite not having western education, was endowed with wisdom and natural

---
[1] Onukaba A. Ojo, *In the Eyes of Time: A Biography of Olusegun Obasanjo*, African Legacy Press, C1997, Pg41
[2] Comrade Lekan Aderibigbe, *Obasanjo for Nigeria*

Early Beginnings

instinct which he was able to instill in his children. As Bankole worked on the farm, so did Olusegun receive lectures and was taught the ways of the world from his father's perspective. Information from the older generation was gradually passed on to the young boy through general conversation while helping on the farm. It was from time spent on the farm Olusegun learnt that only hard work can bring success and that nobody came to the world with money.

He was also taught that some families who were prominent and had money could lose it in the next generation and their children who had enjoyed the privilege of having rich parents would have to work extra hard to keep that money flowing in their family. His father also often told him that anything a man achieved on earth was through the will of God and hard work.

It was during one of these lectures and conversations one fateful day when Olusegun was about nine years old, while he was with his father making ridges and clearing the farmland for planting, that as if he was pushed by the unseen hands of destiny his father suddenly asked: "This school thing can't you go?" And not knowing what it really meant, he answered by saying that he could go if it was his father's wish for him to attend. This was the event that finally changed his life and put him right on the path to his destiny.[3]

There were no schools in Igbogun and anybody who wanted to be educated had to go to Abeokuta or Lagos. Anything that was related to the western world was alien to Igbogun at the time. The only available vocation at the time within the town was farming.

---
3   Patrick Avwenagbiku, *Olusegun Obasanjo and His Foot prints*, Metro Publishers, 2000, Pg3

Activities like carpentry, welding, automobile repairs, masonry etc., were jobs introduced by the Europeans from Britain and these were available only in the cities.

It was at Abule Lani, a neighbouring farm settlement that Olusegun began his education. He started reading, writing and learning arithmetic. In those days in Nigeria, they were taught in both English and the mother tongue and Yoruba was the mother tongue of the southwest of Nigeria. The rote system was the teaching style for arithmetic and mathematics at the time. This was a part time private study.

In 1948 at the age of eleven, he started school at the Saint David Ebenezer School founded by the Anglican Church through the missionaries who brought Christianity to Nigeria. The fees at the time were six shillings in total. He was registered as Mathew Olusegun Obasanjo, taking his father's first name as his surname instead of his grandfather's name, Bankole.

The pre-school proved very helpful at Saint David. He began his formal education in Class One B instead of Class One C which was for beginners. He was promoted to Class One A, and that gave him a double promotion to Standard One. He was at the top of his class all the time up to Standard Four where he did his final examination in 1950.

In December 1950 Olusegun Obasanjo left Igbogun and by January 1951 he got admitted into Standard Five at Baptist Day School in the Owu quarters of Abeokuta in present day Ogun State. The school was mid-sized and was run by the American Baptist Mission. It was a liberal school that placed value on personal freedom, individual initiative and persuasion as opposed to the use of force with Christian morals and values. Olusegun had as his classmates, Abolade Adewusi, Solomon Adewusi, Kayode Ogunremi, Wale Salako, Folaji Ijaola, Lati Dosunmu and Afolabi Sorungbe.

But shortly before the high school examination, his father's farming business crumbled, it was then his father, Obasanjo Bankole, left for Onigbedu, 25 kilometers away after a disagreement with his wife. She was left to take care of her two children. Obasanjo Bankole took another wife by the name Aduke, who had three children but none survived.[4] However, despite the separation of their parents Olusegun and his sister, Adunni Oluwola, survived the difficulty of a single parent (their mother) training.

This was a turning point in the life of Olusegun Obasanjo. He had sat down to think deeply how he would survive and from then on he had to work and do odd jobs to take care of himself and his sister and to continue his education. He sold firewood, sand and did labour jobs on other people's farms. It was a pathetic period but he was not alone, there were many others. Among them were the likes of Moshood Kashimawo Olawale Abiola, an intelligent boy who also fetched firewood and sang and danced for survival during Muslim festivals. Abiola later became a business and political figure in Nigeria. Olusegun did not allow his financial situation to affect his progress in school.

In December 1951, he passed the entrance examination into Baptist Boys High School (BBHS). He also passed the interview and was admitted into Form One A. The future from this moment began and continued to look brighter despite him facing financial difficulties. His upbringing had hardened him. Even though he was

---
4   Olusegun Obasanjo, *My Watch*, Vol. 1 Kachifo Limited, 2015, Pg 23

just fourteen years old, he kept Saint David's motto "Help Your Self" in his mind all the time. The difficulty he was going through had allowed him to mature very fast, exhibiting a sound grasp of life's complexities and an admirable knowledge of the Owu society and its place in Abeokuta and the Yoruba history. The Owu cultural traits were already manifesting in Olusegun through his upbringing and that was how he survived.

CHAPTER TWO

The BBHS Years

Baptist Boys High School (BBHS), Abeokuta was founded on January 23, 1923 by Reverend Pinnock, an American Baptist Missionary in Abeokuta. The school was establish to take care of the educational needs of Nigerian youths of above average and average abilities and also catered for those with little means and those with no means at all.[5]

The school had acquired an enviable status of being a centre of academic excellence within the almost three decades of its existence in western Nigeria. It was referred to as the 'Penny School' by a prominent principal of the Abeokuta Grammar School because the fees were very low as compared with sister schools within the area.

Despite the school fees being the lowest in the town, indigent students like Olusegun Obasanjo, Moshood Abiola and a few others found it difficult to afford the school fees. It was Revered Patterson who as principal of the school between 1925 and 1944 introduced the American system, in which poor students worked their

---
5   Adinoyi Ojo Olukaba, *In the Eyes of TIme: A Biography of Olusegun Obasanjo,* African Legacy Press, 1997, Pg60

way through school. That is, jobs would be given to students for a small fee. This was part time jobs done within the school premises. The students cleaned the gutters, toilets, cut grasses, swept the premises, washed the dishes or waited on the principal and also worked in the library.

Olusegun did all these and finally secured being a library assistant where he monitored books borrowed and returned to the library by students. It was time consuming but he preferred it as it was more dignified than manual labour. The little income he got from these jobs combined with what his mother Ashabi gave him, paid his way through high school.

The school being a missionary school had the fundamentals of Christianity imparted into the students. There were strong emphasis on religious values, integrity, honesty, moral instructions and proper grooming to be responsible citizens in the society.

Olusegun felt comfortable with the way the school was run and with its religious activities because he was born into a Baptist family and he had attended church regularly in childhood. It was at church he had first met Oluremi Akinlawon and Onaolapo Soleye. He was a member of the Royal Ambassadors, a Baptish Church organisation for youths similar to Boys Brigade. He joined many school societies and took active part in their activities. He joined the literary and debating society and the Boys Scouts movement. Olusegun did not have much time to socialise and had to put in a lot of effort to make it through school. Obasanjo was brilliant and that was what won him respect and friendship.

In his report card Rev. Griffin had made good remarks that if he kept up his performance it would lead to a promising future. Obasanjo had distinguished himself by winning many of the school prizes including books, the school uniform and tuition grants. The missionaries gave out the uniform as prizes where they knew students could not afford them.

The period Olusegun Obasanjo attended Baptist Boys High School had been the period nationalism among the African States reached its peak. Colonised countries and peoples agitated for participation in running the affairs of their country and this trickled down to all sectors managed by the Europeans including missionary schools. During the First World War, Africans had discovered that White British and Black African soldiers were the same as the bullets that killed the white man also was the same bullet that killed the black African soldiers, so it was an eye opener that the black man and the white man were not different except only in colour.

It was a period the schools, including Baptist Boys High School, Abeokuta were also being *Nigerianised* towards self-government. This was in expectation of when the British would hand over power to the Africans fully. It was also the period Olusegun Obasanjo dropped his English name Matthew.[6]

Reverend Bennie Theodore Griffin, an American from Texas had started the process of involving Nigerians in the day to day activities of the management of the school. By 1953 when Emmanuel Olatunbosun Akisanya became principal of the school, Mr. Griffin became the business manager and he operated from behind the scenes in preparation for Nigerians taking full control at a future date.

---

6   Dapo Olaosebika, *Olusegun Obasanjo: Father of New Nigeria,* Performers Publishers, 2002, pp 3-5

The period Olusegun Obasanjo spent at the Baptist Boys' High School was a defining moment in his life. It was then he met his pretty, chubby future wife, Oluremi Akinlawon, from the time he set his eyes on her he never let go again. They had met before many times but he never said anything until the 8th of March, 1956. It was in the afternoon and he was wearing an *agbada* on khaki trousers but wore no shoes. In those days, except for those from elite and educated families, many young people did not really bother to wear their shoes all the time especially when they were within their neighbourhood. They would just walk barefooted around casually but Oluremi being a girl from an elite family thought it prim and proper to wear shoes all the time. She stated in her book, *Bitter Sweet* that Olusegun did not wear shoes, not even the 'cheap tennis' sold for 7 shilling and 6 pence.

That day Olusegun told her that he liked her and wanted them to be friends. It was simply a confession but she walked away. Maybe she was shy or she just felt, what audacity from somebody who was not wearing shoes.

However, Olusegun did not give up, he was persistent and used to send letters to her through her younger brother, Yomi. It was a hot chase and Olusegun, being an unyielding person continued until she finally agreed to his advances having realised that despite how rude she had been to him on a number of occasions, he still was not discouraged. It amazed her and she was convinced that a man who could tolerate these insults and jeers must really love her. It was Olusegun's patience that won her over.

Olusegun having found his future wife went back to full concentration on his studies. He wanted to finish his studies as fast as possible and decided to take the London General Certificate of Education (GCE) examination in the fifth form as a private candidate. At the time, students were discouraged from attempting the examination before the Sixth Form because if they passed and left the school before the Sixth Form final year examination it could affect the school's overall performance. Those who disobeyed were not given a testimonial which was so important as it served as a recommendation to any future outing, whether academic or job-seeking.

In 1955 he took the qualifying examination, the London GCE and was successful. He did the examination at Ibadan and passed all the subjects in high grades. Armed with a good London GCE certificate he left Baptist Boys High School knowing fully well the implication of him being denied a testimonial. However, Obasanjo got respectable people to speak for him and finally the principal, Mr. Akinsanya was persuaded to give him the testimonial. He was planning for the university as his next step but knew he had to work to raise the funds.

Olusegun got a job with the famous United African Company, UAC as a clerical staff but the job took all his time as it gave him no time to study. His stay in Ibadan was difficult as there was no fantastic pay from the job, the overtime benefits were not paid in time so he decided to quit.

Olusegun opted for a teaching job at the African Church Modern School at Ago Tailor area of Ibadan where he taught General Science and Religious Knowledge.[7] It was during his time as a teacher in 1957 that Olusegun sat for the entrance examination to the University of Ibadan which was the only university in

---

7   Patrick Avwenagbiku, *Olusegun Obasanjo and His Foot prints*, Metro Publishers, 2000, Pg5

the country then. Unfortunately, he could not afford the fees. At the time he did not know how scholarships were given neither did he know that he could approach the Christian missions for sponsorship. The criteria was that a person given scholarship would come back and work with them for a certain period, with this agreement, sponsorship was approved.

However, as fate would have it, Adedire who was his friend and flatmate at Ibadan bought a copy of *Daily Times* on this particular day and having nothing to do he decided to read the newspaper where he spotted the advert placed by the Nigerian Army inviting interested citizens to participate in the cadet examination.

Having no knowledge of the Army, he took the cadetship examination and passed. The armed forces, the army, police and air force were not given any pride of place in southwestern Nigeria at the time, most parents never knew or had the foresight that it was an honourable job. It was considered a profession for the never-do-wells and most parents did not even consider it an option for their children to serve in the armed forces like the Americans do. I think it was the British who did not encourage or enlighten southwestern Nigeria like they did with the north of Nigeria.

The British had enlightened the northern elites that once they controlled or had a majority in the army they will be in control of Nigeria. However, by independence the easterners were more prominent in the armed forces and held most of the senior positions and titles while the North were more in the rank and file.

Before independence and even two decades after, southwestern Nigerian parents were not willing to release a promising son into a profession they considered dangerous. However, Olusegun got shortlisted, he was interviewed and was enlisted. This had been a very wise decision at the time, he never knew that it was his destiny calling. From that moment on the sky was the limit as he fondly remembered when Chief Obafemi Awolowo had come to address and make a speech at his school where he had declared in his words that the sky was the limit.

He had taken a very big step he knew that family and friends would criticize. The next step was to break the news to Oluremi his fiancée. He visited Abeokuta and quietly broke the news to her. Oluremi was shocked, she jumped up raising her voice in shock, "what happened to your other plans? The scholarship and university plans?" As his fiancée she did not understand how the army was structured, she only remembered the soldiers at Lafenwa in Abeokuta drinking *burukutu* (a highly intoxicating gin) and making noise amongst themselves over the different young girls who liked the men in uniform.

Obasanjo however explained to her that he was not going to the rank and file but would be trained as an officer and he would be able to continue his education within the military structure. His friends, Abolade Adewusi and Moshood Abiola, his school mates at Baptist Boys High School (BBHS) who were working as clerks in Barclays Bank, Ibadan were also shocked. They did not imagine his gentle personality would survive in the army.[8]

Abolade Adewusi kept saying: "Obasanjo a soldier? But after a while everybody accepted and wished him goodluck. His mother however was the last to know

---
8   Oluremi Obasanjo, *Bitter Sweet: My Life with Obasanjo* Diamond Publications Ltd. 2008, Pg 18

because Obasanjo felt she would oppose his joining the army as her only son. When she eventually got to know, she was not keen and excited about the development. It had been one of the most important decisions he had made in life.

CHAPTER THREE

Nigerian Army

Olusegun Obasanjo became a cadet in the Nigerian Army in March 1958. He was sent to Ghana for training, which was the first country to get independence from the colonial masters and government in West Africa. The military training school which was located at Teshie, was the training institution for all cadets in the West African region.

The course was a six months intensive preparatory course described as hell by some cadets that attended the course due to its very rigorous programme where officers were trained in handling weapons, battle craft and physical drills.[9]

The officers were sent in batches from time to time and among those in Obasanjo's batch were Benjamin Adekunle, Patrick Amadi, Foluso Sotomi, Humphrey Chukwuka, Emmanuel Udeaja, Sam Adegoke, Henry Igboba and Jacob U. Esuene. They had both physical and academic training with the objective of achieving leadership qualities as well as individual capabilities. What many Nigerians did not know was that the full

---

9   Abiodun A. Adekunle (ed), *The Nigerian Biafran War Letters: A Soldier Story* (Vol. 1),

training was equivalent to going to the university especially with the overseas training that officers attend. It was a thorough training as it had to do with countries all over the world on aspects of military matters such as defence, wars and the role of the armed forces working together in harmony, that is, they learnt academic courses such as History, Geography etc. They learn where the other armed forces stand in the society, the Police, Navy, Air Force, Customs and Immigration in matters concerning national security. They were taught how to deal and relate with civilians and the control of weapons. It was a training that was comprehensive and made the officers well equipped. The training also brought about competition among the cadets but Obasanjo got on fine.

Benjamin Adekunle had been one of the cadets to fall out with Obasanjo. It was a chemistry that wasn't there – they just did not blend. Benjamin Adekunle was the third generation of soldiers from his family that served in the Nigerian army. Both his grandfather and father had served in the colonial army in Nigeria. The military was therefore not a strange place for him. He had early enough during the training distinguished himself as articulate, composed and brilliant. He was an excellent swimmer and had accused Obasanjo of clumsiness while swimming because he splashed and upset the water too much. These had created an atmosphere of competition between the two men.

The six months training ended in September 1958 and Obasanjo returned to Kaduna. It was not long before he was selected for further training at MONS Aldershot United Kingdom. It was another six months training. Those who attended this short service at Aldershot like

Obasanjo were considered already too mature both in age and scholarship. It was an intensive course in military training. Though short, it was specific and focused.

Benjamin Adekunle on the other hand got selected for the eighteen month regular commission at the royal military academy in Sandhurst, England. Any Nigerian officer who did not go there was considered handicapped as a soldier as it was the most prestigious military training institution and was seen as ranking with West Point in the United States of America. The military training was aimed at developing a cadet's character and leadership qualities, commanding and training and keeping control of those under his command.

It was during this period that tragedy struck, Obasanjo lost his mother, Ashabi, in 1958 and the following year he also lost his father, Amos Obasanjo Bankole. He had become an orphan; it was very painful as they (his parents) were not going to witness his success in life. The promising young man was only twenty-two years old at the time of this heavy loss.

While in Aldershot he enrolled privately in a polytechnic for a diploma in Engineering. By the end of the first session he attempted the exams organised by the society of engineers and passed but it was not rated as that of the Institute of Engineers.

The study period in England exposed Obasanjo to a new orientation as he had never known that racism existed and that people of colour were not accepted. In fact it was simply a matter of being black against the whites. The white Europeans were the superior beings and if you did not belong they would simply tolerate you. It was like a stigma to be black and class was emphasised and racism was pronounced amongst black and white people and if you were a mix you were considered coloured.[10]

He did not like the discrimination he experienced in Britain. However, he made up his mind to succeed, and did not bother about the colour of his skin but what he wanted to achieve on his mission and training overseas. His attitude towards racial slight was to ignore it completely. Obasanjo's six months stay was from late 1958 to early 1959 after which he returned to Nigeria.

The Nigerian Army was established as was in Britain to defend both internal and external aggression against the country. It was expected to serve the civilian government as one of the institutions of defence within the country. When he returned to Nigeria in 1959 he was posted to the 5th Battalion in Kaduna as an infantry officer. He was made a full lieutenant shortly as the army officer's corps was being *Nigerianised*. As Nigeria inched towards independence, recruitment and training was stepped up to boost the number of soldiers. This was the period Nigeria was moving towards self-government.

NIGERIA - INDEPENDENCE, CRISIS IN WESTERN REGION

Olusegun Obasanjo was on training during the period of Nigeria's Independence in 1960. Dr. Nnamdi Azikiwe, the creator of modern nationalism was the most important politician in Nigeria at the time.

Nigeria is geographically subdivided into the following: the North; the East divided into two, Igbo East and non Igbo East which is now known as the Niger Delta; the Yoruba West and non Yoruba West around Benin now Edo State popularly called Mid West. The minorities from

---
[10] John Lliffe, *Obasanjo: Nigeria and the World,* Woob bridge and Rochester, New York, (2011), pg 14

the middle belt area of the north and the Cameroons existed quietly and did not have much voice and were subsequently ignored. The Cameroons later joined French-speaking Cameroon, a costly mistake for both English-speaking Cameroon and Nigeria.

The east and west were envious rivals of each other but, as dominated by Christians, both regions often combined politically against the Muslim-dominated North. They are more *Europeanized* than the north, their watchward at the time were advance and 'emancipation.' Wealth was more concentrated in the western part of Nigeria, which had the advantage of the seaport and became the headquarters for British rule.

However, barely over thirty years after the amalgamation of the north and south in 1914 there was the emergence of a new class of western educated people who moved with the Europeans through trade and studied overseas and this brought a new consciousness among the elite in Nigeria which brought about the formation of political parties and the emergence of a nationalist movement in preparation for self-government.

In 1950 Nigeria had three regional houses of assembly for the east, west and north of Nigeria. The north and west had houses of chiefs more or less like House of Lords in London. Members of the regional assemblies were elected by the people through a combined system of direct primaries and electoral colleges and membership were all Nigerians.

A federal legislature called the House of Representatives was situated in Lagos and served as the Nigerian parliament. It had ninety two members from the north as against fifty-six each from west and east.

This ratio rather than population figures served to protect British interest to an extent, since the north was more pro-British than the southern areas. There were twelve British members, appointed in the old house like a reserve, acting as a check and balance, these could combine with the north any time to hold the balance of power.

The nationalist Nigerians of the east and west wanted to progress further from this framework towards independence. But the desire was compromised by sectional rivalries. The British did not want Nigeria broken up like India where Pakistan was formed. Britain did not want Nigeria to break into three or more independent states and they did not want their former colony which they had nurtured for almost a century to fall into communism at the time.

The east and west had two dominant political parties which agitated for early self-rule, as against the north which pleaded for more time, thereby encouraging the British to stay on.

There were three major political parties: the Action Group (AG) which had a strong base in Western Region and had Awolowo as its leader. The National Council of Nigeria and the Cameroons (NCNC) existed in the three regions but had its strength among the Igbo east. It had Nnamdi Azikiwe as its leader. The Northern Peoples Congress (NPC) wanted more time and had its strength in the Hausa/Fulani north and its leader was the Sarduana of Sokoto, Ahmadu Bello. In fact, all the regions had ethnic-based political parties.

The personality of the leadership of each zone and their relationship with key British officers were the deciding factors of who would eventually receive the mantle of Nigerian leadership. Dr. Zik, as Azikiwe was popularly known, was an explosive man, magnetic and versatile in several fields. He managed a bank and Press - the *West African Pilot*.

Awolowo was an extremely cultivated and intelligent man. He was an intellectual. There was never a breath of scandal about him. He was somewhat principled and rigid; you were either with him or against him. British officials loved him but since he would not socialise and drink tea with them he lost out. He was too blunt and had no diplomatic skills and often spoke what was on his mind which upset Her Majesty's Government at the time. He began to upset the British from 1948 with his discordant melody which was different from those of Britain.

The Sardauna had commanding vigour, intellect and prestige from the religious point of view. Sokoto was a holy city and he was the spiritual head, not only of Muslims in the north of Nigeria but the whole west coast of Africa. The north however, through its good behaviour, was the darling of the British and became the beautiful bride of Britain.

The elections of 1959 in Nigeria had no international observers like the one in Sudan. Sir James Robertson, the Governor General was aware of this but did nothing at the time. The British government treacherously handed over power to the educationally backward north of Nigeria then, after the 1959 federal elections. The elections were allegedly massively rigged in favour of the northern people's congress. They also favoured the north with higher population figure which is still controversial in Nigeria till date.

The Governor General however called on the leader of the northerners, his friend, Sir Abubakar Tafawa

Balewa to form a government even before the results of the 1959 elections were known. This was the genesis of election rigging in Nigeria.

The end result was that Nnamdi Azikiwe, leader of the NCNC, had to settle for the empty post of Governor General, then ceremonial President, but was apparently persuaded that this was really the number one job. He would even be commander-in-chief and could wear the uniform of a field marshal. If Zik thought he was to be the real head of the Nigerian military forces he was soon to be disabused of the notion.

After independence Awolowo did not find himself either in the presidency or prime minister's office but in a small prison cell. Chief S. L. Akintola had emerged as the Premier in Western Region. Chief Awolowo resigned as Premier in 1959 to become leader of the opposition in the federal house hoping he would emerge as President but this did not happen, he lost out. This later led to a bitter quarrel between the Awolowo family and the Akintola family. Awolowo had arrogantly wanted Akintola to report events in Western Region to him as deputy leader of the Action Group (AG). This was resisted by Akintola's wife, Faderera, who said Awolowo was just the party leader and Ladoke Akintola, now as Premier of Western Region, had risen above him.

She once said to her husband: "Why should you be carrying official files to Awolowo at his home in Ikenne? let him report and come here if he wants to know anything." She threw the files into the rain and barred her husband from such trips meant for errand boys. This did not go well with Awolowo and a feud started with Awolowo using his influence as party leader to gain support against Akintola who later left the Action Group.

The Sardauna of Sokoto retained his position as Premier of the Northern Region while the Eastern Region had Michael Okpara elected as Premier.

Thus, the new nation took off on a precarious tripod. There was a structural defect in the house the British had created in Nigeria. The north alone had 55 percent of the federal constituencies which was more than the combined total of the other two regions of east and west. But the excitement of independence which Nigeria had succeeded in getting without any violence on October 1, 1960 subdued all the grievances for the moment.

Congo

Congo became independent at the same year Nigeria got her independence from the British colonial powers. At the time Congo became independent in 1960, the Belgians, their colonial master, had almost destroyed the people both physically and psychologically. The people were left disoriented and had a loss of self-confidence as the Belgians had made them feel inferior in everything they did. The years of subjugation had later triggered of the catastrophe that has plagued the subcontinent of East Africa. The Belgians treated people of Congo like slaves and animals.

The Belgian colonial government had failed to develop and prepare its colony for self-government and independence. The disharmony among its people had led to the first coup in Congo shortly after independence in 1960. Prime Minister Patrice Lumumba had planned to retain Belgian officers in the armed forces which provoked a mutiny. The prime minister was faced with the Congolese army against him and the collapse of the government's administrative sector. The United Nations sent peacekeepers to restore order but had not supported Lumumba or protected him. The opposition leader, Moishe Tshombe, declared secession of the Shaba province which he and his supporters called Katanga Republic, leading to a serious war in Congo.

It was as a result of this civil war that Nigeria had sent its fifth battalion in October 17, 1960 to May 1961 to Congo and Obasanjo was among the soldiers selected for the peacekeeping programme. The fifth Battalion was the first to be selected to Congo and was under the command of Colonel Ironsi. They were posted to the eastern Kivu province with headquarters at Bukavu.

It was a complicated and difficult mission. The Congolese were friendly with Nigerians but once they were seen interacting with the white men they became angry, hostile and agitated.[11] The anti-white sentiment was very high and Nigeria had to send only Nigerian troops. Among the Nigerian officers sent was Lt. Patrick Chukwuma Kaduna Nzeogwu, an independent minded and strong-willed officer. The chemistry between him and Obasanjo was of a similar blend and the two got on very well. It was a bond that seemed like they were from the same parents. They had a lot in common and they abstained from alcohol. The working conditions were tough but the Nigerian troops raised the morale of all, both peacekeeping soldiers and the Congolese soldiers and their people. There were other notable officers like David Okafor, Foluso Sotomi, Ray Mathew Dumuje,

---

11 Adinoyi Ojo Olukaba, *In the Eyes of TIme: A Biography of Olusegun Obasanjo,* African Legacy Press, C1997, Pg90

David Ogunewe, Captain Hilary Njoku, Yakubu Pam, Colonel Johnson Aguiyi-Ironsi, Major Galloway, the British second in command among others.

Congo was an unforgettable experience for Obasanjo. He once came close to a tragic end when he had gone on a survey without much backup as a driver and interpreter to inform the missionaries in one Catholic Church of their need to be evacuated. The priests and nuns agreed reluctantly to a midnight evacuation. However, as he was about to drive off, two Congolese soldiers arrived and arrested him. He was stuffed in the boot of a car and driven off to be killed. However, his earlier efforts at making an impression anywhere he went by getting to know and meet others irrespective of status had stood him out. He was known in Congo as Lieutenant Oba. When the soldiers phoned their superior officers they ordered he should be released immediately.

His colleagues were angry and shocked, describing the Congolese soldiers as ingrates. They immediately apprehended and disciplined the erring soldiers after that incident and since then Congolese soldiers never harassed their Nigerian counterparts again. His fiancée, Oluremi, had been worried when information got home that a Nigerian soldier had gone missing coincidentally at a time Obasanjo's letters had not been regular as before to Nigeria. However, she later got his letter and was reassured of his well-being in Congo.

Nigerian soldiers had the duty to also protect the Belgian settlers and at home the politicians made an issue of the activities of Nigerian soldiers in Congo. They had denounced the use of Nigeria soldiers to kill the Congolese in order to defend European settlers. The Action Group political party had used it against Balewa's conservative government. The crisis went on in Congo till about 1965 when Mobutu Sese Seko became leader through a coup. The name of Congo was then changed to Zaire. He was the defence minister before the coup and his name was Col. Joseph Desire Mobutu. He was alleged to have been backed by the American CIA.

However, Obasanjo had long returned to Nigeria in May 1961 and never returned to Congo. Another batch of Nigerian soldiers were sent for peacekeeping for another three years before they were finally pulled out. Obasanjo had used his allowance in Congo, known as *Dag's Dash* to purchase his first car, a Ford Taurus 17m with the registration number KA 5021. It was a surprise for Oluremi when Obasanjo came to pick her up at school. Seeing him as he suddenly emerged from the car was a big shock for her. As she described in her book: *Bittersweet,* she was excited and grateful to God as the car was a status symbol at the time, not many Nigerians owned one, it was the elites who were doing well that owned cars at that period.

Obasanjo, back from Congo, had been posted out of the fifth Battalion with Nzeogwu. Obasanjo was posted to the Army Engineering Corps in Kaduna as its second Nigeria officer. The first had been Captain Mike Okwechime, while Nzeogwu was posted as a training officer to the army training depot, Zaria. He spent six months and was redeployed to the Army Headquarters as the first Nigerian military intelligence officer.

When Obasanjo joined the engineering unit, Major Shepherd, his immediate British boss, discovered that he was hard-working. His colleagues saw the move as unwise because the highest rank at the Corp of Engineers was Major, whereas the infantry where most of the officers of the "general" rank come from, one stood the chance of becoming a Major General or at least a Brigadier General but Obasanjo was not interested in rank but job satisfaction.

The Nigerian Army Engineers at the time had one Major, a British officer, two British captains, one Nigerian captain and about 110 rank and file soldiers. It was a different organisation from the fifth Battalion. He was inducted, acclimatised and trained as an army engineer officer. Mike Okwechime was Captain while Obasanjo at the time was a Lieutenant. They were the two Nigerian officers in the corps at the time. The corps was seen as the elite group within the army.

They were referred to as three in one because they have full infantry training, they must also qualify in a trade proficiency certificate as a carpenter, bricklayer, welder, vehicle mechanic, plant operator or a driver and they must be field engineers. They are those who set booby traps or disarm and clear them. They also are to build semi permanent bridges, assault bridges for advancing troops, lay and clearing of mines, create obstacles and clear them, etc.

CHAPTER FOUR

Marriage In London

The year 1962 was eventful for Obasanjo as he had been promoted a temporary captain and was going on another course again in London. This time it was at the Royal College of Military Engineering, in Chatham, England. He had taken the bold step of formalising his intention of marrying his sweetheart, Oluremi Akinlawon. He had gone to formally introduce himself to Oluremi's parents, Mr. and Mrs. Akinlawon who received him warmly as their future son-in-law. The Akinlawons were comfortable by the standards in those days. Mr. Samuel Akintobi Akinlawon belonged to an elite group and worked for the Railway Corporation in Nigeria. He was the station master and his post at the time was well revered as the Nigerian railway in those days provided the major link between the north and south of Nigeria. The trains were important as they served as the major means of official travel in the 1940s, the other option was by road and cars which were not yet popular in Nigeria at the time. It was the railway that opened up Nigeria to development. The people and their goods were conveyed from one region to the other by train.

Oluremi Akinlawon's father was a polygamist with four wives and eighteen children. Her mother, Mrs. Alice Akinlawon (nee Ogunlaja) was the second wife. Mr. Samuel Akintobi Akinlawon was good looking and light skinned who spoke three languages: English, Yoruba and Hausa and people had felt he was of Fulani ancestry. He built a one storey house which was among the few of its type at the time. They called the house *onipetesi* and it was also called station master's house. Obasanjo had studied the way of life of the Akinlawon's and had made up his mind along the way to be successful like Oluremi's father or even greater. He had seen Mr. Akinlawon as his role model because he liked his lifestyle. When Obasanjo got to the United Kingdom he started sending money and taking care of Oluremi his future wife.

Obasanjo was a good letter writer, he wrote many letters regularly to update Oluremi on all that he was doing. And it was on March 7, 1963 that Oluremi left for London. Obasanjo had bought her a ticket on the Egyptian airline and had also arranged an accommodation for her.

Oluremi wanted to study nursing but Obasanjo convinced her to study institutional management. There were lots of Nigerians in London all in search of the Golden Fleece western education which was the yard stick to success at the time. England was a new experience for Oluremi: the food, the weather and the British whites at the time. It was a different culture and way of life but she settled down fine.

Olusegun Obasanjo and Oluremi Akinlawon on Saturday June 22, 1963 got married at Camberwell Green Registry in South East London. She was 21 while Obasanjo was about 26 years old.[12] The courtship

---

12   Oluremi Obasanjo, *Bitter Sweet: My Life with Obasanjo* Diamond Publications Ltd. 2008, Pg 25

Marriage in London

had lasted a seven year period. Captain Obasanjo later graduated in July 1963 from the British Royal College of Military Engineering's young officer's course and he returned to Nigeria in August 1963. He shortly served as a troop commander before he assumed command of the Nigerian Army field engineering squadron in Kaduna where he spent eighteen months.

While in Kaduna the Sardauna of Sokoto and Premier of Northern Nigeria had wanted a road built while ignoring normal procedure. He just ordered through the Brigade Commander in Kaduna, instructing all, including Obasanjo, that a road be constructed in the Mambilla Plateau in the Northeastern part of Nigeria. Obasanjo had replied through the Brigade Headquarters that he would not take orders from the Sardauna. He said at the time he would move to the Mambilla only if the order came from the army headquarters in Lagos to which the engineering squadron was directly responsible.

Obasanjo ignored the Sardauna's threats until Lagos gave the go ahead. In those days up North, the Sardauna was treated like a god and when he drove past on the road people had to park and come out of their vehicles kneeling down on the road and paying homage until his convoy passed by.

The Sardauna was offended by the action of this young officer. He had sent Lt. Col Yakubu Pam, one of the senior officers in Kaduna to warn Obasanjo who was seen as a head strong engineer, to be careful. Obasanjo dismissed the threat as he did not owe his office as a soldier to the Sardauna's generosity. He was indirectly sending a message that soldiers could not be ordered around without regard for operational rules and chain command. It was a risky thing up North to disobey the Sardauna in those days.[13]

Then again in March 1965 he was sent to India for training at the Indian Defence Staff College which also had the Army School of Engineering in Poona. Obasanjo again came back with super commendation from the Indian school. This training courses abroad in England and India had kept him away from the tensions that were gradually building up in the army in Nigeria. On his way back from India he stopped over in London to visit his wife who was rounding off her studies.

Before his trip to India Obasanjo had began to invest in property. His first property, a land, was at Oke Ado area of Ibadan. He also bought a second one at Kaduna, a place called Makera. Then he and his close friend, Nzeogwu, got a plot each at Surulere. That was through the Lagos Executive Development Board (LEDB). The good thing in those days was that you were allowed to pay in instalment over a period of time, as it was not a cash and carry business at the time.

Obasanjo had learnt the virtues of savings and investment and was very frugal when it came to money matters. Then first week in September 1964 he did the promotion examination from Captain to Major and had passed. He had become a Major before travelling to India for the course. He however left India at the end of November 1965 en route to London where he spent two weeks with Oluremi his wife. He then left for Nigeria and returned to Kano on January 13, 1966.

On his arrival in Kano he was surprised nobody was there to welcome and receive him. The Army Engineers

---

13 Adinoyi Ojo Olukaba, *In the Eyes of TIme: A Biography of Olusegun Obasanjo*, African Legacy Press, C1997, Pg 99

Marriage in London

Corps normally sent a driver and Land Rover to pick him but nobody came this time. He then took the domestic flight Nigerian Airways DC – 3 plane to Kaduna. It was the same story as nobody received or welcomed him back. He made frantic calls all in futility and then decided to call Nzeogwu who responded promptly and took him to his residence which both of them shared at 13 Kanta Road. Having dropped Obasanjo off, Nzeogwu returned to his office.[14]

Obasanjo had visited the Brigade headquarters where he had exchanged views with Major Keshi who had gone to America for his own training at the American Staff College and later Brigadier Ademulegun, the Brigade Commander who talked about his impending trip to Ghana. Captain Ben Gbulie, a junior officer who was acting as commander of the Engineering Unit had informed Obasanjo that he would have to wait about two days before he could resume back at work. He had written formally to Obasanjo to resume Saturday January I5, 1966.

He was totally in the dark and was oblivious of the impending crisis the country would witness that morning. Nzeogwu had kept mum and had simply tagged the coup "operation Damisa" (lion hunt). Obasanjo knew nothing about it and thought it was just a military practise within the barracks.

---

14 Olusegun Obasanjo, *My Watch*, Vol. 1 Kachifo Limited, 2015, Pg 174

CHAPTER FIVE

Coups In Nigeria

When the British colonial government formed the Nigerian army shortly before independence, the training had been one united military and armed forces, free from ethnic bias and sentiments. It was an army built on strong professionalism designed to defend the Nigerian state as a new nation that was moving towards self-government and independence. The bond was that of camaraderie and genuine friendship. The nationalist feeling at the time had blurred out ethnic lines.[15] It was a training that had made Obasanjo to declare he was a Nigerian and for the Nigerian nation as against the expectation of people from his ethnic background, the Yoruba, wanted of him. He had always been a detribalised Nigerian. The Nigerian army promoted and practiced this quintessential image and its priority was the Africanisation and promotion of the officer's corps. The push for self-government had led to the increase of Nigerian officers in the army from fifty to four hundred and fifteen while the British expatriates were totally withdrawn. This started the ethnic rivalry in the army.

---

15 Olusegun Obasanjo, Nzeogwu: An Intimate Portrait of Major Chukwuma Kaduna Nzeogwu; Spectrum Books, Ibadan, 1987, pg 44

At independence the Igbos dominated the army, having over two-thirds as a result of their high educational background and enlightenment. But after independence, with the north given power by the British, the minister for defence was a northerner and he imposed quotas based on the falsified census figures. He allocated 50% of enlisting of soldiers to the north and 25% each to the east and west.

British colonial leaders had enlightened the north that to gain full power and control over other regions, they needed to increase the number of northerners in the military and so by 1966 41% of officers were Igbo, 33% were from the north and 27% from the west with priority given to the midwest region rather than the Yoruba in western region. The Yoruba were not too interested but cared more about western education but the policy did not go down well with the Igbos.

By 1966 most northerners were junior officers while easterners filled the middle ranks as majors and lieutenant colonels. Then there were other rivalries that had to do with educational background, those with university degrees and those without who had risen through the ranks such as Ironsi and Sodeinde. Those who went to Sandhurst, Mons Aldershot etc.

The better educated junior officers were trained as cadets. They could not tolerate such people like Ironsi, who joined the army as a tally clerk. Ironsi's promotion as commander-in-chief was as a result of the years he spent in the army, making him acceptable to the eastern soldiers. That was the way it was, soldiers from eastern Nigeria were in control at the time as a result of seniority of years spent in the army.[16]

---
16   John Lliffe, *Obasanjo: Nigeria and the World*, Woob bridge and Rochester, New York, (2011), pg 15

Obasanjo had taken no part in the rivalries though he was observing all that was going on. He was wise, thoughtful, reliable and somewhat quiet and clam, and that kept him out of trouble. He was not ambitious and had a personality that did not threaten his superior officers. The army however came under serious strains such as indiscipline, nepotism, over politicisation and ethnicity with the emergence of double standards causing division. The trip to India had kept Obasanjo out of the coup that took place on 15 January, 1966.

The coup of January 15, 1966 had been planned since August 1965 and was spearheaded mostly by Igbo officers in the army: Major Emmanuel Ifeajuna, Captain Nwobosi, Majors Patrick Chukwuma Kaduna Nzeogwu, Chris Anuforo, I.H. Chukwuka, Donatus Okafor, Adewale Ademoyega and Tim Onwuatuegwu. They wanted a change in the leadership of the country. They struck simultaneously in Lagos, Ibadan and Kaduna, bringing about heavy casualty. The Sardauna of Sokoto, Ahmadu Bello, who was the Premier of Northern Nigeria was killed by Nzeogwu, the Prime Minister Abubakar Tafawa Balewa was also killed. The Premier of Western Region Samuel Ladoke Akintola was killed by Nwobosi but he had failed to control the city. The Finance Minister Festus Okotie-Eboh and senior army officials such as Samuel Adesujo Ademulegun, Commander First Brigade Kaduna, Brigadier Zakariya Maimalari, Commander Second Brigade Lagos, Lieutenant Colonel Yakubu Pam, the Adjutant General, Abogo Largema, Commanding Officer of the 4th battalion in Ibadan, Arthur Unegbe, Quarter Master General and Col. Kur Mohammed, Army Chief of Staff. In Kaduna Ahmadu Bello's wife,

Hafsatu, and many others were killed in the coup including policemen working at the Premier's lodge.

The chords of ethnicity, partiality and double standard had reared its head. Major General Aguiyi-Ironsi, the GOC of the Nigerian Army managed to escape, it was believed he was tipped off. The GOC and his wife, Victoria, had earlier attended a party at the Ikoyi residence of Brigadier Zak Maimalari that night.

Gen. Ironsi came later to the Ikeja cantonment to organise a counter offensive against the coup. He consulted with Lt. Col. Yakubu Gowon who was the commander of the second Battalion in Ikeja and Lt. Col. Hillary Njoku, the man Gowon was succeeding in Ikeja. "Some officers have taken up arms against the government." Njoku had quoted Ironsi as saying to him on the phone, "Are you with us or against us?" Njoku's book, *A Tragedy Without heroes: The Nigerian Biafran War* further went on to say Ironsi had unconsciously blurted out, "But they said they would not kill anyone" and within an hour his conscience pricked, him "But they said there will be no blood shed." He had been referring to the yet to be identified coup plotters.

Njoku and Gowon, the two officers with Ironsi when he made these shocking utterances exchanged glances. It became clear he had known about the coup plot and was not in the dark as they had originally believed.

From that moment Gowon became suspicious of Ironsi and kept his observations to himself. The coup had been successful in Kaduna. Nzeogwu led the operation in the north and was in absolute control as he held sway for four days in the entire north.

Lt. Oguchi, the leader of the eastern operation to handle Benin and Enugu had failed to deliver at the expected time. They took control late in the morning of January 15, 1966. His troops seized the radio station but was not able to arrest the premier until much later as the Archbishop of Cyprus, Makarios, was at the premiers lodge but when the Archbishop left they put the premier of the eastern region, Michael Okpara under house arrest.[17]

Lt. Oguchi had acted professionally by avoiding bloodshed as was originally agreed upon. He went on air to announce the army take over and waited in vain for further instructions from his colleagues in Lagos. The bad coordination from other units foiled the coup. One of his responsibilities and orders upon assuming control of Enugu was to dispatch troops to Benin for the Midwest operation but his bad coordination grounded him in Enugu, until Ironsi ordered loyal troops to rout the rebellion.

In Kano, Lt. Col. Ojukwu refused to be involved.[18] Lagos was just as bad as Kaduna, Ifeajuna had shot several senior officers and had killed the Prime Minister Abubakar Tafawa Balewa, but he did not take control and command of the Ikeja infantry battalion and all this lapses led to the failure of the plot. However, nobody can be certain of what was exactly on their minds and if that was how they had wanted the events to unfold. This is because Ironsi had knowledge of the coup, so today, we may assume they plotted the coup but had wanted or agreed Ironsi will take over.

But because the casualty had been very minimal on the coup plotters and eastern region, it was soon

---

17　Adinoyi Ojo Olukaba, *In the Eyes of TIme: A Biography of Olusegun Obasanjo,* African Legacy Press, C1997, Pg 108

18　Ben Gbulie, *Nigeria's Five Majors: Myth and Reality,* Africana Educational Publishers (Nig) 1981, Nigeria, pg 89-96 asserted it was an Igbo coup because officers and politicians from their zones were spared from the killings. Ironsi had taken power from the civilians in Lagos and had consolidated the other southern region. What was left was the northern region controlled by Nzeogwu. There were verbal exchanges with the new government in the south and the lone revolutionaries in the north. Nzeogwu had planned to march on the rest of the country, but was convinced against it. However, it was then Obasanjo offered to broker negotiations between Nzeogwu and Ironsi.

He left Kaduna for Kano on January 17, 1966 in an air force plane flown by flight Lt. Dan Suleiman. He stopped over in Kano on transit and was received by 2nd Lt. Ike Nwachukwu who led him to his commanding officer, Lt. Col Emeka Odumegwu Ojukwu, the son of the Nnewi transport magnate who was very wealthy and influential.

Ojukwu had pedigree and was a graduate of the University of Oxford. His education and background gave him a different kind of personality and this brought out a lot of confidence and show off in him. He was from elite background. Ojukwu subjected Obasanjo to a lot of questions and when he was satisfied Obasanjo was finally allowed to catch the flight back to Lagos.

However, Ojukwu was only being cautious as it was a time of national chaos and uncertainty where nobody trusted anyone. However Obasanjo did not forget the hostile reception he was accorded and considered it a slight on his person.

When Obasanjo reached Lagos, Ironsi and Nzeogwu had already spoken by telephone, Nzeogwu offering his loyalty under certain conditions and Ironsi accepting the loyalty without the conditions. Obasanjo met Ironsi and put the request of Nzeogwu forward which was safe conduct for him and the other coup plotters as condition to laying down their arms. Obasanjo explained that his friend was possibly asking for a pardon or amnesty. Ironsi replied that the request would be considered by the newly constituted Supreme Military Council (SMC), the highest policy-making organ. Before Obasanjo left, Ironsi had made a sarcastic statement asking whether Nzeogwu expected medals for what they had done?

Obasanjo returned to Kaduna January 18, 1966 to discover that Nzeogwu had decided to surrender, he then apologised to Obasanjo for keeping him in the dark. A military attaché Lt. Col. Conrad Nwawo, had been flown into the country to speak to Nzeogwu. He handed over his control of the north to Major Hassan Usman Katsina who had been appointed governor of the region by Ironsi. Lieutenant Colonel Adekunle Fajuyi was made governor of Western Region, David Ejoor for the Mid West and Emeka Ojukwu was the governor of the Eastern Region. Then Lt. Col Yakubu Gowon became the Chief of Army Staff.

However later that day, Nzeogwu announced that Ironsi had accepted the five conditions for submission. He flew into Lagos and got detained and so did the other coup plotters. Almost all the coup plotters were of Igbo extraction and they claimed to have acted in the nation's interest.[19]

What compounded the problem was Ironsi's action and statement that "All Nigerians want an

---
19 Ejindu, Majo Nzeogwu speaks Pg 15

end to regionalism" he proclaimed quite falsely. He had surrounded himself with Igbo advisers when the promotion exercise took place. He had promoted twenty-one officers to be lieutenant colonels in April 1966, the outcome was that eighteen were of Igbo ethnic origin who commanded ten out of the army's thirteen combat units and the coup plotters were neither tried nor released. This angered the northern region and tension started to build up again.

Then again Ironsi made another blunder, he tried to change Nigeria into a unitary state when he introduced the unification decree No. 34 of 24 May of 1966. This led to demonstrations which turned violent with over six hundred people killed, mainly Igbos and southerners. The Emirs warned him that the North would secede unless they returned to a federal structure.

But the Igbo domination theory had seemed to be greatly exaggerated by anti Igbo forces in the country as members of Supreme Military Council were not all Igbo. The nine-member council only had two Igbos: Ironsi and Ojukwu. Lt. Col. Kurubo, one of the members was Ijaw from the southsouth area. Even though the East was seen as one region, it really was not. The fourth member of the SMC was Igbo, he was the federal Attorney General Gabriel Onyiuke. The Inspector General of Police, Edet though an Easterner, was not Igbo, his deputy, Kam Salem, a northerner, the Council Secretary S. O. Wey was a westerner. Lagos military administrator Mobolaji Johnson was a westerner and the permanent secretary in the ministry of finance was a northerner, Abdul Aziz Atta, a northern minority from Okene.[20]

---
20 Adinoyi Ojo Olukaba, *In the Eyes of Time: A Biography of Olusegun Obasanjo*, African Legacy Press, C1997, Pg 115

There were twenty-three federal permanent secretaries but only three were Igbo. The north had eight and the midwest had seven while western Nigeria had five. But probably what happened was the disposition of few Igbo officers and government officials of Igbo extraction who cornered Ironsi, alienating other groups from him.

There were also complaints about employment vacancies where Igbo heads of parastatals were accused of discriminating against non-Igbos. The belief was that all available vacancies were given to Igbos and they were accused of nepotism even though this had happened with all groups in Nigeria.

The tension in the Northern part of the country was further heightened by the alleged attitudes of some Igbos living in the north. It was said that offensive display of posters showing the head of the all-powerful Ahmadu Bello, the Sardauana of Sokoto, who was dead under the military boot of major Nzeogwu. Northerners were allegedly ridiculed and insulted by the Igbo traders.

The same allegations were made in the barracks in the north where the wives of southern soldiers began intimidating the wives of northern soldiers, especially when they were fetching water at the public pump. It was alleged that southern wives would push away northern wives, saying "get out, let us take our water first, after all, we are now in charge" and the women were pestering their husbands and asking, "when are you going to hit back to redeem our image?"[21] It was said that the northern civilians began to scoff at their sons in the army calling them cowards for not avenging the deaths of their leaders. This led to the mobilisation

---

21 Yususf in Usman and Kwanashie: Inside Nigeria History pg 74

for a counter coup. It was Major Murtala Muhammed who was the second most senior northern officer at the time after the coup, that continued to call for the trial of the coup plotters who were about One hundred and thirty in number.

When this did not happen, he coordinated the northern effort for a counter offensive, and it was this revenge that later made him the hero of northern Nigeria.

The onslaught began five days after the Unification Decree No 34 of 24th May 1966. The 29th of May, 1966 was a day political violence erupted in the Northern city of Kano and like fire in the dry season it spread and engulfed all the northern states: Katsina, Sokoto, Maiduguri, Bauchi, Kaduna, Zaria, etc.

The order was revenge and vengeance by northerners who carried out the act to an over kill, thousands had to flee to Eastern Nigeria. The northerners were satisfied that they had payed back blood for blood. The easterners counted their material losses and brooded in the gloom of the bloody massacre.

This development led to fear, animosity, distrust, suspicion and anarchy, the stability of the country became very shaky with rumours of another coup coming on the 3rd of August, 1966. The chief of staff to the Head of State, Brigadier Baba Ogundipe and Chief of Army Staff Lt. Col. Yakubu Gowon had tried to reach out and give advice on many occasions but they were denied access to the head of state by Njoku.

However, Obasanjo remained a reliable and loyal friend to Nzeogwu and they wrote letters to each other even when Nzeogwu was in prison. This led to suspicion within the military and in the post-coup interrogations Obasanjo was questioned by security agents who continued to doubt his knowledge of the coup. This led to screening of the letters Obasanjo wrote to Nzeogwu in prison.

Following the crisis in the North after the May 1966 riots, Ironsi toured many parts of the country including the northern region, appealing for calm and pledging to resolve the grievances of the northern region concerning the January 1966 coup. Ironsi had arrived in Kaduna on the 20th of July, 1966 where Obasanjo was stationed. There were rumours of the possible act of mutiny in the barracks and also at the cocktail party that was held for Ironsi and officers had to be searched for weapons before they were allowed into the venue. However, the northerners in the army continued to kick everywhere against Igbo officers or anybody from the south.

In Ibadan the fourth battalion refused to obey the Igbo officer who was the new commander. This brought about a change in the army that was already divided. The army had to replace the Igbo officer. The rumours of a counter coup continued. Murtala Muhammed now declared they would not allow sergeant majors to take over and control the army.

On July 28, 1966 Obasanjo was in faraway Maiduguri to search for a site to build a military barracks for a detachment of soldiers that were to be deployed and stationed there as a result of the May riots. Obasanjo again did not know the army had been thrown into another crisis while out there. Ironsi, in continuation of his reconciliatory tour had gone to Ibadan on July 28, and while there, Adekunle Fajuyi who was governor of western region hosted his guest to a state banquet.

Murtala Muhammed was in Ibadan earlier on that day to coordinate the final stages for the coup. He had gone back to Lagos after midnight which was the day of the coup on the 29th of July 1966. The northern soldiers at Abeokuta garrison had reacted with violence to a minor misunderstanding with an Igbo officer and this lead to a full scale mutiny where several Igbo officers were killed. The coup had begun at about 1a.m. and by about 3 a.m. early morning of 29th July, 1966 the Head of State, Ironsi, was alerted in Ibadan along his host, Governor Fajuyi. Frantic efforts were made by phone to no avail, the northern soldiers had gained control.

General Ironsi had been warned about the coup by his ADC Lt. Bello and was actually given the date but he took no action. Bello had been loyal to him despite being a northerner.

Both the Head of State and Governor refused to move from the government house, probably they felt it was going to be a palace coup where nobody would be killed as he had willingly surrendered. The irony was that it was Major Theophilus Yakubu Danjuma, a member of Ironsi's entourage and Lt. William Walbe, the officer in charge of Ironsi's security that effected the arrest of Ironsi and Fajuyi and their ADCs.

Danjuma later exonerated himself that he had later handed them over to Walbe whose soldiers killed them in the bush at Iwo road. There were about forty Igbo officers killed and another one hundred and twenty from other ranks.

With General Ironsi dead Brigadier Baba Ogundipe who was the Chief of Staff Supreme Headquarters was now the most senior officer in the army but he knew the northerners were not ready to obey any southerner and being that the coup that had just taken place was a northern coup, he did not attempt to show any interest to be the new head of state. He travelled to London and was later made Nigeria's high commissioner to the United Kingdom.[22]

It was on the 1st of August, 1966 that debates were made whether the North should break of from the Nigerian Union. This was quashed on the intervention of the British High Commissioner and American Ambassador in Lagos along with senior permanent secretaries who advised Murtala and Gowon not to secede. They grudgingly agreed to remain within a united Nigeria and chose Gowon who was the most senior officer from the North as Nigeria's second military Head of State in August 1966. This choice had opposition, as the coup leaders preferred Murtala Muhammed because he was the one that spearheaded the coup.

Those who executed the coup were Murtala Muhammed, Martin Adamu, Shehu Musa Yar'Adua, Muhammadu Buhari, Pam Nwatkom, Ibrahim Babangida, Jerry Useni, Ibrahim Bako, John Longhem, Gaba Duba, Shittu Alao and Musa Usman. However, Murtala Muhammed agreed that based on seniority Gowon should be allowed to rule, a decision he later regretted.

---

22 Adinoyi Ojo Olukaba, *In the Eyes of TIme: A Biography of Olusegun Obasanjo,* African Legacy Press, C1997, Pg 120

CHAPTER SIX

Genocide On The Igbos And The Aburi Report

After the death of Ironsi, Lt. Col. Gowon, a thirty-two year old officer from the north, became the new head of state. And as he was yet to settle down, the North continued with its savagery and violence against non-indigenes, especially southerners from Eastern Nigeria and what today is Southsouth in the Niger Delta. Even people from other regions who shared resemblance with Igbos were also killed. Gowon continued to sue for peace to douse the flames of ethnic hatred and mistrust which the army had ignited and fuelled as innocent men and women vanished daily but his effort was not very successful because he was a Christian and from middle belt area of Nigeria.

It seems pertinent to ask whether the lives of between 30,000 to 50,000 Igbo/eastern civilians already killed with about two hundred Igbo army officers were not enough compensation for the deaths of three Hausa civilians and four army officers killed in the alleged Igbo coup of 15 January, 1966. It may equally be interesting to know the answers to the following questions:[23]

---
23 Emefiena Ezeani, *In Biafra Africa Died: The Diplomatic Plot*, Veritas Lumen, London (2012), page 36

Did the Igbo or easterners as a people know about or take part in executing the January 15, 1966 coup? Did the Igbo or easterners commit mass murder on 15 January 1966 or thereafter? What was the justification for the killing of the people of eastern origin since the Hausa counter coup plotters on 29 July, 1966 had avenged the killing of those that were killed during the first coup of 15 January 1966 which included Aguiyi Ironsi, the highest ranking army officer along with other Igbo officers but still went further with killings of hundreds of innocent Nigerians of Igbo ethnic origin from southeastern Nigeria? The Hausas and Fulanis and other tribes in the North had used all sort of weapons like short guns, matchet, cutlasses, daggers, and poison arrows in their slaughter of the Igbos.

Kaduna was burning with violence and unrest when Obasanjo returned from Maiduguri via Jos on July 30, 1966. Although Igbos were the main targets but non-Igbo Easterners were also being attacked. One Captain Ogunro was mistaken for an Igbo man and was slaughtered in his pyjamas by a murderous mob.

During this period, Oluremi, Obasanjo's wife had returned from England and while alone at home the phone kept ringing and when she picked it, some unknown men were asking for her husband's whereabouts which she however volunteered no information. Then an exodus of southerners began to leave the north for their own regions as nobody felt safe again. The army had become so undisciplined and the life of a non-Northerner became cheap and meant nothing to the northern people.[24]

---

[24] Oluremi Obasanjo, *Bitter Sweet: My Life with Obasanjo*, Diamond Publications Ltd. 2008, Pg 40

Obasanjo had gone to the house of the air force commander. Lt. Musa and informed his wife he was in town. He arrived home with escorts provided by Hassan Katsina (Lt. Col.) the Governor of the Northern Region. Katsina had predicted confidently that Obasanjo be protected as Nigeria was going to need him in the future. I guess he had noticed a leadership trait only the wise could spot about Obasanjo, being a detribalized, trust-worthy and a treasure to the nation.

The chaos continued and later became genocide as the North wanted to wipe out all Igbos and southerners and when the threats were too much, Obasanjo knew it was time to relocate from his residence in the barracks. The rumour flying around was that the officer with a red Peugeot 404, that is, Obasanjo, should be killed.

Obasanjo and Oluremi had sought refuge in the flat of one Mr. Egungbohun and his wife he was a junior staff at the post and telegraph corporation in the clerical quarters of the corporation in Kaduna. They had stayed for six days in a tiny dingy room waiting for sanity to return.

Obasanjo now made a call to Governor Hassan Katsina who was very glad that he was alive and was relieved to hear his voice. He ordered that they leave town immediately until the situation had cooled off. They were sent to Maiduguri where there was no crisis with the assistance of Abba Kyari and Lt. Col. Muhammed Shuwa, the acting brigade commander and the Governor. The three had arranged for a plane that flew them to Maiduguri but due to shortage of fuel in the plane they had to stopover in Kano where they spent one night. They were warmly received in Kano.

The next day they got to Maiduguri. Abba Kyari had contacted a Maiduguri based businessman, Mai Deribe, who saw to the comfort of the Obasanjos and assigned to them a Mercedes Benz car for their movement around town. Unknown to major Obasanjo and his wife in Maiduguri there was panic and fear in Abeokuta over their safety. The rumour was that they had been killed. Oluremi's parents were already being ridiculed and mocked that their daughter had been slaughtered with the soldier to whom they had sold her for money.[25] Oluremi's mother had to travel to Kaduna at the peak of the crisis where a cousin, Adolphus Ogunlaja, informed her that they were alive and safe and were in Maiduguri at the time.

They eventually returned to Kaduna when the violence subsided but it was still an atmosphere of apprehension and uncertainty, so he eventually sent Oluremi to Lagos and on the 27th of April, 1967 Oluremi Obasanjo gave birth to their daughter, Iyabo. Obasanjo remained in Kaduna till January 1967 and he was the most senior Yoruba officer left in the north as others had returned to the Western Region. The military officers and civilians from Northern Nigeria continued to meet and have secret meetings in Lugard hall, Kaduna.

Meanwhile, Governor Ojukwu of the Eastern Region did not accept the appointment of Gowon as Head of State and commander-in-chief of the Armed forces of Nigeria. He said with the death of Ironsi, even though it had not been officially announced, the proper procedure was to make the next most senior army

---

25 Adinoyi Ojo Olukaba, *In the Eyes of TIme: A Biography of Olusegun Obasanjo*, African Legacy Press, C1997, Pg 125

officer the head of state. Either Brigadier Ogundipe or Colonel Bassey should have been chosen but since the North was at war with the southern people of Nigeria, they did not accept and would not execute a coup only for a southerner to come and take control. It was the North who had done the revenge coup and so they would have to install a northerner as head of state. The situation continued and Ojukwu would not recognise Gowon.[26]

Then Gowon pleaded for peace and reconciliation as he was a very wise and peace-loving officer. He released political detainees and prisoners which included chief Obafemi Awolowo and Anthony Enahoro who had been jailed by the Balewa government in 1963 for treason. The event became a celebrated case in the history of Nigeria as the "treasonable felony trial."

The genocide continued and officers from western region of Nigeria complained, questioning the rationale and wisdom of their continued stay in the North. This was at a time the conference of regional representatives was holding in Lagos where they recommended many things including the posting of military personnel to the barracks of their various regions of origin. There were four senior western officers: T.B. Ogundeko, E Akinfenwa, Oluleye and Obasanjo, they had agreed to meet with Governor Katsina over rumours of planned attacks on westerners on October 22, 1966. At the last minute Obasanjo pulled out, pleading for patience and when they got to Governor Katsina, Olusegun dismissed the rumour. It was this act that saved the Nigerian army from disintegration and also Nigeria from breaking up. The officers from western region

---
26 Ibid pg 127

held on to their posts as soldiers of the Nigerian army despite the Unrest in the North. Obasanjo and others agreed to stay until they were officially reassigned.[27]

Eventually Obasanjo was reassigned to Lagos as the Chief Army Engineer. The job was a position held by his former boss, Col. Okwechime, an Igbo officer who had returned to the East following the July 1966 Genocide. Ojukwu refused to come down south and preferred the long range discussion with Gowon who wanted the Nigerian federation to remain. Ojukwu however was too smart and intelligent. His oxford pedigree had put him a century ahead of others. He had realised and seen the future of Nigeria and like a Nostradamus he understood the North and its people very well and had seen the problems which Nigeria still faces today right from the 1960s.

Ojukwu wanted a confederation or the Eastern Region's independence from Nigeria. He refused to attend federal meetings in Lagos because northern troops were in the west. Chief Awolowo who had become the Yoruba leader in western region had asked for the removal of the Northern troops from western region. Gowon had agreed to this and the troops were withdrawn to Ilorin and Jebba. This moves made no difference to the situation. Then on the 4th of January 1967, Lieutenant – General Ankrah who had just over thrown the Kwame Nkrumah's civilian government made an attempt to mediate. He had invited Nigerian military leaders to Aburi in Ghana. The meeting lasted two days and the outcome and resolutions were as follows.

---
27 Ibid pg 128

"We the Supreme Military Council solemnly and unequivocally declare that we:

(1) Renounce the use of force as a means of settling the present crisis in Nigeria and hold ourselves bound by this declaration.

(2) Reaffirm our faith in discussions and negotiations as the only peaceful way of resolving the Nigerian crisis.

(3) Agree to exchange information on arms and ammunition in each unit of the army in each region and on the quantity of new arms and ammunition in stock.

The death of General J.T.U Aguiyi Ironsi and Lieutenant Colonel Adekunle Fajuyi was formally announced, thus making Lieutenant Colonel Yakubu Gowon's new position clear.[28]

The meeting also resolved that decisions made concerning and affecting Nigeria as a whole would not be taken without consultations with other regions. The federal government had published the report verbatim. The federal permanent secretaries who later studied the Aburi report, made their recommendations to favour the overall interest of Nigeria.

Below is the summary of recommendations:

(a) If the adoption of the title 'commander-in-chief' declares the post of 'supreme commander' vacant, serious instability would result from political and military manoeuvres to fill the post.

(b) The creation of area commands without any unified and effective central control of the Nigerian army has serious political implications: internally, because of the

---
28 Dr. R.B. Alade, *The Broken Bridge*, the caxton Press Ltd, Ibadan (1975), pg 4

vulnerable position of the commander-in-chief or supreme commander and the status of minorities externally, because no single authority is vested with the power to use the army for defence against external aggression.

Acceptance of the Accra meetings decision would require amendments to the armed forces acts and the Constitution.

(c) To avert possible repercussions the determination of the fate of soldiers in detention should be done after assessing the possible reactions of the rank and file of the army.

(d) The decision to appoint or approve appointments of federal public servants, will not only paralyse the federal public and police service commissions, but will also create regional loyalties among federal public servants.

(e) The decision that displaced persons should continue to receive their salaries till the end of March, 1967, should be considered for economic reasons.

(f) The vesting of the executive powers of the Federal Military Government on the Supreme Military Council with the introduction of the element of consent of the regional military governors makes the federal military government subordinate to the regional military government, and this amounts to accepting confederation. The powers of the federal government as contained in the exclusive and concurrent lists should be restored as recommended by law officers.

(g) The Ad Hoc constitutional conference should stand adjourned indefinitely and the immediate political programme announced by the supreme commander of the nation on 30th November, 1966 should be implemented.

(h) There is a clear need to associate reputable civilians with the federal executive council as previously recommended and the nation should be so informed.

(i) If the intention of the Accra decision is to restore to the regions the constitutional powers which were taken from them before January 1966, the supreme commander should instruct the law officers to list the relevant decrees for repeal.

Cabinet office
Lagos
20th January, 1967[29]

The leaders came out of the peace conference with different interpretations of the agreement they reached there. The leaders returned to Nigeria with each side implementing their version of the Aburi declaration.

The Eastern region felt the Aburi agreement had granted the regions a provisional confederation and began taking unilateral measures that were in conflict with the central and federal government in Lagos.

It was also at variance with the permanent secretaries decree No 8 of 1967. Ojukwu felt that the Aburi agreement had been violated and many Easterners insisted that "on Aburi we stand" and without Aburi there could be no Nigeria. Ojukwu announced edicts that brought about the confiscation of federal properties in his region. payment of federal government dues and taxes to his treasury, impounding of Northern Nigerian produce enroute Port Harcourt and the hijack of a federal plane flying from Benin to Enugu. To climax all these he

---
29 Ibid. pg 6,7

ordered non Easterners to leave the region without their belongings. They continued to build a sovereign state apparatus, setting up their own armed forces that had been quietly built up as against military action from the federal government.

On the 1st of May, 1967 Awolowo led a delegation consisting of western region Obas and some prominent elites which included Sir Adetokunbo Ademola, the federal Chief Justice of Nigeria but they failed to convince Ojukwu from pulling out of the Nigerian union. Awolowo had during this visit blown hot air, threatening that if by acts of omission or commission the East was allowed to secede from Nigeria, he and the Yorubas from western region would do the same.[30]

It was a promise Awolowo never kept, but how could he? The military was back in power and this was not a civilian dispensation and government. Then he would have to get senior Yoruba officers like Obasanjo, T.B Ogundeko, E. Akinfenwa, Oluleye etc., to agree with him but at this time Obasanjo was not interested, he was not a politician and did not want Nigeria to break up. Obasanjo was a reliable well-trained military officer and gentleman who wanted to adhere to the military training and standards he had gone through. This had caused a frosty relationship between him and Awolowo. How could Awolowo follow through with pulling out of the Nigerian union without the Yoruba officers in agreement? It was impossible. He had just been released by Gowon from prison wherein the Balewa government had put him having accused him of treason. He would not make trouble or cause any problems that would endanger his

---

30 Adinoyi Ojo Olukaba, *In the Eyes of TIme: A Biography of Olusegun Obasanjo*, African Legacy Press, C1997, Pg 125

life or send him back to prison. At this period, Awolowo was already working for Gowon, the new Head of State, as an adviser. The Igbos felt Awolowo was a traitor for not keeping his words.

On May 27, 1967 Yakubu Gowon declared a state of emergency in the country and announced the creation of twelve states out of the four regions. Brigadier Adeyinka Adebayo had a meeting with Ojukwu but made no impact as Ojukwu was not going back on his stand. The state of emergency had caught Ojukwu unawares as it reduced the size of the eastern region of which he was the governor.[31]

On May 30, 1967 he rejected the twelve state federal structures which had automatically cancelled the regional system of government and he declared the secession of the Eastern region from Nigeria, declaring it the Republic of Biafra. This was backed by the Consultative Assembly of Eastern region. Gowon on the federal side responded decisively, ordering mobilisation. The war began on 6th July 1967.

---

31 Comrade Lekan Aderibigbe, *Obasanjo for Nigeria* pg 226

Chapter Seven

Civil War Years

The Nigerian civil war began in second week of July 1967. The federal government declared the Onitsha Bridge closed but a few people who wanted to get back to the east still managed to cross to the other side. The federal government mounted a blockade of the Eastern states. The rebel army with its 8th brigade on the 9th of August, 1967 crossed the Niger Bridge heading in two directions.

One detachment headed for Benin on getting to the Midwest while the other went towards Southwest for Ughelli, Warri and Sapele. Another set of soldiers headed for Auchi Northwest and some crossed the Niger River further north to Ilushi. The rebel troops that went to Benin disarmed the Nigerian troops and took over the armoury, airport and radio station. They were firmly in control within a period of ten hours.

The Biafran troops broadcasted from Benin, announcing their take over of the region. The leaders of this campaign were Col. Victor Banjo, Major Emmanuel Ifeajuna and Major Alale. More Eastern soldiers on the rebel side arrived the border between the west and mid-west on the Ofosu River and along the Akure Benin road they were on the Eastern side of the Osse River. On the Northern part they occupied Ibillo while North West area they were east of Idogun town.

The federal government sent troops to the borders to prevent infiltration of rebels. Ore junction was very strategic as it led to Ondo, Okiti-pupa, Ijebu Ode and Benin. The Biafrans came with their own locally made armoured tanks called "Red Devils", military trucks and motorcycles all with inscription of B.A. (Biafran Army). They also had artillery. People residing near Ofosu River, Ore and the Europeans who were working on telecommunication network and extensions workers of Borini Prono took to their heels, moving to Ijebu Ode which became a beehive of activities. Journalists from Britain, America and France had arrived to get information for their home countries and the international press. The hotels everywhere were fully booked. It was called catering rest house at the time.[32]

The first attack took place at the Ofosu River. The federal government troop defeated the rebel troops who pulled back only to regroup again from Benin. The second encounter was fierce and the 19th and 20th of August 1967 were tense moments in Ijebu Ode town and western Nigeria with tension hitting Lagos.

The rebels got to many places, even close to Lagos by Epe with the aid of canoes but were intercepted by federal troops before they could advance into Lagos. Others went north wards infiltrating areas like Ondo town and the boundary between Akure and Owo.

---
32 R.B. Alade, The Broken Bridge, pg 11

The rebels attempted to get into Lagos through Ore-Ijebu Ode road but the Oni Bridge was broken and they could not cross-over because of the river, in fact, a lorry load of soldiers had ignorantly driven straight into the river. The rebels and their mercenary officers were driven back towards Benin at the end of August. If the bridge had not been damaged, Lagos might have been captured with only seven hundred troops in defence.

Fighting took place at Idogun, a town not far from Owo, where the secessionist had gained control but were dislodged by federal troops. The Biafran Army blew up the Agbanikaka and Owan bridges on the Akure-Benin road. The Biafran rebels had problems within themselves as reports of mutiny among the secessionist troops in Warri reached Ijebu Ode.

Colonel Murtala Muhammed led the troops of the second division of the Nigerian Army advancing south from Okene. The rebels put up a strong resistance but were eventually overwhelmed and defeated at Ukpilla, the cement town and Ibillo. Also at Auchi, Sabongida Ora, Ekpoma Uromi and Ehor, federal troops prevailed, entering Benin about 6pm on the 20th of September 1967 amid jubilation from the Midwesterners.

A lorry load of secessionist troops from Biafra drove through the Sapele-Benin road unaware that the federal troops were in Benin and they were eventually surrounded and captured in front of the General Hospital. This was because the day before, Major Okonkwo, the rebel administrator of Midwest, had already proclaimed the republic of Benin not knowing that within hours he would be defeated.

Major Ogbemudia was named military administrator for the Midwest after federal troops gained control. The rebel invasion of the Midwest on August 9 1967 rattled everybody including Obasanjo. Nobody had expected that Ojukwu would go that far. Obasanjo along with his other colleagues in Ibadan moved fast to the west against the rebels, mounting road blocks at Ore, Ifon, Irua, Sobe, Igbotako, Irele and Okitipupa.

He ordered the army's 11th Battalion then stationed at Iwo road, Ibadan, under the control of Bajowa, to commandeer vehicles and seize rifles from the police to halt the rebel incursion from Akure. Despite Biafran soldiers taking control of the Midwest there were those who sympathised and wanted Col. Victor Banjo and his libration Biafran soldiers to have unimpeded access to the region and Lagos. They were however marked as anti-Nigeria elements. Gowon had told Obasanjo, alerting and warning him of the radicals. Among them were the journalist Bisi Onabanjo who later became civilian governor of Ogun State in the second republic, the lawyer, Bola Ige, and the playwright Wole Soyinka who were described as being subversive. Obasanjo had given an account of the incident in his book *My Command*. Soyinka proved and lived up to the description of being a radical.

Soyinka, Obasanjo had said, was Banjo's emissary. The poet and playwright was reported to have told Obasanjo that Victor Banjo was ready to pay any price to be allowed into Ibadan and Lagos with his rebel forces. Obasanjo allegedly turned down the offer to Soyinka's disappointment. The news got to Gowon and Soyinka got arrested and imprisoned. Soyinka said that Obasanjo did not report accurately what transpired, that he only delivered a message as opposed to his putting pressure on Obasanjo to concede to the request of the rebels.[33]

Soyinka said he simply delivered a message from Victor Banjo for an unimpeded passage for the rebel libration forces through western region to Lagos. Soyinka said he neither attempted to persuade Obasanjo to change his mind nor promised him material inducement to make him do so. He said he was implicated as being a part of the rebellion. This incident made many Yorubas to hold grudges against Obasanjo.

Obasanjo toured border areas assessing troop's performance and issuing the necessary instructions on the need for proper coordination between the fire men at the frontline, being Chief Engineer. He also paid regular visits checking that engineers gave the troops the necessary technical support.

Benin, the mid-western state capital, was recaptured by the federal forces from Okene on September 22, 1967 after some fierce battles that left heavy casualty on both sides. Col. Murtala Muhammed, the commander of the second division that flushed out the rebels out of the Midwest unilaterally appointed Major Samuel Ogbemudia as military administrator of the state when Gowon appeared indecisive on the matter.

The loss of the Midwest was devastating to the Biafrans. The leadership was desperate to find scapegoats for the setback. Lt. Col Ojukwu became paranoid and suspicious of some of his men claiming they were planning to overthrow him in a coup.

A sham military panel was set up, where a kangaroo judgment was given and on September 24, 1967 four

---
33 John Lliffe, *Obasanjo: Nigeria and the World*, Woob bridge and Rochester, New York, (2011), pg 15

secessionist officers were executed in the Enugu army barracks ostensibly for disobeying orders, and for alleged subversion and plan for a coup against Ojukwu. They were Lt. Colonel Victor Banjo, Major Alale, Major Emmanuel Ifeajuna and Samuel Agbam, a former career diplomat for Nigeria and political scientist.

The capture of the Midwest gave some courage to Murtala Muhammed's second division who had attempted to cross the River Niger twice but failed but now made a third attempt from Idah where they succeeded. They went on to capture Enugu the Biafran capital but this did not end the war as it went on for another three years.

Lt. Col Ojukwu's Biafra was vanishing from September 1967 to mid-1968 as Benin, Asaba, Onitsha, Nsukka and Enugu had been occupied and captured by federal troops. Lt. Colonel Benjamin Adekunle, the General Officer Commanding the 3rd Marine Commando Division arrived Bonny Island on the 25th of July, 1967 and also took over the village of Peterside opposite Bonny.

The centre of the oil industry was blockaded both by sea and by land. Rebel forces tried in vain to recapture the area several times but the federal troops held on. However on the 20th October, 1967 the third marine commandos, along with the navy and air force captured Calabar. This eventually helped the advance to Port Harcourt and northern part of the Southeastern state.

The capture of Ikang, a coastal town in Cameroon border south of east Calabar was executed on the 18th of November 1967. And by the 13th of January 1968 federal air and ground units had taken over secessionist rebel fortified positions along Port Harcourt channel.

The Gowon-led federal government announced it had killed twenty-three white mercenaries on the 3rd of February 1968.

However, Calabar, due to communication difficulties was cut off from the southeastern state. Ikom to the North could not be reached since it had no link road to Calabar to the west. Calabar was cut off by the Cross River over which a ferry carried traffic to Oron which has direct road links with the vast interior. Biafra had a strong garrison there with heavy fortification to resist federal government troops.

Despite this, the 3rd Marine Commandos launched fierce waterway attacks since it was a riverine area from Calabar. They captured Oron and drove west wards to Uyo and southwest wards to Eket. Eket and Uyo were captured and by 24th March 1968 Ikot-Offiong was liberated. On 30th March, 1968 the important road junction town of Ikot Ekpene was taken. By 1st of April 1968 Abak was also captured. Aba, the Biafran stronghold was also captured.

Federal troops were in control of Ikot Ekpene town while the Biafra secessionist controlled Ikot Ekpene district. The fighting was a tricky one as there were inter marriages between the Igbos the and the Southeasterners now known as south south.

Secessionist counter attacks were frequent and many refugees were unreliable as they were confused on whose side they wanted to belong. Adekunle's Third Division was renamed Third Marine Commando because of the gallant display it had shown in the riverine areas of Bonny and Port Harcourt where they gave the military operations different names like operation OAU (Owerri-Aba-Umuahia) and "operation tiger claw."[34]

Benjamin Adekunle, the slim war commander had become an instant war hero. He was courageous, daring, controversial and unpredictable. His handling of the battle front had taken him to the height of national and international fame, he was idolized and called the "Black Scorpion."[35] A name parents called their children when playing action games.

As the war progressed with the capture of Enugu, the 3rd Marine Commando Division at the end of May 1968 had killed several mercenaries including an Italian named Giorgio Norbiatti.[36] They consolidated their position on the 23rd of June 1968 in Port Harcourt, as the important towns of Bakana, Abonnema, Degema and Nembe in the Rivers State were captured. The federal troops continued to make progress and within another five days Yenagoa and Ahoada had been taken.

Secessionist propaganda was so strong that many inhabitant of the areas were caught unawares when federal troops captured many towns. After the capture of Enugu Obasanjo travelled to Lagos to brief the Head of State on the happenings that took place in the rebel - held areas and the general war situation. He had suggested the need for an Igbo civilian administrator, to set up and oversee the day to day administrative running of the Biafran capital of Enugu. Gowon agreed to his idea and asked Obasanjo to look for a competent person.

---

34 Adinoyi Ojo Olukaba, *In the Eyes of Time: A Biography of Olusegun Obasanjo*, African Legacy Press, C1997, Pg 125

35 Godwin Alabi-Isama, *The Tragedy of Victory*, Spectrum Books, Ibadan 2013, pg 417

36 Frederick Forsyth, The Making of an African Legend: The Biafran Story, Penguine Books, (1969) Pg 132

The meticulous Obasanjo lived up to the task, contacting his long time friend, Dr. Jacob Ade Ajayi, an accomplished historian who was already the acting Vice Chancellor of the University of Ibadan. Ade Ajayi had a Citroen DS car, one of the best cars in the world at the time, immediately he bought the car with hydraulic suspension, the car became the talk of the town and this enhanced Ade Ajayi's popularity. These created a trend as other professors and lecturers started going for the Citroen Dsuper, Ds 23 cars and it became status symbol at the time.

Obasanjo had noticed all these peculiarities as he was such an observant military officer. When Dr. Jacob Ajayi recommended Ukpabi Asika, Obasanjo had never heard of or met him, although he knew many university lecturers through personal networking and the "town and gown" forum. One of Asika's senior colleagues in the department, the eminent political scientist Billy Dudley was for instance a good friend of Obasanjo who was impressed by his intellectual wit and inclination.

Dudley designed a course called military science which he persuaded Obasanjo to teach his political science students on a part time basis. But envy crept into the matter when Obasanjo was lecturing at the most prestigious university in Nigeria, leading one officer from the army headquarters in Lagos to halt it, saying it was revealing some military secrets and unduly radicalising the students.

Students of the course among who was Andy Akporugo who later became a successful journalist had later declared Obasanjo's lectures as fantastic and not prejudicial to state security or posed any threat whatsoever to the military establishment or made students more radical than they already were. However, Obasanjo stood out and this was noted in the army as academics were respected. They now knew he was an all rounder able to fit anywhere.

So, Obasanjo recommended Ukpabi Asika, a thirty-one year old radical political science lecturer who had been against the secession of eastern region from the Nigerian union.

Obasanjo introduced him to Gowon and even though the head of state was skeptical of his ability to perform, Mr. Ukpabi Asika lived up to the bill. He started work and persuaded the Igbo people to get resettled and carry on their trade and normal lives. Then the refugees started returning back to town.[37]

The immediate assignment of Asika was civil administration, the resettlement of displaced citizens, maintenance of justice, electricity and water supply, dissemination of information on Radio Nigeria, Enugu, and that of entertainment. It was also to establish health services and postal services.

The water supply was restored to many important areas. Electricity was also restored and went off at midnight for security reasons. The restorations were done and carried out by people who were sent from Lagos, Ibadan and the Midwest.

The court and prisons regained their functions. The policemen returned to their duty posts and guarded important buildings assisting both the army and civilians.

---

[37] Adinoyi Ojo Olukaba, *In the Eyes of TIme: A Biography of Olusegun Obasanjo,* African Legacy Press, C1997, Pg 145

Postal services were restored and letters began to reach Enugu on a daily basis and many labourers were employed and paid as they cut the grass restoring the town to its normal looks.

Drinks and food became readily available and the China Town had been restored as goods like shoes, bicycle tyres, cloths, watches, staple foodstuffs etc. became available though more expensive than in other parts of the country. The Central Bank was renovated and so was Kingsway Stores. The refugees and children suffering from kwashiorkor were fed and they became healthy again. Travellers were given free return flights in the Red Cross planes bringing relief materials to Enugu from Lagos.

Mr. Ukpabi Asika recorded a broadcast which was relayed to the Igbo people at least twice a day, on radio Nigeria Enugu. It started,

> This is a public service announcement to the Biafran soldiers. Don't be dead when peace returns. Yes peace, your special envoys are now talking and seeking peace. They may yet find it. Why not wait and find out before you decide. If you should die it will be too late if you are dead. Come on over. Don'tretreat from the advancing federal troops just show them you are no longer fighting. Show your hands. You may even hand over your weapons to them. You will be quite safe.
>
> It may not be fun at first being a captured person but you are not really a prisoner of war you will have three meals a day. You will see a doctor any time you need one. You will rest and sleep soundly at night we will try to make it more comfortable but any how you are better alive than dead. At least you can judge for yourself. Yes come on over and be a living witness to peace.[38]

---
38   Mr. Ukpabi Asika's Appeal Broadcast, Radio Nigeria, Enugu

Hospitals were built which consisted of three bungalows built of mosaic stone walls streaked with white intervening paint between the place. Only few beds could be seen as the windows were splashed with black paint to protect/shield the lighting at night so as to avoid being sited by the enemy planes at night.

The soldiers on the federal side were proud of the first division of Nigerian army. Those in the third division, the crack marine commandos led by the "black scorpion," colonel Benjamin Adekunle, were just as proud of their division and on 4th September, 1968 Lagos announced the capture of Aba, an administrative capital of rebel government by the 3rd marine soldiers. On the 16th of September 1968 Owerri was captured by the first division and the 22nd battalion called Jet 22 and the 21st battalion called the mig 21. These two battalions had the reputation of never withdrawing even against fierce rebel onslaught. They spearheaded the capture of Nsukka and Enugu. The rebels feared them and whenever they advanced the rebels disappeared into hiding.

Asika continued with his job but social readjustment called for patience and understanding. The escape from rebel-held villages to federal liberated towns exposed the refugees to new social order and conditions. The psychological change resulting from the loss of their property, family and friends required a lot of patience for them to readjust.

The refugees needed moral support, resettlement, encouragement and counseling. Women had suffered a lot with their children and many were ill, hungry and emaciated. There were lots of children that had become so thin and bones and their hair had turned red as a result of malnutrition. Their faces, feet and abdomen swollen with bodies riddled with scabies. Many were almost lifeless not able to hold up their heads. Many had developed sores on their mouths and buttocks as a result of diarrhea and malnutrition. The women and children wore tattered clothes that were so dirty as a result of not having soap to wash and when soap was available there was no money to buy it. Sleeping and walking in the same cloths for weeks allowed skin diseases to develop.[39]

There was shortage of salt as the Biafrans had used the available measure for making bombs. The Biafran army propaganda had brainwashed the people and when the federal troops asked them to surrender and return home, many stayed back in the bush believing the federal troops would kill them.

The reason was that many times there were bad eggs in the federal troops who still wanted to kill the Igbos and that was done several times when air planes had dropped bombs in the market place where people lined up for food. Hundreds were allegedly killed.

Those who dared to come out discovered it was a different story, they were given food, shelter and medical attention. The word started to spread and the refugees became confident and started returning from their hideouts in the bush back into the city.

Life was gradually returning to the liberated cities. The Igbos had a good reason for the war after the genocide against them in the North after the coups of 1966. But the other ethnic groups of the then South Eastern

---
39   R.B. Alade, *The Broken Bridge*, Pg 60

Nigeria (which is the south south today comprising the Efiks, Ijaw, Ibibios, Annangs did not want to be forced into "Biafra" and wanted to remain within the Nigeria union.

The success and fortunes achieved by the federal government in the war had by early 1969 begun to suffer some form of humiliating reversals. In March 1969 Owerri slipped fast from federal control, the situation was really bad that all the celebration of past victories started tumbling like a pack of cards.

Biafra had an equipment called the Red Devil which was like farm equipment made by the French. They were covered with welded materials which made them bullet proof and served as tanks. By April 25, 1969 federal troop began to withdraw from Owerri which was a serious setback.

CHAPTER EIGHT

Humanitarian And International Organisations

Nigeria's domestic problem had spilled outside her frontiers. The international community did not understand fully the ethnic problem, how to intervene and by which side to stand. The British were mischievous in their own little contributions. The secessionist propaganda in Western Europe and America had tremendous impact. They had powerful radio, they used news handouts to foreign correspondents in different world languages while the federal radio in Lagos was not clearly received in Enugu let alone outside Nigeria. The Biafra secessionists had internal press agents in America, Britain and France to name a few countries. The Nigerian government had published a statement at the time in a popular American newspaper and it cost them £6,000 pounds.

It was then the federal government in September 1968 appointed Mr. Sam Epelle to handle external publicity and telex link was established with London under a consultant by name Mr. David Russell.

Biafra propaganda began effectively in August 1967 for the following objectives:

1. To tell the "Biafran" story to international audience.
2. To stimulate more foreign interest in "Biafra" by creating a more intelligent curiosity to journalist of high caliber.
3. To build up a higher level of publicity and good will for "Biafra" to foreign countries.
4. To demonstrate to the outside world that they have the military capacity to preserve their territorial integrity.
5. To show that their decision to assume independence was irrevocable.

They allowed free passage and hospitality for representatives of the world press such as:

New York Times The Washington Post NBC film Crew	America
Le Monde French TV and Radio Crew	France
The Irish Press (Ireland)	from Britain Commercial TV

They also extended free passage to German Radio and TV, the Swiss press and the propaganda effort effectively got sympathy from East African countries. This had cost Ojukwu several thousands of pounds but nearly turned the world press against the federal military government as Nigeria's side was scarcely heard.[40]

Mercenaries were engaged under tremendous financial undertaking. France had long been assisting Biafra and had so admitted in early August 1968 before the Addis Ababa peace talks. Biafra also engaged agents from all over the world black market to procure arms and ammunitions for them. The intermediaries bought weapons at exorbitant prices and risked their lives to deliver the weapons to Biafra which was rebel – held territory. The plane that crashed in Gavoa, Cameroon Republic had revealed the identities of the gun runners and their business.

Meanwhile, the currency change in Nigeria had affected Biafra and made it difficult for Ojukwu to finance the war. The foreign businessmen then exploited the situation. A plane was seized in Togo at the time with millions of old Nigerian currency notes. These led to many of the rebel agents panicking and coming into Nigeria by whatever means to exchange their cheaply bought notes for new ones. Ojukwu then printed the new Biafran currency.

President Nixon had just emerged as the president of USA and wanted to have reliable figures of the situation on both federal and secessionist held territories. He had sent Professor Clyde Ferguson Jr. to assess the situation. The recommendation was for aid to be sent by land, water and air corridors to enable relief to reach those desperately in need.

Ojukwu however, for political and military considerations, refused daylight relief flights. There

---
40   R.B Alade *The Broken bridge* 1975 Pg 64 as explicit

were figures and pictures of deaths as a result of starvation which aroused world sympathy. Churches and relief organisations in secessionist-held areas gave figures of 1,000 to 10,000 people mainly children dying daily from starvation but these figures were exaggerated to arouse world sympathy. If the figures were true, then, it meant that in the first two years of the war 7,300,000 people would have died while in reality the population of Biafra was about 5 million people while that of the Eastern region, including Biafra had been calculated to be 12.4 million from census figures at that time. The federal government also added to the problem of relief materials getting to rebel-held areas. They were reluctant to open air corridors through which arms and ammunition could be smuggled into "Biafra" so the disagreement continued at the expense of innocent civilians in rebel-held territory.[41]

The relief from world agencies like ICRC had to be done by road through Enugu, Port Harcourt and Calabar. Several countries continued to send relief in form of food, and organisations like the Oxfam, Save the Children Fund, UNICEF, the World Council of Churches and later Caritas International, an Italian based charitable organization and the International Committees of the Red Cross which had its headquarters in Geneva. Also medical and nursing personnel from Scandinavia, America, Germany, Britain and Thailand came to Nigeria to help the sick and hungry people.

The international community continued to send help via Sao Tome and Portugal in routine weekly flights which came to the secessionist-held area on the notorious gun trail. Pope Paul got entangled in

---
41 Ibid

the controversy when he agreed in an interview that Caritas International, an Italian based Catholic relief organisation sent in relief by all means available. The statement was interpreted that even arms carrying planes flew in disguised as relief aircrafts.

This led to protests against the Pope's involvement in the Nigerian war. The World Council of Churches had also been very vocal in their support for relief supplies being airlifted to Biafra.

The opposition put up by some prominent Nigerians prevented a resolution being raised at the conference of the World Council of Churches in Uppsala, denouncing Nigeria for the civil war against the Biafrans. The Nigeria press the *New Nigeria* of 6th July 1968 read thus:

> We cheer the decision of the federal government that the air force should seek and destroy all aircrafts engaged in unauthorised mission to Ojukwu. This decision shows a marked contrast to the pitiable helplessness which the government seemed to display in the face of foreign organisations masquerading in the guise of humanitarianism.
>
> Oxfam impetuously decided to follow the gun trail from Lisbon to send relief to Ojukwu. The international Red Cross has not been as indiscreet. But that does not mean that it has not been trading with Ojukwu as if "Biafra" is a sovereign state.
>
> All the do-gooders have got a dangerous proposal to beguile the government. They wish to have an air strip somewhere in the East central state set aside and freed from Bomb raids for the so called many flights".
>
> There can be no guarantee, however, cast iron it may look, that the runners may not take advantage of it.

> There is ample evidence to suggest that as the basis of all his feverish humanitarian activities like the pro Ojukwu lobby and the profit motivated air line sharks also have captured the relief business for their more sordid ends.

The type of food brought in by the international organisations was also a problem as many villagers were not accustomed to rolled oats from America. However there was tinned rice, fish and powdered milk and suggestions were made to the federal government to send local food. This sent a panick to the rebel areas that the food will be poisoned.

However, thousands of tons of relief materials came into Nigeria both on the federal and secessionist side, even the Nord Church Aid from Scandinavia sent relief. The federal government alleged that money sent to Biafra by relief agencies including the Red Cross was being used to buy arms. This was denied by the Red Cross.

The crisis got the Americans worried so much that Senator Edward Kennedy in his first Senate speech wanted the problem of starvation in Biafra to be tabled at the United Nations General Assembly which opened in the last week of September, 1968. According to him, the argument that this was an internal affair had to fall by the way side.

He recommended that the General Assembly should direct the Secretary General U. Thant to bring about what he called "mercy agreement" in Nigeria so that all outside governments and agencies could participate and contribute to the relief programme.

Then Canada's foreign minister wrote to U. Thant saying that Canadian public opinion as well as that of other countries could not understand how the UN could fail to concern itself with the prevention of starvation in Nigeria. The relief problem became a matter of concern in other African countries which prompted Dar-es-Salam and Tanzania to raise money for food and medical supplies for Biafran war victims. The South African government had sent food and medical supplies worth (₦12,000) to Biafra.

The International Red Cross chairman, M. Samuel Gonard, said that in the months of September and October 1968 that 12,000 tons of relief supplies were brought into Nigeria. They were responsible for feeding 1,250,000 people as they had 250,000 in the "Biafran" held territory. They were able to execute this feat as they had six aircrafts in operation from Fernando Po that took materials to the Biafran territory.

The Nigerian government was not happy at the time as the war continued unabated, straining the relationship with the ICRC. The government had threatened to shoot down any aircraft flying at night. The Nigerian government continued to warn humanitarian organisations of the risk of flying planes at night because it was providing cover for gun runners for the secessionists.

The World Council of Churches at the end of November 1968 gave 150,000 dollars for relief to Biafra including 2,000 tons of stock fish from Norwegian churches in both Nigeria and Biafra. The United Nations World Food Programme provided food supplies worth one million dollars to be distributed throughout Nigeria and Biafra. The joint church aid was a combination of Christian churches.

They formed the organisation for aid to civilian victims of the Nigerian civil war. The Catholics, Jewish and Protestant churches were involved. They operated branches in thirty-five countries and the headquarters was in Scandinavia where its activities were coordinated. They had twelve air planes which made several trips to the Uli air strip to drop relief materials. Pastor Mollerup coordinated the flights from Copenhagen.

One of its pilots, Count Carl Gustaf Von Rosen, was involved in supplying weapons with relief materials. He was investigated and sacked. He later went on to play a vital role in the formation of the Biafran Air Force.

Then sometime in January 1969 another diplomatic exchange between Nigeria and the United States government took place when the U.S Government intended to sell eight planes, the C 97 Strato freighter cargo air craft with 18 ton capacity, for the bargain price of $4,000 dollars, the Red Cross and Joint Church Aid got the planes.[42]

Mr. Joe Iyalla, the Nigerian Ambassador, protested to the State Department and General Gowon asked the U.S Ambassador in Lagos for clarification from his government. The Gowon-led government felt the sale of the planes would directly and indirectly increase the arms carrying capacity of the Biafrans. The statement declared:

> Caritas had admitted that they give space in their planes for rebels, this therefore would indicate that the United States intention was to allow Caritas and other rebel supporters to donate their plane, entirely to the rebels for the traffic in arms.

---
42 Frederick forsyth the making of an African legend – The Biafra story Pg. 237

The Nigerian government felt the use of these planes would be the prolongation of the war. Inspecting the planes did not satisfy the federal government.

The U.S. government declared the planes were offered based on humanitarian considerations and not political support for Biafra. This triggered a reaction from six university professors at Ibadan and Lagos. They criticised the United States governments that the offer was a means of keeping the rebellion alive and warned Nigerians against, "the true face of Americans and their Western European allies and their intention to impose a NATO solution to our crisis on the people of this country."

The letter was signed by Dr. O. Aboyade, Dr. D.O. Ekong, Dr. E.U. Emovon, Dr. Essien Udom, Dr. A.L Mabogunje and Dr. T.M. Yesufu. The (ICRC) Red Cross had difficulties and hitches when on the 21st of December, 1968 the government of Equitorial Guinea suspended flights by the organisation to the Biafran held territory. The Red Cross suspended its right from Fernando Po because it took along petrol to Biafra. The allegation was petrol was being used for military purpose but this was denied as the petrol was used for generating electricity in the hospitals and also for vehicles carrying relief materials.

The Nigerian government continued its displeasure with the Red Cross and by February 1969 when the Red Cross airlift from Cotonou began, the first three flights had to turn back due to difficulties in landing at Uli airstrip.

This was resolved but the Nigerian press and radio were critical, for example, Radio Kaduna reproached Republique du Dahomey (now Republic of Benin) for taking over the dirty job of providing the international Red Cross with a base to resume its illegal flights, saying it was hard to see and reconcile with Dahomey's support for Nigeria. Dahomey denied any wrongful act and invited the federal government to send inspectors who would check what they were taking to Biafra and that it was purely humanitarian.

However, the United States continued to be of assistance on humanitarian grounds. President Nixon in February 1969 appointed Professor Clarence Clyde Ferguson Jr., a Rutgers university law professor to seek ways of getting more food to civilian victims of the war. They continued to work with the Red Cross, OAU and other international organisations, agencies and governments. The White House statement recognised that political and military issues had complicated relief efforts but Nixon declared that it should be within the conscience and ability of man to give effect to his humanitarianism without involving himself in the politics of the dispute.[43]

The federal government offered Obilagu air strip, captured from the Biafrans and now controlled by federal troops, for the landing of food and relief materials, then the goods would be delivered by road through the land corridors into secessionist territory. The offer was rejected by Biafra for security reasons.

The external affairs minister of Canada spoke in Toronto that food and medicine were on the way to Biafra but observed that the leaders there were responsible for delays in getting the relief materials to the starving population because they preferred to receive arms.

---
43 Ibid

The federal government on the 5th of June, 1969 had intercepted a Red Cross DC6 near Eket in South Eastern Nigeria. The plane was ordered to land for checking but when it refused the government ordered that it should be shot down. After the incident, Red Cross relief planes did not fly into Biafra thereby resulting in reduced arms traffic.

Chief Anthony Enahoro, a first Republic Federal parliamentarian said genuine relief efforts had to be separated from humanitarian activities which included the shipment of arms. He said operations of relief agencies had been counter-productive in that, Biafra had gotten an estimated £50 million pounds and over in direct and indirect foreign exchange from the activities of voluntary organisations and the money had been spent on arms. Enahoro added, that by indirectly prolonging the war, more lives were lost, thus cancelling out the value of saving lives through relief operations.

Meanwhile federal fortunes in the war had by early 1969 began to experience a series of reversal. The federal government began to lose grip of Owerri around March 1969 when rebels were encircling the town. The town of Umuahia had fallen to the federal government troops but no one could celebrate as federal troops were forced out of Owerri. This was a serious setback. This was a disgrace to the third marine commando in the hands of Biafra. The federal troops experienced desertion, looting, self-inflicted injuries and acts of indiscipline were on the rise.

The Biafran war had polarised the world. The British colonial master who had created the geographical expression called Nigeria by merging the North with the South wanted Nigeria to remain a single entity. Nigeria was Britain's largest trading partner in Africa so there were economic implications and considerations.

The British did not know whether Biafra controlled by Ojukwu would remain loyal, preserving the economic relationship they had with Nigeria. Britain decided that the devil she knew was better than an angel she did not know and wanted the union they created to stay intact, thereby giving support to the federal government

The Soviet Union also gave support to the Gowon-led federal military government and sold her weapons and military equipment. The Secretary General of the United Nations, Mr. U Thant, refused to get involved declaring the situation a civil war where they had no role to play.

The Lyndon Johnson administration in the United States was unsympathetic with Biafra despite support from liberal Americans. The administration was fighting an unpopular war in Vietnam. They towed the British line since Britain supported the U.S. on the Vietnam War. Despite this setback, propaganda was used, photographs of bony swollen-headed children with distended tummies were flashed across the world and the war got a comparison with the Nazi holocaust.

The Igbos who were predominantly Christians wanted to be free from the repression of the largely Muslim, Hausa-Fulani group. Biafra got recognition from Tanzania in 1968, followed by Zambia, Gabon and Ivory Coast and also the West Indian nation called Haiti. Militarily the war was being prosecuted with shocking sloppiness and unprofessionalism as rampant incidents of chilling atrocities was committed against the rebels and unarmed civilians.

In Lagos everything was going on fine. Residents and visitors could not feel the war going on in Eastern Nigeria. In 1969 Gowon got married to his wife Victoria Zakari, a nurse, in a state wedding.

Back in Ibadan the Obasanjos lived in peace, Iyabo was growing up as Mrs. Obasanjo took a job at the Premier Hotel, Ibadan's prestigious hotel, as housekeeper. She later moved to the University of Ibadan Guest House. Her salary was reasonable as she bought her first car while working at the Premier Hotel through a car loan.

On November 1968 a second child was born and named Olubusola. Obasanjo continued to visit the war front to supervise the engineering unit and oversee the soldier's welfare and needs.

Obasanjo's star had risen and started to shine and he was like a light bulb with moths flocking to it. There were men who visited him for friendship and business as he had become important in the army and women also flocked around him which led to new relationships. However, he did not allow his wife to be disrespected by anybody.

CHAPTER NINE

Taking Command

The 9th of May, 1969 was the beginning of the end of the war. The Biafran commandos crossed into Agbor and Kwale areas in the Midwest Benin and killed eleven men working for Agip, the Italian oil company. Eighteen others were abducted and taken to Owerri.

At the military headquarters in Lagos, Col. Hassan Usman Katsina, the Chief Of Army Staff and Gowon decided to change officers even though Gowon had wanted some, like Benjamin Adekunle to remain to finish the job.

Gowon summoned Obasanjo to Dodan Barracks, he was now a full colonel. He was informed about his impending deployment to the 3rd Marine Commando Division as its commander. He was aware of the problems in the units and knew how enormous the task of achieving success was.

On the 13th of May 1969 the federal government officially announced changes in the commands of all three divisions. Col. Benjamin Adekunle of the 3rd marine commandos was replaced by Colonel O. Obasanjo, Chief of the Nigerian Army Engineers. Col. Adekunle was reassigned to head planning and training division at the military headquarters in Lagos.

Col. Mohammed Shuwa was made the military secretary while Col. Bisalla replaced him at Enugu. Colonel Haruna of the 2nd division replaced Col. Rotimi as Quartermaster General. Then, Col. Rotimi was re-assigned to command the Ibadan Garrison organisation.

The federal troops on the government side with all its gains in the two-year old war seemed to have rolled back as the Biafrans acquired sudden vigour and impetus. Adekunle the Black scorpion was tired. Though he had done very well and became a hero in the war, his achievements seemed to be in disarray as the foreign intervention continued to arm the Biafrans.

Gowon knew deep down it was not his fault for the setbacks and had been reluctant to replace the field commanders but advisers insisted on change of leadership. When Gowon agreed he and the advisers decided they had to replace Adekunle with another Yoruba officer because they needed delicate balancing of ethnic sentiment. Gowon then called Adekunle on phone at Port Harcourt where he said "come back home, you are tired, come and rest."

Adekunle had done a good job, after building a formidable division but he however protested to be allowed to finish the job. He felt the army headquarters was starving him of arms and good fighting men. Adekunle felt reports about his style of command was unfair, blaming him for the atrocities of his men and officers under his command who were accused of unruly and brutal behaviour as opposed to other federal soldiers. He denied charges of harshness and being psychopathic.

His argument was that a simple mistake by careless soldiers could lead to huge losses of men and materials which would be devastating. His men feared him and saw him as a terror. I guess it was all psychology because his office door had a warning which said "Enter at the pain of death."Obasanjo had taken it off immediately he took over. His fire brigade approach to battle which had paid off at the onset came under fire, not because of his fault but because the international agencies through relief materials had been arming Biafra with food and weapons. Adekunle was successful as he followed his instinct and not military textbooks in fighting a war. He had done the job but had not consolidated the victory as Biafra still continued to resist the federal troops.

However, when Colonel Olusegun Obasanjo took command, there were initial hiccups but then he got his groove. He was thirty-two years old as at on May 16, 1969 when he left Lagos to Port Harcourt, the headquarters of the third marine commando. As he was about leaving for his new assignment the newspapers interviewed him, responded in his usual humble manner, promising to do his best to ensure a quick and decisive victory for the federal government.

The press reported him as being "publicity shy", and "camera shy". They saw him as the opposite of his predecessor whose remarks often brought out his mercurial personality. Benjamin Adekunle was earlier in Lagos to handover to Obasanjo. They had spent about fifteen minutes at the VIP lounge of the Ikeja Airport going over the final points.

Gowon had wanted the handover to be at Port Harcourt to ensure a smooth transition but Obasanjo knew it would be dangerous and in his wisdom said there are never two ambassadors from the same country assigned to an office at the same time. It was like saying again you cannot have two kings in the same palace. Obasanjo argued the new one resumes only after the departure of the former. That was why they met in Lagos on neutral ground.

Obasanjo flew to Port Harcourt shortly after in the same executive Hawkker Siddeley 125 jet that had brought Adekunle. He arrived Port Harcourt to a colourful reception ceremony. The young naval officer who was the military governor, Alfred Diete – Spiff (now the Amanayabo of Twon-Brass)and his entire cabinet had come to welcome and receive him at the airport. A short address was made to officers and men of the division, Obasanjo called for cooperation discipline, loyalty and hard work.[44]

However, there were mixed reactions. While some officers in the command were bitter about his appointment with some threatening to quit, many others hailed his arrival.

By the report of a poll that was conducted by the *Daily Times* it turned out that Obasanjo was one of the most respected officers in the whole army. Some others described him as open-minded, fearless, an officer who knows his job and likes it, others said he knew what he was doing etc.

On the 17th of May 1969, the day he started at his new post he was already there by 8a.m. and got officers embarrassed as they came in late. Three days at his new posting he launched an attack on Ahoda, some 15 miles from Owerri which ended up in a disaster, the Biafrans were still strong and determined in this

---
44   General Olusegun Obasanjo, My command Pg 65-8

region. Anyway, Obasanjo was still learning to be an infantry and field commander as he was more of an engineer in the engineering unit.

However it was Alani Akinrinade and Alabi Isama, the military strategist who recommended they could put him as commander since in his Ibadan Garrison he was the infantry commander there. They had in fact both visited Obasanjo before he was finally chosen to replace Adekunle. They brought him their proposal in Ibadan on how to end the war in thirty days with their strategy designed by Alabi Isama. They had brought and explained operation pincer 1, operation pincer 2 and operation pincer 3. They said pincer 1 could not be used because it would be too bloody and they opted for operation pincer 2 which was to deal with Biafra's centre of gravity as well as their communication between East and West, operation pincer 3 was designed as a back up for pincer 2.[45]

However, Obasanjo tried out his own idea and when he was ambushed with little casualty he tried other options ending up with Operation Tailwind which eventually ended the war. Akinrinade had kept on mentioning his name to Gowon as the best option. He had obviously noted something different and special about his personality which many others did not probably see. There was the option of Bayo Onadeko, Oladejobi, Duke, Captain Olajire and Sotomi, Oluleye and Olutoye but Akinrinade and Alabi Isama asked for Obasanjo and this pressure convinced Gowon to choose him.

Despite earlier challenges Obasanjo got moving with his new assignment and within the first month

---
45 The Tragedy of Victory Brigadier General Godwin Alabi Isama

of his arrival at Port Harcourt he met all the officers in the battalion and divisions, heard all their complaints and had taken down notes meticulously and drew up an organisational chart and welfare plan for the command.

He discovered that the soldiers were overworked that their salaries were delayed, and that the commando girls posed a threat to discipline and confidence among officers. He also discovered looting of goods, the delay of materials like hardware, uniforms, boots etc. and that soldiers were deserting by faking injury. He sorted out all the ills and got rid of the commando girls hired for the sexual needs of officers. Contractors who had been inflating their supplies got their prices slashed.

He requested the Central Bank to reopen along side other commercial banks which was done promptly. He continued to work hard and within a short while victory was at hand. The federal government on the other hand also did its job and on the 13th of September 1969 the federal government entered into an eight-point agreement with the International Committee of the Red Cross (ICRC) over relief flights.

The terms went as follows:

1. All relief flights shall take place in daylights hours.
2. A federal government inspector shall join two inspectors appointed respectively by the government of Dahomey and the ICRC to inspect relief consignment from Cotonou.
3. The federal government inspector has the right, acting alone to exclude from any flight any cargo or passenger who do not form part of genuine relief action.

4. The federal government shall call down for inspection in Lagos any aircraft it wishes, whether or not the aircraft has been inspected at Cotonou.
5. Relief materials shall be as agreed by the national commission for rehabilitation.
6. Only agreed relief personnel shall be entitled to board the aircraft
7. Hours of flight shall be between 9am and 5pm.
8. These arrangements shall be without prejudice to military operations by federal forces.[46]

As negotiations were being held with Gowon on the resumption of flights by the ICRC who had 11,000 tons of relief materials stock piled, two old United States warship sailed into Lagos: the Dona Mercedes and Dona Maria. They were to open the water corridor up to the Cross River. The governments of Southeastern and Rivers States objected and refused their passage for south eastern state, it had security implications and could be exploited by the Biafrans; it was then eventually used by the federal government.

The federal government was satisfied with its eight-point agreement with the ICRC but Biafra rejected the terms and agreement on military grounds, because federal jets could follow the Red Cross planes to launch attack on Biafra and this led to world reaction.

British and American newspapers hailed the federal government's concern over the relief flights and accused Ojukwu of starving his people for military and political reasons. The *Washington Post* editorial on Monday 8th September 1969 said while everybody else

---
46 Frederick forsyth The making of an African legend, The Biafra story Pg. 233 R.B. Alade The Broken bridge Pg 80.

was vacationing this summer, the secessionist regime of Biafra went about its now routine business starving "much of the responsibility for this calamity which has gone on for so long that few people outside the area pay much attention to it any longer, falls upon the harsh imperatives which halted all relief flight of the international committee of the Red Cross after early July."

Nigeria insisted as it had right to do, that relief cargoes must touch down in its territory for inspection but "Biafra's leadership regarded fulfillment of that demand as an acknowledgement of federal authority and it preferred to starve its own people instead."

Nigeria has magnanimously abandoned its earlier inspection demand. General Gowon, its leader, says Nigeria will allow food planes to fly into Biafra direct from Dahomey, he claims only a right to call down planes for inspection.

The Biafran Chief, Colonel Ojukwu, evidently is willing to accede to even more suffering and death rather than accept the new Nigerian stand. The world humanitarians were asked to be fair and appeal to Ojukwu.

The war had already continued into the third year but more people on the Biafran side started to shift support to the federal side, including Nnamdi Azikiwe. Obasanjo's wife, Oluremi, had their 1st son Nov. 4 1969, while Obasanjo was at the war front.

The Biafran relief problem was discussed again in London on the 16th of November 1969. The Prime Minister Mr. Harold Wilson who spoke at the Lord Mayor's banquet at the Guildhall said if Ojukwu tonight would agree to day light flights, the worst of the starvation and hunger could be ended within a week. He expressed surprise that Ojukwu was rejecting the agreement between the federal military government and the ICRC for mercy flights to his territory refusing to allow food passage under proper safeguards to go along road corridors. Mr. Wilson had said." The obvious conclusion would be that food supplies were being sacrificed to arms running. It might mean a starving people were used as pawns in his political and military struggles."

He said the tragedy in Nigeria was of great concern to the United Kingdom and Commonwealth. All appeals to Ojukwu fell on deaf ears as he still refused day time flights into Biafra. An Israeli, Mr. Abraham Mendenz, who was twenty-eight years old was interviewed by a Dutch newspaper called *Algemeen Handelzbald* said he had discovered arms in the Red Cross planes put there by an official for his private business.

Obasanjo, having taken over from Benjamin Adekunle, and the success on the federal side of drastically reducing the arms coming into Biafra, victory had begun to shine on the federal side. Obasanjo, within three months had faced the secessionist between the months of July and August as they attempted to recapture the town of Onitsha. They had put all their effort into recapturing Onitsha but their efforts were futile. They launched another attack middle August and it was a disaster for the Biafran side with over a thousand soldiers dead.

It was a loss from which they never recovered despite the new delivery of sophisticated weapons. Obasanjo was now convinced it would be better to advance on a broad front to Umuahia joining the first division and he then will cut of Biafra in half before turning to face Uli from the west. By the 4th of December he went to discuss with the first division to coordinate their efforts with his, but the divisional commander advised against moving before 15th of December. Obasanjo however ignored the advice, built up his supplies to advance northwards along Owerri and Oguta axis towards the strategic Uli air strip from where Biafra got all her supplies.

The 3rd marine commando had started a serious offensive against secessionist troops in Ikot Ekpene area and by about the 22nd of December had cleared the area and successfully linked with the troops of the 1st division which moved southwest from Umuahia. A whole brigade of secessionist troops were cut off and overwhelmed leading to the liberation of thousands of refugees numbering about 70,000 of southeastern origin and another 20,000 from Rivers State.

Federal troops followed this success up, crossed the Imo River west of Aba and Umuahia and drove west wards to within 6 miles of Owerri town. This led to capture of road towns like Okpuala and the road bridge over Imo River at the town of Owerrinta between Aba and Owerri. The 3rd marine commandos had held Obecha, the oil town of Oguta.

By 2nd January, 1970 federal troops continued shootings in owerri. In effect federal troops encircled the secessionists who were in the area around Nnewi on the East bank of the River Niger to orlu on the northern front.

On the 11th of January, 1970 it was announced that Owerri, the largest town held by the secessionist had fallen to federal troops, the day before Arochukwu and Otutu and Ohafia had been captured and liberated by Obasanjo's 3rd marine commandos and Col. Shuwa's

1st division troops. There were three coordinating links between these two divisions.

Ikot Ekpene and Umuahia, Ikot Ekpene and Aba and Ikot Ekpene and Bende, these coalitions cut Biafra in half slicing off about one quarter of the remaining land area. This deprived them of their large food growing area.

Obasanjo's federal troops then pushed on from Owerri and Obecha and bombarded the Uli air strip with artillery and aircraft and also attacked across the River Niger. The 122 mm Howitzer long range Russian guns then came to play and by 11th January 1970 the relief agencies that worked in Biafra knew the war was over, evacuating their personnel by suspending all flight, to Uli. The last plane that left carried 106 joint Church Aid workers out of the Biafran territory.

Col. Ojukwu on the 11th of January, 1970 announced he was flying out of Biafra to seek peace with the promise to return soon. This was announced in a tape recorded morning broadcast.

Lt. Col. Phillip Effiong from the Efik tribe told his troops to surrender and disengage in an orderly manner. It was joy and victory for Nigeria when Col. Olu Obasanjo spoke on radio Biafra which the federal forces had captured and to hear Mr. Okonkon Ndem, the favourite powerful secessionist broadcaster proclaim "long live United Nigeria." The radio station was re-christened radio Nigeria. The civil war was over and thirty months of the monstrous nightmare was over.

The nation needed reconciliation, resettlement rehabilitation and progress. The Igbos had taken note of Obasanjo's humane behaviour when he had always insisted soldiers must never shoot defenseless civilians or anybody at all who did not carry arms. However, were he irresponsible as had been done by others before the civil war began, he would have asked his men to continue killing defenseless people in a macabre celebration of victory.

Gowon at midnight on January 12, 1970 announced the end of the civil war, thirty gruelling months with about a million people dead and at a cost of 1.4 billion dollars.

Obasanjo's commendable leadership was officially acknowledged in Lagos on January 13, 1970. He received congratulatory message for victory and success from the Commander-in-Chief and the Chief of Army Staff, Brigadier Hassan Katsina.

In Owerri on January 14 1970, Obasanjo met the Biafran team of Phillip Effiong, Patrick Amadi, Patrick Ajwunah, David Ogunewe, Biafran police inspector, General P. Okeke, Louis Mbanefo, M.T. MBU, Eni Njoku and Chike Obi. They left in convoy for Port Harcourt en route Lagos.

CHAPTER TEN

Military Rule 1970-1975

Obasanjo was re-deployed to Lagos as army commander of the engineering corps in 1971 while Lt. Col. Theophilus Yakubu Danjuma took over in Port Harcourt. Before leaving he had become critical of Diete Spiffs government as they were reluctant to return the property of Igbos after the war. Obasanjo thought it unfair he declared he did not fight a war to reduce the Igbos to serfs in Nigeria. He was unhappy that Rivers State and its people were holding on to what did not belong to them.

The Rivers people held church services, parties, cultural display as send off in honour of the departing GOC. They were appreciative of his good leadership. Individuals like Ken Saro Wiwa also held parties in honour of Obasanjo. The most memorable legacy from the war front in Port Harcourt was a lady by name Gold Oruh who was a journalist that had come to interview Col. Obasanjo. They fell in love and a relationship started which ended up in marriage that produced two lovely children.

The people of Abeokuta and the Alake of Egba land trooped out to welcome the war hero. There was a long convoy of cars and buses and the little town burst into life, cheering and hailing the soldier. It was then the Alake in council conferred him with his first ancient Egba chieftaincy war title of *Jagunmolu*.

After the reception he returned to Lagos. His achievement at the war front and his capture of Biafra earned him respect and popularity among his peers and subordinates, bringing his status to an icon and moving uptown. Obasanjo had returned to peace time soldiering and had become a Brigadier, commanding the corps of engineers in Lagos.

The next five years from 1970 to 1975 were quiet for Obasanjo except in his private life. Success had come with its challenges; friends, relations and casual acquaintances began to visit the Obasanjos. Oluremi noticed a change in her husband – he became what she called a new man. The humorous, quiet and reserved man she knew before the war had suddenly become intolerant and ruthless to her; he had become unfriendly, impatient and leery of human intentions, she went on further to say his success had gone into his head.

But on the other hand Obasanjo did not believe the war made him a less responsible husband. It had not affected his family life or human relations. If any one had changed at all, he believed it was Oluremi who did not know how to handle their new social status. Suspicion and petty squabbles ate up into their romance when it should have been their greatest moments.

Obasanjo accused her of trying to isolate him from relatives and friends which he resented. Mrs. Obasanjo forgot her background here. Oluremi came from a polygamous home, as a daughter of Abeokuta's famous station master. Her father was a polygamist who had four wives and her mother was the second wife. She had forgotten that her father was Obasanjo's role model as a child and her husband was unconsciously acting like her father as he had become a man of the people.[47]

Obasanjo was a Brigadier in the army and lived alone in Lagos while his wife remained at Ibadan and had just recently given birth to their second son, Olugbenga – Obasanjo's fourth child on November 20, 1971.

Then Oluremi's father died on January 10, 1972 and Obasanjo played a big role as he handled the burial programme as if his own biological father had died. After the burial ceremony he asked Oluremi to move to Lagos. She agreed, but that he would have to find her a job as good as the University of Ibadan Guest house job. He got her a job with the Ibru's, the famous Urhobo family and she was put in charge of the guest houses for the menu preparations.

Then in November 1973 the fifth child was born, named Dayo but he passed on after two years. Then again on September 24, 1975 the Lord blessed the Obasanjos with another child who became the fifth surviving child.

The relationship between Obasanjo and Oluremi had become strained due to the interference of other women. Obasanjo had become so powerful in the army, government and society and was glowing like a bulb that attracted moths to it. There was definitely no hiding place for a gold fish even if he was cautious with spending money.

He later married Taiwo Martins Obasanjo, Linda Obasanjo and more were to come later. The marriage between Obasanjo and Oluremi became strained because Mrs. Oluremi Obasanjo during her younger

---
47 Oluremi Obasanjo Bitter Sweet, My life with Obasanjo Pg. 4

days had hoped for a monogamous marriage like Mr. and Mrs. Akisanya who were her role models at the time. Mr. Akisanya had been the principal of Baptist Boys High School, Abeokuta. Their relationship was harmonious and their conduct had convinced Oluremi that monogamous marriage was beautiful. However, she loved Obasanjo with a passion and did not want any other woman sharing him with her. That was why the relationship became strained by 1974 when other women came between them. Despite their differences, the marriage remains intact till today. Oluremi remain the first wife of Olusegun Obasanjo.

On the official side Obasanjo continued to work in the army, building barracks for the soldiers all over Nigeria as they were expected to quit running the government by 1976 when Gowon promised to hand over the government to civilians.

Major General David Ejoor had become chief of army staff while Ukpabi Asika was in his sixth year as East Central Administrator. He had worked successfully for a united Nigeria and had become very powerful and influential in the Gowon regime. History had vindicated him when the Biafran dream project failed.

Obasanjo had never lobbied for appointments and promotions but whenever he felt cheated over a selection process of officers for military courses he kicked. This was a time Brigadier Iliya Bisalla and Mohammed Shuwa had been selected by the Army Headquarters to attend senior officers course at Britain's Royal College of Defence Studies in 1974. They sidelined Obasanjo and selected Mohammed Shuwa. Obasanjo felt as their senior he was the right candidate to go. Then he had contacted Asika who diplomatically solved the problem by speaking with Gowon who in turn did what was proper. The Royal

College of Defence Studies was founded in 1927 but was originally called the Imperial Defence College until the name was changed in 1970 to reflect an international status as a result of its operations with NATO countries. Nigeria began its relations with the College in 1961 when it started sending Nigerian officers there for training. It was a yearly course with about thirty countries participating with about 75 – 80 students attending yearly.[48]

The College was designed to prepare the selected officers and officials for high responsibility in the direction of management of defence and security or other related areas of public policy. According to its charter the course was designed to train officers in defence and security issues in relation to the North Atlantic Treaty Organisation (NATO) and in the global security and strategic arena. Obasanjo did well as usual and returned to Nigeria after a year.

He had gained some new educational and military training but had also found happiness all over again on this trip to London in a new way where destiny had mapped out a new relationship with Stella Abebe. Then sometime in January 1975 Gowon announced his new cabinet reshuffles and Obasanjo emerged as Federal Commissioner for Works and Housing.

General Gowon was a handsome and dynamic young gentleman who had carried huge responsibility of unifying the country together during the civil war. He had performed creditably well as a humble and hard-working officer but as the norm in Nigeria, all political leaders faced their public criticicm no matter their good intentions for the nation. They said his government was visionless and the most corrupt but

---
[48] Adinoyi Ojo Onukaba *Olusegun Obasanjo in the eyes of time* Pg 193-5

till date every regime and government carries that tag today.

Obasanjo continued to work hard and had introduced the land use decree which vested the ownership of all land in the state as the property of the state government. This took effect by 1979. He also tackled the professionals whom he felt were over charging the government with their ten percent consultancy fee, engineers, architects, surveyors etc. He scaled down their fees to between 4-6 percent. The professionals were displeased at the time but the reduction saved the government huge sums of money.

Obasanjo did execute projects like highways, bridges and inner ring and state roads. He initiated the satellite town housing estate, the Durbar Hotel and 1004 flat complex in Victoria Island in Lagos.

He had also done the brave when the Nigerian government felt the American embassy was too close to the cabinet office in Lagos. He asked them to relocate which the American did not want to do and with the matter dragging on for two years until he drafted soldiers from the engineering corps to seize the building.

The government had offered them an alternative building but American diplomats did not respond until Obasanjo used the military force. He defended the action at the time affirming that Americans would not tolerate such impudence in their own country. He was accused of igniting a war between two countries. The matter was eventually resolved diplomatically behind the scene. Today almost forty years after, the American Embassy is still at Eleke Crescent (what is now known as Walter Carrington Crescent - renamed in honour of the American Ambassador) in Victoria Island Lagos.[49]

---
49 Ibid Pg 170-2 John Lliffe Obasanjo Nigeria and the world

The Gowon administration advanced economically by the huge oil revenues available during the oil boom that Nigeria witnessed at the period and embarked on a heavy structural development of the country. The government mapped out a six-year plan before handing over to a civilian government which was from 1st October 1970 – 1st October 1976.

They also made arrangement to repair and alleviate the problems of the country and people affected by the civil war. This was to go along with re-organising the armed forces.

The second national development plan also included the creation of additional states, reviewing the revenue allocation formula, conducting a national population census, tackling corruption, preparing the country for the formation of political parties and installing popularly elected civilian government for the states and the federal government. Gowon went on to establish the Nigerian Enterprise Promotion Decree in 1972, giving Nigerians opportunities to express themselves more in business areas controlled by foreigners.

Apart from these, the Gowon-led administration changed Nigeria's right-hand drive system to left hand - drive. The changing of decimal system or weights and measure to the metric system was also done. He then introduced the naira and kobo, scrapping the pound sterling. The government also introduced the Universal Primary Education (UPE) which allowed the compulsory free education scheme at the primary school nationwide.

In 1975 a crisis hit Nigeria with a corruption scandal involving Mr. Aper Aku, a TIV anti-corruption crusader who swore to an affidavit in court, accusing police commissioner Mr. Joseph Gomwalk of corruption. The head of state at the time exonerated him. Another crisis brewed, this was an allegation against the federal commissioner for communications Mr. Joseph Tarka by a loud and flamboyant anti-corruption crusader, Mr. Godwin Daboh, a fellow TIV. It was the press that brought the "Tarka must go" campaign. This spilled over to the Nigerian universities with demonstrations. Then the slogan came "If you Tarka me I will Daboh you."

However, the impunity of members of the cabinet and governors, including the permanent secretaries were heading in a dangerous dimension. The ports were congested with over 450 ships carrying 20 million tons of cement.The government had ordered too much cement at once and the facilities at the port could not handle the quantity ordered. The government was paying demurrage of ₦500,000 naira per day. To add to the problems, the 1973 census figures were irregular and this also led to series of protests.[50]

The government had also neglected agriculture and concentrated on the wealth from crude oil. Nigeria became a food importer when it had exported food to other countries before the civil war. There were so many mistakes in the government as they were still inexperienced in managing a developing nation. We cannot really blame them today as the country keeps learning.

Murtala Muhammed was very critical of the government that he went to advise Gowon to change his leadership style to regain public confidence and save the military from humiliation. Obasanjo knew things were bad in the country and did give his concerns at a private

---
50 Ibid Pg 44

audience with Gowon. He avoided discrediting and criticizing the regime he was serving in. He pleaded with the press, both at formal and informal meetings, to soft pedal on their criticisms of the government.

Murtala was less cautious as he was blunt, aggressive and often rude to Gowon, he could not stand Gowon's gentle style over crucial matters. Muhammed was extremely popular in the North and among Northern officers in the armed forces for leading the counter coup and the killing of the Igbos. He had become an icon and Gowon could not touch him for fear of offending the "Kano Mafia" who seemed to control Northern Nigeria. If Gowon had been a cruel, vicious and a tyrant like some other African leaders, Murtala Muhammed would have been eliminated silently.

In 1971 Obafemi Awolowo had become the federal commissioner for finance and vice chairman of the Federal Executive Council, making him the most powerful civilian in the Gowon team. Murtala had approached him to speak to Gowon to improve the financial situation of the country by curbing the corruption going on, but Awolowo could not do much as he was not the Head of State.

The government had planned to reduce the size of the army from 250,000 to about 150,000 but this was not done; only about 50,000 soldiers were retired despite the recommendation of the demobilisation committee that consisted of Obasanjo, Murtala and Danjuma.

Murtala Muhammed had resented Gowon's emergence as head of state during the 29 July, 1966 coup and had regretted till his death for not opposing his selection. He felt Gowon before assuming the nation's highest office had never commanded any unit in the army that was higher than a platoon, making him limited in experience. But the animosity had started since 1966 when the 29 July coup took place, when some powerful leaders in the North had set the two men against each other. Northern extremist saw Gowon, a Christian minority, born and raised in Wusasa, Zaria as an outsider. Murtala Muhammed, a Fulani Muslim was from Kano and these powerful groups felt he should be Head of State, saying afterall, the coup was staged to restore political power to the (Hausa-Fulani) North.

And from 1966 – 1972 their relationship had been strained. Murtala had approached Col. Obasanjo back in October 1969 while leading the third marine commando and other divisional commanders to engineer a coup against Gowon from the battle field. He wanted Obasanjo and his other colleagues to hold Lagos to ransom by refusing to stop the war unless Gowon agreed to be replaced by a presidential commission of three officers who would govern by consensus. Obasanjo politely refused because such plan when executed would jeopardise the federal effort at stopping the war and giving Biafra an advantage. He promised to speak with Gowon after the war. When the war ended Murtala Muhammed was not given any special post in the new government and was left at the signals corps. Joseph Garba's reconciliation efforts only brought temporary relief from the time the war ended and the trauma was over.

Nigeria's economy began to flourish as a result of crude oil sales. Five years after the civil war ended crude oil contributed to 99 percent of the country's revenue. It was the paradise of oil wealth Nigeria had become a member of the Organisation of Petroleum Exporting Countries (OPEC) in 1971, thereby creating a leverage at the international world market for oil producers. The Arab-Israeli war in 1973 where the Arabs imposed an embargo on crude oil sales to the west had given Nigeria a bigger share to its oil quotas, which automatically triggered a price increase. Nigeria's oil was the substitute for the oil bought from Middle East countries. This was a time of boom for Nigeria as the country produced 2.3 million barrels a day.

The economy was awash with oil money and there was unlimited cash in supply. The governors and leaders in various sectors became arrogant and irrational and lost focus of what to do with the funds. There was rural urban drift as people headed from the villages and rural areas to the city in droves, ignoring agriculture.

The governors had become uncontrollable and lost direction in the management of funds and public affairs. Gowon aggravated the situation when he failed to honour his promise in 1971 where he declared that the country will return to civilian rule by 1974. He had cancelled the hand over date, offering no alternative date, implying an indefinite military government.

However, the economy later started facing problems as inflation increased along with the award of salary bonuses known as Udoji Award which was named after Jerome Udoji, who presided over the review and increase in civil servant salaries.

Then early in 1975 Gowon after the Commonwealth Heads of State/Government meeting which he attended in Jamaica went for a state visit to Grenada, an Ireland of about 90,000 people. Gowon had committed Nigeria to pay the salaries of all Grenadan civil servants granting it a loan of five million and also sending Nigerian police officers to train the Grenadan police. This was not a bad idea but back home Nigerians saw this as reckless show off as it's own people were far from solving their own problems.

As laudable as some of these programmes were, they ended up with poor implementation as most government policies. However in 1975 everything would change again.

Chapter Eleven

Stella Obasanjo

Mrs. Stella Obasanjo was born Stella Abebe on November 14, 1945 in the city of Warri in present Delta State Nigeria. She was the first child of the seven children born to Dr. and Mrs. Christopher Abebe. They were upper middle class elite family; very quiet and reserved.

Dr. Abebe was the first indigenous chairman of the United African Company (U.A.C) which was a blue chip and multinational company. The family was very comfortable and the children lacked nothing. Dr. Abebe was a disciplined man who lived a quiet conservative life style.

Stella attended Our Lady of Apostles Primary School, Yaba, Lagos from 1955 to 1959. In 1960 she enrolled in St. Theresas College, Ibadan, and later passed the West African School Certificate Examination in 1965 and then completedthe A Levels/HSC in 1967. She proceeded to the University of Ife where she studied English from 1967 – 1969. However, she did not finish the degree before she relocated to England where she got interested in insurance and enrolled for a degree from 1970-1974. She also trained as a confidential secretary at Pitmans College, London.

After her A levels she went for a teaching job at Holy Child College in Lagos before going to the University of Ife in 1969 to study modern language. She however did not like the course and stayed only a year and half since she could not change the course.

While waiting to begin on her next plan of action, her father got her a temporary job with United Insurance Company (UNIC) in Lagos. It was from her job experience she got interested in insurance. They promoted her to take a course in insurance and she started taking part time classes in professional insurance, then came the Part I Professional Insurance Examination in which she did very well. It was her success in the examination that prompted UNIC Insurance to send her for additional training at their headquarters in London in 1971.[51]

Before she left for London, as destiny would play its game, she met Obasanjo in 1971 in Lagos. She was twenty-six years old and was still single. It was through Mr. Ndalugi and Mr. Bayo Ajao, a businessman that she first met Obasanjo. This was shortly after the war when Obasanjo's profile was rising already as he was the commander that brought the civil war to an end after he took over from Benjamin Adekunle. Obasanjo had told Ndalugi that he liked Stella but since he was still married he treaded cautiously. He knew her parents and liked their family. Then in 1974 when Obasanjo went on course through the army at the Royal College of Defence Studies destiny again brought them together.

Obasanjo had always socialised with select crowds of Nigerians hosting a good number of friends, relations

---

[51] https://en.wikipedia.org/wiki/stellaobasanjo Encyclopedia.com http://biography.jrank.org/page/2978/obasanjo-Stella.html Stella Obasanjo biography.

and his colleagues passing through London or visiting. He had done this to avoid a lone ranger kind of life and that was what kept him up to date on the happenings around him and the world.

He would discuss with different categories of people and hear their views on different subjects and happening around the world. This actually prepared him for greatness. Victor Ndalugi who was Managing Director of Vono products, the company that made mattress beds and furniture had just resigned to set up his own business and was among Obasanjo's visitors. In fact he was staying there and had called Stella to come down and pick her letters and other gifts sent by her parent. She collected the address: Number 6, Park Square West. Then she came along with her friends, Willie and Juli Murray Bruce who also knew Ndalugi. Willies father, Murray Bruce, had also worked in the UAC but in the Kingsway departmental stores, Murray Bruce left Kingsway and bought Yaba stores, renaming it Domino Stores.

They had met Ndalugi alone at home but shortly after Obasanjo arrived he renewed his interest. This was three years after their first meeting and she was now twenty-nine years old while he was thirty-seven years old. She had again resisted the relationship on the excuse he was married and also that he was much older than she was, but it was the normal resistance a well-brought up lady often put up to an aspiring suitor.

It was her looks, the colour of her skin, eyes and the way she carried herself that struck Obasanjo and every time he saw her his heart did seem to skip.[52] It was like a feeling that something was missing in his life. He also

---
52 Adinoyi Ojo Onukaba, *Olusegun Obasanjo, In the eyes of time* Pg. 197-199

knew her family and adored them. He tried harder by sending her money which she returned and also invited her for a tour of some European cities.

Then she reported him to her brother, John, who was a medical student in London, the idea was for him to come and see the man that was chasing her. Her brother immediately took to Obasanjo and he encouraged him to capture her.

The Alake of Egba land, Oba Oyebade Lipede was visiting London and he stayed with Obasanjo. He had just been installed the new Alake of Egba land and Obasanjo had a party for him. Stella was invited and with pressure from her friends she did attend, making it her second visit to Obasanjo's house and she enjoyed the party. After that her attitude changed and she started considering his proposal.

Then on July 29, 1975, few weeks after Obasanjo had returned to Nigeria, she heard of Obasanjo's elevation as the new Chief of Staff Supreme Headquarters (i.e. the Deputy Head of State so to speak). All this while, she had finished her studies but she did not want to comeback to Nigeria. Her father also had become chairman of UAC, making him one of the most powerful men in corporate Nigeria.

Dr. Abebe visited London in 1976 and felt Stella should return home. She at first resisted but he convinced her to return with him. By the time Stella arrived in Nigeria Unic insurance company had changed the company, hired new staff and things were done differently. Since she was not bonded to them she opted out of going back to work there and remained in her father's house planning what to do with her life.

Then Obasanjo started calling to ask her for a lunch date but she kept refusing, sometimes her parents picked up the phone and innocently passed it to her.

It was Ndalugi and Ajao that informed Obasanjo that Stella was back in Nigeria. She had confronted Ndalugi and Ajao that the man is married and they told her he was divorced. Then Obasanjo invited her to another party which she attended along with her friend, Grace Odiri. It was a joint birthday party for his three children. It was after the party they got married in 1976.

After the assassination of Murtala Muhammed, Obasanjo became Head of State. Obasanjo was Head of State but there was nothing like the role for first ladies. He had always tried to keep his family out of the spotlight because he had always felt government is about serious business not showing off with family members. He gave them what he felt was enough for their survival and education.

When Obasanjo handed over they both returned to Ota farm where they retired from the military life. Stella had stayed home to raise her family and was a housewife attending to all Obasanjo's needs taking care of the home front and sometimes giving advise on the management of the farm when her opinion was needed.

They travelled together occasionally and it was not until 1999 that she became a public figure as first lady, when Obasanjo became civilian president which was his second coming to run the affairs of Nigeria.

The office of the first lady had started with Victoria Gowon. She was not very visible and had performed minimal ceremonial functions. She hardly appeared in the public eye but was visible with state functions like when you had other heads of states visiting Nigeria from around the world. After General Gowon was overthrown in 1975 the office went into oblivion until Mrs. Maryam Babangida emerged in 1985 as first lady of Nigeria. She brought up a pet project to keep her in the limelight called Better Life for Rural Women. The focus was to uplift women in the rural areas of Nigeria.

Then came Mrs. Mariam Abacha with her Family Support Programme. Then Justice Fati Abubakar, wife of the Head of State, Abubakar, came up with Women's Rights Advancement and Protection Alternative.

Stella Obasanjo had to force her husband, the president, to allow her to be an active first lady. He had announced initially that there would be no first lady project but emissaries were sent from all over to plead with him before he gave the nod for the position of the first lady to be recognised. Stella Obasanjo then came up with her own project called Child Care Trust. It focused on the less privileged children.

Mrs. Obasanjo said at the time that she had always believed that disabled children could live productive lives and contribute to national development if given the necessary assistance and support. Their talents and skills can be developed and enhanced by early treatment and management of the condition. What made her special to Obasanjo was Stella's efforts during his incarceration by the Abacha government that falsely accused him of planning a coup. Stella went all over the world meeting world leaders to intervene on behalf of Obasanjo so that General Abacha would get him released. Obasanjo never involved in coups or plots to overthrow any government and he had been outside the country when the accusations started. He boldly and confidently returned to Nigeria because his hands were clean. However they said he was guilty where there was no offence and guilt. When Abacha died and he was released he was thankful to all and grateful to Stella.

At the peak of Obasanjo's first term in 1999-2003 both the president and first lady had their profile up town. Stella was so beautiful that some people called her "Baby Doll." Complementing Obasanjo, the two were a fantastic match. The famous Bill Clinton visit to Nigeria with Stella dancing with Bill Clinton at the dinner and ball party at Aso Rock villa made her more popular. Then the president and Stella on another occasion did go shopping in a normal store in Abuja and everybody was excited watching on television, marveling and wishing they were at the shop to meet them one on one.

Then after Obasanjo came in for a second term successfully, many of his enemies became bitter that they launched an attack on Obasanjo's first daughter, Iyabo. Iyabo's convoy was shot at, killing the two children of her friend who she was sitting with in her own car. The children had innocently wanted to see what a tinted car would look like riding inside it. This wicked people threw the nation into mourning as many people were sad about the incident.

The enemies not satisfied again planned another attack that would hit Obasanjo badly and they neatly hatched their plan two years later.

Stella was turning sixty years when they plotted again. It started with close friends asking her to do cosmetic surgery so she could look forty years old on the day. Stella Obasanjo was a very beautiful woman and Obasanjo was not complaining about her looks. She was advised to go for cosmetic surgery to take away some lines from around her eyes and ageing marks.

She did their wish, appeared on television with dark goggles protecting her newly done surgery as she did say on television at an event where she announced she would only stay briefly. Then they encouraged her again to do her stomach to crown her looks so she can be slim like a young girl. Then again under pressure she agreed, not knowing that danger awaited her. The plan was already hatched as her friends who had houses and apartments abroad where the surgery was to take place had recommended the cosmetic plastic surgeon. It was only a simple procedure, almost 100% safe but sinister motives had been planned for the Doctor to do a bad job that would bring death.

On Monday 17th, 2005, she went to Spain for the surgery, a tummy tuck to flatten the stomach in Marbella but never to return. The doctor was bought by enemies in Nigeria, to sabotage the operation. The surgery took place at a private health clinic in Puerto Banus Marbella, Spain on 23rd October 2005.

The surgeon identified only as AM in court was sentenced to one year imprisonment in September 2009 on a charge of causing homicide through negligence. He was disqualified from medicine for a period of three years and ordered to pay £120,000 approximately in compensation to Stella Obasanjo's son. Prosecutors requested two years jail term and five years disqualification.

A request for compensation for the Nigerian government was also rejected. The physician had misplaced a tube designed for a liposuction procedure into Mrs. Obasanjos abdominal cavity, thereby causing a punctured colon and lacerated liver which led to her death two days after the surgery.

The nation mourned her death because Stella was a different kind of first lady. She had her style. She was simple and was not loud and extravagant and she helped lots and lots of people who came her way.

CHAPTER TWELVE

Military Rule 1975 - 1979: Obasanjo Emerges Emperor

A new dawn began on July 29, 1975. It was the day commemorating the day the northern officers did a counter coup in 1966 but this was nine years after in which another coup was taking place. The chief conspirators were Lt. Col Joseph Garba and Shehu Musa Yar'Adua. Others were Abdullahi Mohammed, Ibrahim Taiwo, Muhammadu Buhari, Ibrahim Babangida, Lieutenant Colonel Muktar Muhammed, Alfred Aduloju and Ibrahim Alfa. The coup was very successful and was called a palace coup, where there had been agreements to shed no blood.[53]

Gowon was far away attending an Organisation of African Unity (OAU) Heads of State meeting in Kampala, Uganda.[54] He was aware of the coup as his intelligence officers warned him before it was hatched. By the early hours of July 29 the coup plotters were in control of such strategic locations as the Airport, the national radio, the Ikeja cantonment, army barracks,

---
53 Adinoyi Ojo Onukaba pg 216
54 Elaigwu Gowon Chapter 13 Olufemi Ogunsanwo, General Yakubu Gowon, The Supreme Commander Pg 98

Bonny camp and other military installations in Lagos. it was swift.

Joseph Garba who acted as spokesman formally announced the end of Gowon's nine year rule and clamped a dusk to dawn curfew on the nation. They closed all the land, air space and sea borders. They declared the day work free and appealed to the public to be calm and law-abiding.

This was coup number three in Nigeria. The reactions were however mixed. The Gowon loyalists were not pleased, but were handicapped and could do nothing. Murtala Muhammed was away in London but flew in that very day from London to attend a meeting with senior officers.

As highlighted earlier, Gowon was privy to the coup as he was warned by Obasanjo who said he heard a rumour of a coup. Abdullahi Mohammed had warned him of the coup and in return he had notified Gowon. Obasanjo commanded no troops being in the engineering department but he was respected for his civil war efforts.

He was never ambitious and power-driven and that was the master key that got him to the top. Obasanjo however remained glued to the newspapers and television until he was invited to a stormy meeting. The coup plotters had agreed they would appoint others to run the affairs of Nigeria, people who they felt could perform and be trusted. They said they would hand over to three Brigadiers and demanded Murtala be invited to be head of state even though he was junior to Obasanjo.

Obasanjo said he was ready to serve as second in command provided he had substantial responsibilities.

They wanted the supreme military council to have a veto power over the triumvirate decision as they did not want another over-powerful Gowon. But Murtala became loud, refusing to be head of state on such an arrangement where his hands will be tied, he wanted to run Nigeria as he saw best. When he was not in agreement they asked him to excuse them, Oh, it was a trick from the North to test how ambitious Obasanjo was going to be and his reactions to their offers.

Garba then offered Obasanjo the position of head of state. But he was wiser than a tortoise and said he could accept the triumvirate option as he, representing the Yoruba together with a Northerner and Danjuma a middle belt representative. Obasanjo said he was neither stupid nor overambitious enough to accept such an offer on such conditions. What part did he play in the coup to dictate or jump at a carrot dangling with dangers lurking around it.[55]

Abdullahi Mohammed intervened convincing Murtala to accept and that if he refused they would announce the terms of his refusal where he finally accepted. The coup plotters now announced they will not be a part of the government.

Obasanjo cleverly vetoed the suggestion realising it would lead to another coup within a short time. Obasanjo had gained power again without seeking it. He became Chief of Staff, Supreme Headquarters.[56] Garba became commissioner for external affairs while Yar'Adua became commissioner for transportation. The new government decided to retire officers above the rank of Brigadier, cancelled the census in an

---
55 Adinoyi Ojo Onukaba Pg 218; John Lliffe *Obasanjo Nigeria and the world* Pg 43.
56 Obasanjo – *Not My Will* pp 11-14.

announcement by the new Head of State, Murtala Muhammed because of the disputes in the true population figures.

Obasanjo had kept a low profile and did not make himself visible but was the brain and work horse behind the regime. Murtala and Obasanjo solved most of the problems that had affected the previous regime of Gowon like the "cement Amarda" where they imported too much cement at a go, thereby causing congestion at the port with 20 million tons of cement to be offloaded from 450 ships. Some of the ships were eventually diverted to Ghana to offload.

The Murtala/Obasanjo regime introduced and implemented a low profile in the management of Nigeria's economy and in the conduct of government business. Obasanjo was investigated concerning corruption many times but they later discovered that he got many of his assets through due process. Properties were often acquired through process of down payment. You could pay in installments of up to four to five times as agreed by the seller which is not done today where it is cash and carry.

The new government continued to make reforms, downsizing on the army and civil service. There was a purge where the super permanent secretaries that managed the economy were sacked, it was called "Operation Dead Wood." The universities too were affected at the time and many people lost their jobs as a result of revenge and witch-hunting. Obasanjo later admitted the process degenerated into callousness and sadism. The result was the loss of skilled economic managers.

However, Obasanjo said that rather than relying on some civil servants and politicians, as Gowon had done, they turned to other groups and professionals who served on advisory commissions. The members were picked from the universities thereby bringing professors, political activists and technocrats who were considered as egg heads and making them a think tank for the Murtala government.

Murtala and Obasanjo did a lot of things within the first three months of being in office and they worked tirelessly all round the clock, brainstorming on state matters till as late as 3 a.m. in the morning of the next day.

The government of Murtala had thought about the need to create additional states. Then on August 7, 1975 a four-man committee was set up with justice Ayo Irikefe emerging as the chairman and by 3rd January 1976 Murtala announced the recommendations of the committee and seven new states were approved Ogun State being among the seven with its capital at Abeokuta. Justice Irikefe had recommended Ijebu ode but Obasanjo changed it to Abeokuta being the former colonial headquarters of the area.

The government continued to work, setting up task force to tackle inflation and hoarding of goods and also to check astronomical rents charged by landlords on their tenants in Lagos and major cities in Nigeria.

Human rights abuses by the former government of Gowon where there were about fifty detainees in prison custody on trumped up charges like civil war crimes etc were revisited. These people were released unconditionally with no case to answer.

Then on the 11th of August, 1975 Justice Akinola Aguda was appointed to head a seven-man panel whose role was constituted to find a new capital for Nigeria. Lagos had played the dual role of both federal and state capital and due to the congestion and chaotic traffic situation Abuja was approved as the new federal capital to be effected within a decade. It was during the government of Gowon that the idea had come like Brazil's Brasilia but it was Murtala and Obasanjo, the action men, that implemented it.[57]

The government was so dynamic that they solved the immediate traffic problems and the government also worked on infrastructural expansions. In Lagos, apart from building new bridges, they temporarily introduced the odd number–even number policy that solved the problem of traffic congestion. Monday, Wednesday and Fridays were for the odd numbers while Tuesday and Thursday were even number days. It was a system which restricted vehicles from going to the Island on those days between 6a.m. – 6p.m. but after 6p.m. you were able to drive your car to any point without hindrances. But trust Nigerians, they buckled their belts tighter and bought an extra car or two to beat the system. It was the days of Champaign Taste, there was oil money and things were good, as cars were affordable. There was a car loan scheme and things were working fine. Middle class and students were given bursary (scholarship grants) so life was good, everybody wanted to go to the university as Nigeria's future was promising. The government was taking care of things and progress was visible.[58]

---

57 Olusegun Obasanjo *Not My Will* pg. 17-18
58 Adinoyi Ojo Onukaba, *Olusegun Obasanjo, In the eyes of time* Pg 124.

Then on 1st October, 1975 the government setup a Constitution drafting committee headed by the legendary Rotimi Williams, one of Nigeria most respected lawyers which drafted a new constitution for Nigeria.

Obasanjo, in a television interview on October 26, 1975 gave reasons why the government churned out many policies within three months. He said the second republic Constitution was not going to be a document imposed on the people but one of consensus. He identified three defects in the old Constitution which include ethnic politics, the concept of winner takes all and institutionalised opposition which he said the government would keep out of the new Constitution. He also announced that within four years Murtala would hand over to civilians, putting the date at October 1, 1979.[59]

In January 1976 another promotion within the army took place. Murtala became a full General while Obasanjo and Danjuma became Lieutenant Generals. Those senior to Danjuma in the army kicked but were pacified with the explanation that the promotion came as a result of the position he was holding at the time.

The government continued to work on dualizing roads and building infrastructures all over the country. Murtala and Obasanjo had a special relationship unusual to many it seemed. One moment they would be yelling at each other and within a few minutes later they would be laughing. They never disagreed to the point of holding grudges against each other. Obasanjo was more sober and reflective while Murtala

---
59 New Nigerian 6th October, 1975.
   Olusegun Obasanjo *Not My Will* Pg 20

Muhammed was tough, aggressive but charismatic. Obasanjo often called him "Muri." While Murtala and Obasanjo both had volcanic tempers but one often allowed the other to have his way when they got to crossroads in a decision block. They often did what they felt was best for Nigeria as a nation.

Obasanjo made himself accessible and people did not have to book an appointment to see him. He always had a good working relationship. High ranking officers such as governors, federal commissioners and senior military officers never had to book an appointment to see him. The government of Murtala Muhammed was reconstituted with three powerful arms of government in the military structure.

The Supreme Military Council (SMC) became the highest policy-making body with 22 members with the head of state as chairman. Service chiefs were the new members while the military governors were excluded in the new arrangement.

The governors were accommodated in a lower body known as the National Council of State (NCS) which was in charge of policies on the concurrent list, those involving both centre and states and the head of state also chaired its meetings.

The third tier of authority at the centre was the Federal Executive Council (FEC). This took care of the implementation of policies. States had a similar organ known as State Executive Council with the governor as chairman. The Chief of Staff Supreme Headquarters CSSHQ became very powerful. This was Obasanjo's new position and so the governors and Police Service Commission were under his office. This turned him into an emperor, the power behind the throne. He became the second most powerful officer and citizen in Nigeria. From then on there was no going back, his profile began to rise despite his humble nature.

Then on Friday February 13, 1976 tragedy struck. Murtala was assassinated by dissident officers who attacked his car in Lagos traffic on his way to work at 8a.m. in the morning, this was the fourth coup. Then at 8:30a.m. one of the coup plotters detailed to assassinate Obasanjo mistakenly shot another officer called Colonel Raymond Dumuje who looked like Obasanjo.

That day colonel Olu Bajowa had an appointment to see the second in command, Olusegun Obasanjo at his home at 36, Lugard Avenue, Ikoyi which had been his residence since he was appointed commander of the engineering corps. Bajowa had gone there on behalf of disgruntled majors, lieutenant colonels and colonels who had fears their careers in the military was coming to an end with the plan of the government to trim down the size of the armed forces. Obasanjo had calmed him down that whoever was retired would be assisted in settling down to civilian life.

Bajowa left Obasanjo's residence only for a junior officer named Omowa to rush in five minutes later in tears, narrating how he had seen General Murtala Muhammed's dead body in his black Mercedes Benz car near the petrol station, opposite the federal secretariat complex in Ikoyi.

Obasanjo in shock found this hard to believe, wondering why anybody would want to kill Murtala Muhammed. Then came in more people, Akanni Amodu, Obasanjo's senior at the Baptist Boy's High School and then staff members of NEPA who lived opposite Obasanjo in their official block of flats.

Then Col. Dimka and his group took over the NBC studio at Ikoyi and went on to address his fellow country men, denouncing Murtala a hypocrite and announcing the overthrow of his government along with all its top functionaries by group of "young revolutionaries." He announced closures of all seaports, airports and borders.

Obasanjo woke up to the reality that he was a target as second in command, which implies that his house was not safe. He went into hiding in a safe place armed with his pistol and telephone book. It was only elites that had telephones at the time. Amodu's house did not have one so he opted for S.B. Bakare's house, "Ijesha lodge," where nobody suspected he could be.

He made telephone calls from S.B. Bakare's bedroom to the police Inspector General M.D. Yusufu asking of the situation of things and where Danjuma was as head of the Army. He was relieved to discover that Danjuma was rallying troops who were loyal to the Murtala regime in which he served and that gave him assurance that he was not a participant in the coup. He had been a target but the coupist ordered to assassinate him failed to do so. Second Lieutenant Lawrence Garba was instructed not to launch an attack where there were many officers.

Danjuma that morning was in the company of the Chief of Naval Staff, Rear Admiral Michael Adelanwa, Staff Officer Colonel Alabi Isama, and Colonel Domkat Bali of Staff Headquarters. They should be all thankful to Alabi Isama today who had given them a ride in his speed boat to the office that day. He had saved their lives.

Failure to assassinate Obasanjo and Danjuma brought the coup to a quick end. However as Danjuma, Obasanjo, MD Yusuf, Colonel Muhammadu Buhari had continued to work frantically to get cooperation and loyalty from all the army formations, the army boss, T.Y Danjuma, then sent for Colonel Ibrahim Badamasi Babangida who was Commander of the Recce Squadron and ordered him to secure the Ikeja cantonment and bring back some armored cars. The Ikeja cantonment was the most strategic military installations in the city of Lagos and until you had this secured you had nothing as it also controlled Ibadan and Abeokuta. Danjuma had instructed he goes in a motor bike to beat the traffic. This he did. Babangida spoke to Dimka to give up at the NBC radio and television station at Ikoyi and when he refused Babangida advised him to escape and he left him and later returned to Danjuma.

Danjuma got mad when the report got to him and he sent him Babangida back but Dimka had however escaped. Babangida only got verbal spanking from Danjuma, his Godfather. Whereas it was a court marshall offence but the press boomed a different story he stormed the place to dislodge the gun totting Dimka and his troops. The coup was eventually foiled and thirty-nine officers who participated in the coup were executed including Dimka and Bisalla.[60]

Murtala Muhammed was buried according to Muslim rites within 24 hours and a curfew was imposed the day he was buried in Kano. The press did not publish any photographs and the press down south was asked to abstain from writing and making media

---

60 Adinoyi Ojo Onukaba Pg 20.

statements about his successor. There was tension in the North as their hero who avenged the January 15, 1966 coup carried out by the Eastern Soldiers had died in the hands of assassins. The radical Islamic teacher, Abubakar Gumi, with his inciting statements almost provoked another crisis in Nigeria when he aroused emotions calling the assassination of Murtala – a Christian coup. After the civil war the Yorubas had replaced the Igbos as objects of rivalry and suspicion in the North of Nigeria and Gumi's statement sparked of rumours that Yoruba induced the middle belt Christians in the military to carry out the coup which was such shallow thinking. It was the Emir who saved the day when he cautioned and warned trouble makers not to start any ethnic conflagration again, concluding that Obasanjo had been Murtala's very close confidant and friend.[61]

After the Murtala coup and execution of Dimka and the other coup plotters, nobody tried any nonsense, for the fear of Obasanjo was the beginning of wisdom. Disgruntled and ambitious soldiers kept their ambitions in the cooler until Obasanjo handed over to a civilian government in 1979.

---

61 *Newswatch* 2 November 1992 Pg 14 John Lliffe, *Obasanjo Nigeria and the world* Pg 49.

CHAPTER THIRTEEN

Obasanjo Becomes Head Of State 1976-1979

Before Obasanjo was sworn-in as head of state, the ruling elite up north contemplated sidelining Obasanjo by installing another northerner to replace Murtala Muhammed. It was the conservatives in northern Nigeria along with Theophilus Danjuma and Joe Garba that swiftly used their wisdom to overrule such idea believing it would trigger an unrest similar to the civil war.

The best option was to do the proper thing by giving power to the next in command. Lt. Col. Shehu Musa Yar'Adua was chosen as his deputy. Obasanjo became head of state and maintained a low profile throughout. He was intelligent and had the ability to secure full support in decisions and implementation of policies within the Supreme Military Council. He was transparently patriotic, very wise and continued to show willingness to learn new things. He was a shinning star as he never made any attempt to bid or force himself into positions of authority and power. It was his destiny at play, share hard work and luck.

Obasanjo continued with many of the Murtala Muhammed policies they had fine tuned together in the first six months of Murtala's administration.[62] It was not until a year after that Murtala's pictures were removed from most offices around Nigeria and replaced by that of Obasanjo.

Obasanjo tackled the problem of inflation and agriculture which was on a decline as oil had taken the spotlight. However, with the population increasing at the time to over 70 million, Obasanjo had cautioned that Nigeria had good potentials to become a great nation but that it was not a rich one.[63]

He worked with determination to get the budget balanced without too much deficits. The government kept its low profile by reducing unnecessary spendings, they avoided capital intensive projects and concentrated on agriculture, health, education and housing.

The economic managers at the time had preferred a stronger currency as opposed to a devalued currency. This had kept Nigeria's economy more stable and predictable and had kept the inflation down. Foreigners from mostly the developed countries had forgotten the fact that African economies were not production-based or driven, meaning, we were not inventing or making finished products as our economy and exports remain unprocessed so it was not wise to allow the currency to float and be determined strictly by the forces of demand and supply.

Operation Feed the Nation was a success, only mischievous people felt it had no impact. I can categorically say that those who tried it discovered it

---
[62] Liman Ciroma in Weekly Trust 18 September 1998 John Lliffe – Obasanjo Nigeria and the World pg 56.
[63] Daily Times 1 April 1976

worked, having your own small garden to grow food. People who grew banana and plantain discovered they only bought plantain in the market three months in a year. They were self-sufficient for nine months even giving out excess to their loved ones. Those who tried it can attest to the fact that the programme helped a lot of Nigerians.[64]

The government did irrigation schemes and built dams around Nigeria to help peasant farmers.

Towards the end of Gowon's regime to the time Obasanjo took over from Murtala, the oil boom was over. There was fluctuation in the oil price around the world. OPEC (Organization of Petroleum Exporting Countries) had caused an energy crisis in Europe and America due to the increase in the price of oil fixed by the cartel. This forced the industrial countries to look elsewhere for cheap oil which they found in non-OPEC member countries and the exploration of new oil fields in Alaska Mexico and the North Sea.

OPEC however fought back, cutting its output and forcing members to reduce production while maintaining the fixed price. This affected Nigeria's daily production output and made her oil the most expensive around the world because the light Bonny crude favourite to the west was expensive to produce due to the marshy terrain of the Niger Delta.

Nigeria had to break OPEC prices by cutting the price of oil to stay in business. However, before he left office Nigeria and OPEC[65] countries along with other oil producing countries enjoyed another oil boom as the Iranian revolution took place in 1979. Iran erupted

---
64   Olusegun Obasanjo *Not My Will* pg 80
65   Petroleum Economist, November 1977 Pg 454.

denouncing western values and lifestyle and opted for a government system, based and tilted towards religious beliefs.

This kicked up the price of oil as Iran stopped doing business to the united states and its western allies and Nigeria's oil price rose from about $12 dollars to as high as $40 per barrel as a result of the closure of the Iranian market.

Obasanjo had also revisited the policy of nationalisation and indigenisation which was first introduced during the Gowon regime but then Obasanjo took interest and further expanded the idea. He nationalised the oil industry including British Petroleum and changed the Nigerian National Oil Corporation into the Nigerian National Petroleum Corporation (NNPC) but foreign interest remained for expertise. Obasanjo had commissioned the LNG liquefaction plant at Bonny which cost 4.5 billion dollars in which the NNPC financed 60% of the project cost.

The (Festac) Festival of Black and African Arts and Culture took place in Lagos in January 1977. It was an unforgettable cultural and artistic event featuring drama, music, poetry and all forms of visual arts and till date, it remains one of the most memorable events in Nigeria with the IPI Tombi musical group and stars like Mariam Makeba. Chief Awolowo was pleased and the Nigerian *Tribune* wrote of Obasanjo's brilliant performance. Oppositions to his policies levied against him allegations of corruption but non of them can be substantiated.[66]

There were some economic crises when the price of oil dropped and inflation was high but the situation was

---
66 Obasanjo March of progress Pg 108 Soyinka - you must set forth Pg 230

salvaged by austerity measures. Then students' protest, in April 1978, the "Ali must go" riot where tuition fees went up and meal ticket was raised from 20kobo to 50kobo rocked the nation but soon after, another oil boom stabilised Nigeria's economic deficits with the Iranian Revolution. Then the Land Use Decree was one of the unforgettable policies introduced and it was added to the 1979 Constitution. It has continued to raise controversy till date. It was designed to discourage land hoarding and speculation.

The land use decree was made in March 1978. The decree gave the federal and state governments the right over all lands in Nigeria. Previous owners of undeveloped lands were given certificate of occupancy. The southern part of Nigeria was not pleased where land ownership belonged to different families. It was seen as the abolition of private property in land.

Then Obasanjo had started a romance with America in October 1977 when he paid a six day official visit to the United States. The Americans had not shown much interest in Africa but the trip gave Obasanjo a new experience and exposure on the international level. At the White House banquet in his honour he justified armed struggle and urged the United States to put political pressure to end apartheid in South Africa by using sanctions. He had said it was one of the powerful options to coerce the South African government to act.

Two weeks later Nigeria got the coveted seat on the United Nations Security Council. Then Jimmy Carter came on a State visit in April 1978 along with his wife to Nigeria. It was the first time a sitting American president would visit Nigeria.[67]

---

67   Comrade Lekan Aderibigbe Obasanjo for Nigeria pg 231.

Obasanjo on the other hand had a cold relationship with Britain resulting from the refusal to send Gowon back to Nigeria to answer questions about his knowledge of the coup where Murtala Muhammed was killed, and also on Britain's policy on other African countries like South Africa and Zimbabwe who were yet to get independence. However, Britain continued to be one of Nigeria's strongest trading partners.

On the 21st of September, 1978 General Olusegun Obasanjo lifted the ban on political activities in Nigeria. Then in 1979, through the promulgation of a decree establishing the Federal Electoral Commission (FEDECO) as part of government programme for the transition to civilian rule, the electoral commission in 1979 conducted the elections where five political parties participated. They were the National Party of Nigeria (NPN), Unity Party of Nigeria (UPN), Nigeria People's Party (NPP), Peoples Redemption Party (PRP) and the Great Nigeria People's Party (GNPP).

In August 1979 Alhaji Shehu Shagari of the National Party of Nigeria (NPN) was declared the winner in the 1979 presidential elections. Alhaji Shehu Shagari polled 5,688,587 votes while Chief Obafemi Awolowo scored 4,916,651 million votes. Awolowo had 25 percent of the total votes cast in 6 of the 19 states. Shagari had 25 percent of the total votes cast in 12 states.

Shagari thereby won 25% of the votes in only 12 states and 20% in the 13th state. The Law has stipulated that whoever was to emerge should have 13 sates. Then the NPN now argued through its lawyer, Chief Akinjide, that what was meant by the clause (122/3rds) twelve two-thirds implied that the winning candidate needed 12 states and two-thirds of an extra state and needed one sixth of the votes of the 13th state which was enough to present the winning ticket and presidential candidate.

When the electoral commission took the matter up with the Supreme Military Council they refused to interfere, telling the commission to take the appropriate decision since it was a democratic election and democratic means should be used to solve the problem. Any agrieved party was asked to seek redress in the court.

On August 16, 1979 the electoral commission declared Alhaji Shehu Shagari the winner, four days later Obasanjo met party leaders and told them in a diplomatic manner that he had no power over the Electoral Commission, urging them to follow due process and constitutional procedures. Awolowo went to court and the Supreme Court upheld the electoral commission's decision by six votes to one.

The Chief Justice declared that even if it was not having 13 states Shagari's election was the closest to meet the requirements. He had more states and more votes. The southwest did not forgive Obasanjo due to Awolowo's loss at the court and Awolowo declared Obasanjo an enemy, believing that he had deprived him of his ambition to become president of Nigeria.

But what really happened was that Eastern Nigeria had not forgotten the civil war. They had declared war on Awolowo long after the outbreak of the war. They believed he used his wisdom to defeat the dream of Biafra because he had been the adviser to Gowon who taught him how to defeat them. First, he was blamed for changing Nigeria's currency and secondly for advising that they block the transportation of food to Biafra even though this was not totally true. This rumour had gone round at the time and lots of people believed without knowing the truth about Awolowo's innocence.

The 1979 election was just nine years after the civil war ended. The people of the East had sent word around that they must not vote Awolowo for the wickedness he caused the Biafrans. They still carry the pains of how they starved and ate lizards, snakes, dogs and anything possible and in some areas they ate freshly killed human beings. They never forgave him. He had insisted on picking an Easterner as his running mate, hoping that would pacify them but it did not. The word was passed quietly around the country through the traders all over Nigeria. They said when Ojukwu had declared Biafra before the civil war started, Awolowo betrayed Ojukwu by not declaring the independence of western region and if he had done same there would be no war and the North would have gone their way. It would have brought three independent nations instead of the forced marriage we have till date that still stands on shaky grounds.

The Yorubas did not allude to this and went about blaming Obasanjo for giving power to the North. Awolowo had got most of his support from western region.[68]

Chief MKO Abiola had gone with his wife, Alhaja Simbiat, to visit Chief Awolowo at Ikenne, his country home, as the elections were still about to start. They were to spend the night in Awolowo's house then as they deliberated on various issues and they came to a heady argument. Chief Abiola had advised Awolowo

---

68 The Nation Vol 07 No 2293 Saturday November, 10 2012 civil war victims. Horrifying tales we fed on raw cassava tubers, rats and lizards.

to pick a northerner as running mate which would be an advantage as they will get lots of votes from both North and South West along with a few from the East. Chief Awolowo had insisted on an Easterner and Abiola felt his strategy was wrong. The argument was strong and Awolowo's countenance changed and the Abiola's felt uncomfortable, thereby leaving his house at Ikenne at late 11p.m. at night. Abiola and Simbiat decided to leave as the cordial reception they got on their arrival was no longer there. It was after this incident that Abiola decided to join the NPN. However, as the Yorubas blamed Obasanjo, he had asked them if the scores were the other way round would they accept Shagari to be sworn in as president with 4.9 million votes as against 5.6 million votes? Obasanjo threw his arms up and heaved a sigh! "I wonder why people would want to do unto others what they would not like others to do unto them."

However on October 1, 1979 the Head of State, General Olusegun Obasanjo handed over power successfully to President Shehu Shagari as the new civilian president. This was the end of thirteen years of military rule in Nigeria.

It became a Guinness book of records accomplishment as the first military head of state in Africa to hand over power willingly to a civilian president and to successfully conduct the election that made it possible.

It was noted all over the world and this was a new beginning for Obasanjo internationally as a statesman.

Cartoon Punch

Feb 13th 1978—Sept 30th 1979

From Kenny ADAMSON &
Omoba on behalf of the
Punch Cartoon Dept

Gen. Obasanjo
— News Report

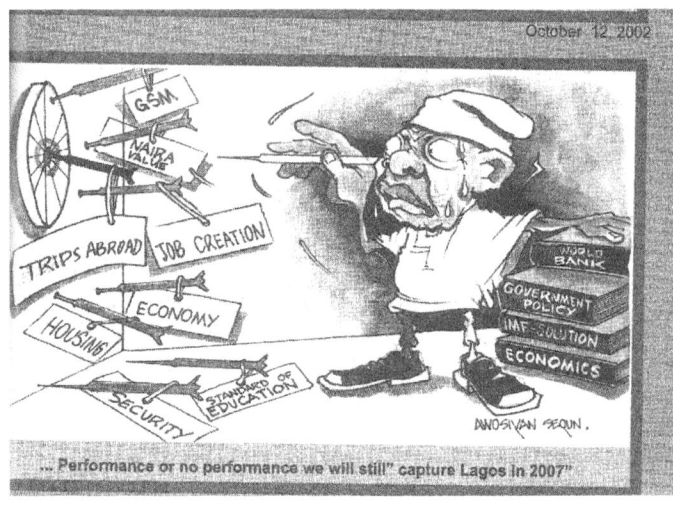

Obasanjo at his poultry farm in Ota

Also at his farm in Ota

Being sworn in as civilian President in 1999

Obasanjo with Bill Gates

Obasanjo with Canadian Prime Minister

With Bashar-al-Assad, Syrian President

With other former heads of state in Aso Rock

Obasanjo coming out from the presidential Jet

With the General Overseer of Redeemed Christian Church of God, Pastor Enoch Adeboye and his wife

Obasanjo with Obama

With George Bush

Receiving President Bill Clinton

With Andrew Young

Obasanjo with Jimmy Carter and Professor Olikoye Ransome Kuti

Obasanjo with wife, Bola

At the White House with Bill Clinton

With Italian Prime Minister Silvio Berlusconi

With Queen Elizabeth

With George Bush

With former Heads of State

Obasanjo with President Buhari

With Chinese President Hu Jintao

With French President Jacques Chirac

With Jimmy Carter

With Junichiro Koizumi Japanese Prime Minister

With Koffi Anan

Obasanjo with the late Gaddafi and others

With Lula da Silva

Obasanjo with Iyabo

Obasanjo and wife,
Oluremi as a loving father
with his family

Some of Baba's children

Obasanjo with his loving wife, late Stella

With Prince Charles of United Kingdom

With Fidel Castro of Cuba

With Tony Blair

Addressing the Nation as a military head of state

CHAPTER FOURTEEN

Retirement From The Army

Obasanjo was forty-two years old when he retired from the army as Head of State. He was still young and had the best years of his life ahead of him. He had retired but was not ready to retire to a rocking chair. On his arrival at Ota farm and with his intention to go fully into farming, the vendors of the land he acquired earlier in Ota started another game and were singing a new song that they had sold the land too cheap for him in 1975 when he bought 230 hectares of land from the family at ₦200 per hectare.

The family now said they sold the land to General Obasanjo at the price because of fear that he would confiscate their land if they refused to sell.[69] It has always been the problem with buying land from private families because once they are broke and after a few years down the line and you don't start work on your land, they start reselling to other parties the same land that they had already sold to the first buyer. There are cases where a land can be sold to five different people if the buyer do not start development on it immediately.

---
69 *Nigerian Tribune* 14 and 22 October 1979

They began to encroach into the land, leading to many court cases but later the case was settled between the three families contesting the land.[70]

Once Obasanjo settled down and the farm had been put in a functional order he roared daily on the farm like a tractor from one end to another. He later became a spokesman for modern farmers.[71] The farm had fish pond, poultry, crops, vegetables, seed production, cassava processing, livestock feed production, poultry hatchery, broiler, meat and egg production. It also included cattle rearing, piggery, mush room cultivation etc. The products were sold in markets in Nigeria and also exported to African countries, Saudi Arabia, Europe and the United States.

Obasanjo farms also supplied the universities and their staff were also given special discounts to encourage patronage. Temperance Enterprises Ltd. had been changed to Obasanjo Farms Nig. Ltd. The farm got bigger and better, housing a red brick personal house for the General; it also had meeting rooms, canteen, a bar, a discotheque and the fifty-room Temperance Hotel.

This new farming vocation kept the retired General busy. He had elite visitors and businessmen visiting and the ventures had inspired others in Nigeria to emulate and join the farmers association. Chief M.K.O Abiola did heavy investment in Abiola Farms Ltd. to the tune of over ₦40 million Naira, Chief Francis Ellah in Rivers State and many retired generals, including Alani Akinriade, followed in the farming culture.

---

70   *Newswatch* 14 August 1989 Page 15
71   *Newswatch* 12 January 1987 Pg 14.

Then suddenly came the urge for intellectual prowess. He had once in the late 1960s lectured at University of Ibadan and there was the burning desire to educate the public and university students about the happenings in Nigeria, both past and present.

Then came the book *My Command* in 1980, it was his war memoirs, all that happened in Nigeria after independence and the Biafran war and the roles he had played. The book sparked a controversy instantly, bringing Obasanjo's name into the public domain again, some said he had praised himself while trying to criticize others. However, that was expected considering the fact that Benjamin Adekunle had become an icon and hero of sort with the 3rd Marine Commando Division. He was a terror to the Biafrans and the Black Scorpion was a name recognised by all and the international community.

Obasanjo had replaced him and within six months, as the gods have always been kind to Obasanjo, the war ended. The success of fitting into the large shoes of Adekunle ended victorious for Obasanjo so it was only natural that a lot of people envied him.

Despite his successes he had always remained level-headed and humble – the war had been a nasty experience and there was no reason to show off. The critics believed he was uncharitable to his predecessor in office, Murtala Muhammed, because Obasanjo had mentioned Murtala's futile and disastrous assault on Onitsha, concluding it was a grave and calculated risk to bring his predecessor down. The book instigated other Nigerians to write about the civil war.[72]

---

72 Obasanjo My Command Pg 42 57-8

My Command was a book he simply published about his experience during the 30-months Nigerian civil war but as it turned out, some felt he had given so much credit to himself by blowing his own horn but as humble as ever he simply said at the time:

> I have written my own story and account about my command not theirs. Any one who disagrees with any portion of the book is free to write his.

Then Alexander Madiebo, a Biafra's army commander published his own book about the Biafran side in 1980 titled: *The Nigerian Revolution and the Biafran War* and did not mention Obasanjo in the book. It was a political move to ignore or omit his name from the war because, to them who wanted Biafra, it was Obasanjo who had stopped their ambition by bringing the war to an end.[73]

It should be noted that whoever goes to the war front is often seen as a war hero even though we may assert that a sitting president takes the glory where the war is successful. Adekunle the Black Scorpion was a hero during the Biafran war. He had done exploits, winning some and losing some. But a war is never fought by one soldier but when there is success the commander takes the glory of the battle front.

From the moment the book was launched, Chief Bola Ige who was the Governor of the then Oyo State which included today's Osun State had denounced the book expressing his bitterness that Chief Awolowo was not allowed to emerge president, because the elections were rigged. He however forgot that the civil war ended only nine years earlier and the Igbos were not happy with Awolowo which made them to vote en masse for NPN because Dr. Alex Ekwueme, their son, was Vice

---
73 Madiebo: Nigerian Revolution

President to Shehu Shagari. The easterners were against Awolowo despite making Chief Phillip Umeadi his vice presidential running mate, they preferred to go with Shagari, so technically speaking, Awolowo only had the control of southwestern Nigeria.[74]

This was what currently had made the Action Congress of Nigeria (ACN) merge with Congress for Progressive Change (CPC) to get huge votes from the North where we now have APC as the outcome of the merger of the Tinubu/Buhari ticket. General Adeyinka had at the time asked Obasanjo to withdraw the book believing the book could divide the army and destabilise the country due to the controversial nature of the contents. The reality was that the soldiers were not interested in such a thing anymore.

At this period General Adeyinka Adebayo wrote in the papers that it was not a time to claim credit for anything and the war was not fought by one man. It was fought collectively. He then pointed out the battle at Ore which he, Obasanjo, lost during Banjo's invasion of the midwest. Ibrahim Haruna who was mentioned in the book that his second division had no effect during the war had condemned Obasanjo, saying he endangered the army by urging the removal of Northern troops from the western state before the war. Obviously he had no clue to the reasons why the troops were moved out. It showed he did not know the politics going on at the time and of course Benjamin Adekunle was bitter but the blame should have been put on Gowon as Obasanjo, an Engineer, was not even ready to go to the war front.

---
74 Sunday *Concord* 9 November 1980,
    National *Concord* 21 November 1980.

Alabi Isama revealed in his new book *The Tragedy of Victory* that when they had put his name forward and they informed him, Akinrinade and himself were not initially well disposed to the development as many soldiers in the administrative sections were not ready to go to war. Anyway Obasanjo tested the ground asking why him? First, he knew it would cause a rift and second, it was a dangerous mission but he had always been outwardly fearless even if within there were fears he never showed it. He took the job at the time and delivered to the disbelief of many, what Gowon thought was another one year and half, had ended in six months. However, Obasanjo had told his critics to write their own books thus ending the controversy behind his book.

While this had died down he continued to work and act as a watchdog on how the civilian government was being run and had often written letters to Shehu Shagari, encouraging him to manage the economy prudently as the politicians were on spending spree. The senate had been in dispute with Shagari and had delayed the budget over their allowances and salaries inflating their take home pay to about ₦88,000 which was equivalent of $150,000 dollars as the Naira was stronger than the dollar at the time.[75]

The politicians became reckless. It was so bad at this time that they degenerated to branding champagne bottles with their names like the famous "The Adisa Akinloye champagne" which was the new world fashion of doing things. President Shehu Shagari was a grade two teacher and was not versatile enough to handle the presidential throne.

---
75 *New Nigerian* 15 November 1980
   My Command Pp 30-4

The Nigerian throne is designed for a strong-willed and disciplined man like a lion, who can enforce compliance. President Shehu Shagari had given more priority to the police force. He probably felt Nigeria was not at war and had favoured the police force with more funding while reducing that of the army.

Shagari had retired six senior officers, including former coup leader Joseph Garba, who was just thirty-seven years old. President Shehu Shagari had seen the military as the only threat to his stability.[76]

In 1980 General Olusegun Obasanjo (rtd), Nigeria's former Head of State was conferred with the highest award of the land - Grand Commander of the Federal Republic (GCFR) along with Chief Obafemi Awolowo and other honours given to different Nigerians from the political, business and academic circles. Also in 1980 General Obasanjo received Doctors of Letters D. Litt (Honouris Causa) from Howard University, U.S.A.

That year also he bagged Doctor of Law degree (Honouris Causa) from the University of Maiduguri and another Doctor of Laws Degree (Honouris Causa) and a Fellowship of the Institute Of African Studies University of Ibadan (U.I) Nigeria. Then in the month of May 1982, Alhaji Shehu Shagari, President of the Federal Republic of Nigeria shocked the nation with the presidential pardon granted to former Head of State General Yakubu Gowon who was implicated in the 1976 Lt. Col. Bukar Dimka-led military coup where the then Head of State, Murtala Muhammed, was assassinated. And the icing on the cake was the inclusion of Lt. Colonel Chukwuemeka Ojukwu who

---

[76] Africa Confidential 30 January 1980 Pg 1,
West Africa 9 June 1980 Pg. 1039.
Newswatch 16 May 1994 pg 14

had gone on exile after the civil war abandoning his Biafran state and dream. The return of Ojukwu was received with a tremendous welcome, the airport was jam-packed as he got a heroes welcome as peoples from all over the country wanted to catch a glimpse of him. It was a plus for the Alhaji Shehu Shagari government.

However, the politicians were reckless, defying and behaving in an obstructionist manner. The 12 states governed by opposition parties had on many occasions acted like separate or independent states outside Nigeria. They were not working in symbiotic relationship with the federal government and were obstructing the NPN programmes and even obstructing the visits of the president to their states.

Then came the Chadian crisis from where a civil war was going on. The borders between Nigeria were being attacked by the Chadians. Shagari did not know what to do when Nigerian personnel, soldiers, custom men, immigration along with civilian casualties were being killed. The president did not act swiftly. This led Major General Buhari to take the bull by the horn, taking responsibility to act by retaliating, organising his men to counter the offensive which was done successfully.

This had led to a fall out within the presidency and the army at the time and giving president Shagari a vote of no confidence. The military had lost respect for Shagari's leadership and carefully waited for the right opportunity to take the government from the civilians who had been democratically elected for a four year period.

The 1983 General elections were held in which Alhaji Shehu Shagari of the National Party of Nigeria was re-elected for another four year-term as president of the Federal Republic of Nigeria, defeating once more Chief Awolowo of the Unity Party of Nigeria (UPN), Dr. Nnamdi Azikiwe of the Nigerian Peoples Party (NPP), Alhaji Aminu Kano of the Peoples Redemption Party (PRP), Alhaji Waziri Ibrahim of the Great Nigeria Peoples Party (GNPP), and Dr. Tunji Braithwaite of the Nigeria Advance Party (NAP) who was a new entrant in the political race.

The NPN having won again brought protests and discontent with the other political parties, declaring that the election was massively rigged. Obasanjo had avoided the re-inauguration giving his judgement that the democratic system had given politicians the loop hole to be corrupt. He went on to say the government operated an assembly hall cabinet with 36 ministers for 18 ministries. He accused Shagari government of wasting the external reserves he had left for them during his military regime on frivolous things including food they could grow in Nigeria. He was most peeved by the fact that all the laid down programmes he made for them to carry on and execute were all ignored and Shehu at the end had nothing to present. They were just in government spending money.

By the 31st of December, 1983 there was a palace coup and Shagari was overthrown. The military government that emerged was headed by Major General Buhari as head of state while his deputy and second in command was Major General Tunde Idiagbon. There were mass arrests and trial of former political office holders and on 3rd January 1984 the new federal military government ordered all brigade headquarters to impound the passports of people who held political offices since 1979. Shehu Shagari was brought to Lagos amidst heavy military security guard. Awolowo's passport too was seized along with other politicians who contested for political offices, it was a blunder of the regime. Then Shagari was put under house arrest while Alex Ekwueme was sent to Kirikiri maximum prison. If the president, a northerner who was the major actor was put under house arrest why will you send his deputy who had ceremonial functions to kirikiri maximum prison? Many people have not forgotten and forgiven General Buhari about Awolowo's seized passport.

Then they went on to search Awolowo's home on orders of the federal government. His country home at Ikenne and the Park Lane home and office at Apapa, Lagos were thoroughly ransacked, carting away many files and documents including his blue prints on how he wanted to govern Nigeria. This later came handy for the government as they continued the super permanent secretaries' style of governance maintaining a balanced budget and keeping the value of the currency at a higher level as against other world currencies, including the dollar. The high exchange rate where the naira was stronger than other foreign currencies had checked inflation and there was price control. The government was a promising one because they were disciplined and focused.

They had introduced the War Against Indiscipline (WAI) in Lagos on 20th March, 1984 and they had changed the currency on 23rd April, 1984. It was the sixth time of changing the currency in Nigeria and this was announced by Tunde Idiagbon at about 7p.m. in a televised broadcast to the nation, stating the currency will get new colour with effect from April 21st, 1984. It caught all unawares as it was done in secrecy, it was done to fish out fakers of Nigeria's currency, to stop sabotage by currency traffickers within and outside Nigeria, and to check the amount of money in circulation and to establish a strong economy for Nigeria.

It was a corrective regime that had tried to put things right. Major General Buhari had put a check and balance on fundamentalists of every shade and colour. The Muslims were ordered to remove all the loud speakers in their mosques, especially those mounted on the outside. He asked churches to do same. He ordered that Friday prayers for Muslims should be done inside the mosques and that nobody should pray outside the premises of the mosques and if the mosque was full the people who cannot get in should go elsewhere or pray in their houses or offices. He ordered that there would be no more blocking of roads thereby interfering with the freedoms of others. He said he wanted no noise pollution of any kind as both Christians and Muslims pray quietly inside their mosques and churches without disturbing others. Some people were happy while others were displeased. He did the right thing so today even Muslims know they have to be careful with him as he does not tolerate extremism, using the name of religion to perpetrate violence. He put the Sultan, Emirs and other Muslim leaders in check.

But despite all these achievements, their advisers allowed them to make some mistakes. They had rocked the boat in 1984 when Chief MKO Abiola imported newsprint materials for his *Concord* press newspaper business. The government had announced earlier that it would not release money for the importation of newsprint materials, that is, the selling of foreign exchange to individuals to import through the CBN

(Central Bank of Nigeria). The government said that if an individual had foreign exchange overseas they could import the materials so long as it was their own personal funds. Then Chief MKO imported his newsprint with his foreign exchange and as soon as it arrived at the ports they seized it.

It became a double standard and there was an uproar. They pleaded with them but they did not budge. This caused disaffection. Then came the case of the drug traffickers in 1984 where some young boys were caught with drugs and convicted by the appropriate tribunal set up at the time. There were pleas from everywhere for leniency. It was the first celebrated case and an eye opener to the drug trade/business around the world and Nigerians were taking part where the rewards made people millionaires over night despite its criminal and illegal nature.

Buhari had ordered they be killed, they were shot dead by firing squad under the Miscellaneous Offences Decree of 1984. It was from this moment people fell out with the government. People screamed that it was too harsh a law and despite all the pleas from everywhere Buhari and Idiagbon turned a deaf ear to the pleas. People believe the actions of those boys was youthful exuberance. Then two journalists by name Tunde Thompson and Nduka Irabor were convicted and jailed by Buhari/Idiagbon regime under the Notorious Decree 4 of 1984 for a news publication government did not like. The government had been promising but Nigerian's don't like draconian laws and became fed up.

The people of Nigeria don't want to loose their freedom or be gagged by anybody or government so the people began to grumble until the 27th of August, 1985 when the Chief of Army Staff, Major General Ibrahim Badamosi Babangida (IBB), toppled the administration of Major General Muhammadu Buhari and Idiagbon in a palace coup. Tunde Idiagbon had just broken the law they made that children should not be going to Mecca on pilgrimage but he had taken his son while General Buhari was in Daura, his country home, for the Muslim Sallah.

General I.B. Babangida became the new head of state with Commodore Ebitu Ukiwe becoming his deputy. Babangida was charismatic and smiled a disarming smile that captured his audience. It was a relief from the unsmiling stern-faced General Tunde Idiagbon and the blank-faced head of state, General M. Buhari, who were not much different but wanted to change Nigeria. General Babangida was more relaxed-looking, friendly, witty and intelligent. He was flexible and was not too rigid with the way he did things.[77]

General Obasanjo had declared simply that he was a nice man. He set out immediately to release political detainees that had been detained by the Buhari regime. Shehu Shagari, Alex Ekwueme, former governors which included Onabanjo, Jakande etc were also released. They also released Abiola's newsprint materials etc.

Then in December of the same year an alleged coup was said to have taken place; some debunked it while others said there indeed was a coup and security breach. The minister of the Federal Capital Territory and a member of the Supreme Military Council (SMC), Major General Mamman Vatsa and some highly skilled military officers were arrested over an alleged military coup attempt on

---
[77] John LIiffe Obasanjo: *Nigeria and the World* pg 103.

the Babangida administration. It seemed at the time to be a phantom coup as Major General Vatsa had just hosted a very colourful ceremony which enhanced his popularity. He had hosted the annual convention of the Association of Nigerian Authors held in Abuja. He was a member and also a poet. The occasion was very successful as at the time the Babangida administration was still trying to settle down and probably they got uncomfortable. It had been predicted to the brothers, as they called themselves, when they went to meet a powerful seer earlier in their career who had told them the names of five presidents that would emerge from the North after Obasanjo and Shagari were out of the way. He had told them Babangida, Vasta, Buhari, Abacha and Abdulsalami will govern the country but he did not tell them when and how each one would become president and on what circumstances.

Three renowned Nigerian authors who were professors: J.P. Clark, Professor Wole Soyinka and Professor Chinua Achebe were at the seat of power in Dodan Barracks to beg for Vatsa to be spared. Babangida promised he would consider and look into the matter only for a few days later the Minister of Defence and Chairman Joint Chief of Staff, Lt. General Domkat Bali had appeared on television to announce that Major General Mamman Vatsa and other coup convicts had been shot for treason by firing squad. This was done despite mercy pleas by all Nigerians and in fact, the whole world was in total shock and bewilderment. I guess he never slept well after the incident because it had never been forgotten as the matter continued to come up. The main reason was because of the closeness of Babangida and Vasta.

Retirement From The Army

Then in January 1987 Obasanjo was back in the news as he had written a new book on his good friend in the army, Major Chukwuma Kaduna Nzeogwu, who along with his colleagues staged the first coup in Nigeria on the 15th of January, 1966. The book was launched on the 15th of January, 1987, exactly twenty-one years after Nigeria's first coup and in remembrance of Chukwuma Nzeogwu.

It sparked off with a barrage of verbal attacks on Olusegun Obasanjo. The book was simply called *Nzeogwu*. Nzeogwu had died on July 29, 1967 while the civil war was going on. He had murdered many civilian and military northern leaders during the first coup in Nigeria.

Obasanjo had declared immediately that he would not mind the book being criticised or even scandalised but he got everything he had expected. The January 15, 1987 book launch was to commemorate the day the first coup was staged and an end to the civil war.[78]

The Northern elites fired a barrage of verbal attacks with Umaru Shinkafi taking the lead. Shinkafi was Chief of Intelligence in the regime of Obasanjo, he had said in the *National Concord* that

> General Obasanjo's decision to write the book is in my view unfortunate, to himself as a former head of state around whom the lethally wounded North, the pervasively disturbed west and the tragically hurt East rallied during his sojourn in Dodan Barracks.

Shinkafi went on to say that Obasanjo had allowed "a minor matter of friendship" to rock his standing and the book to detract from the authors "colossal name."

The date of the book launch evoked many memories and was also the "Armed forces remembrance day." It

---
78 Ademiluyi, *From Prisoner to President*, Pg 45.

was a day that echoed mixed feelings. The Niger State government revoked the certificate of occupancy of Obasanjos 5,000 hectre farmland in Niger State.

General Obasanjo watched with calm, the storm he had created with philosophical calmness. As usual he declared he has told his own side of the story and history and posterity will judge his actions.[79]

Then in February 1990 another book was released: *NOT MY WILL*. It covered the Murtala/Obasanjo regimes of 1975 to 1979 and immediately the book was banned through a court injunction as Justice Elias, a former Chief Justice of the Supreme Court of Nigeria had sued Obasanjo, University Press Limited, the publishers of the book and *Newswatch* communication limited for serialising the book in the magazine for the contents on pages 97 and 98 where Obasanjo had questioned his integrity and management of the judiciary.[80]

However, the book had slipped into all bookshops nationwide and it became an instant hit as everybody rushed to grab copies. This was the third book that became controversial and sensational but in all honesty the truth had been spoken.

How could Justice Elias break the ethics of the legal code? The book had the author, Obasanjo, acknowledging his legal competence and brilliance but how does a judge and chief justice preside over a case involving his brother concerning a land matter? He got so carried way by the case and had forgotten he could not be a participant in the judgement.

NOT MY WILL at this point only shed light on the rot in the judiciary and how certain judges had to

---
[79] *Newswatch* 23 February 1987 Pg 27.
[80] Patrick Avwenagbiku, *Obasanjo and his foot prints* pg 71-72.

be shown the way out due to corruption. The book focused on the administration of the Murtala Obasanjo regime and it clarified issues concerning the burning of Kalakuta Republic belonging to the afrobeat musician, Fela Anikulapo Kuti. It also spoke about Awolowo and his ambition to rule Nigeria. The book fully dissected Awolowo on pages 181, 182 with Obasanjo stating that Awolowo's major ambition to rule Nigeria despite his control of the western region was not possible:

> What he had been struggling in vain to achieve since then and until he died had come my way unsolicited, I had done my best as I know how to; I had voluntarily left the stage while the ovation was high for others to play their part.

NOT MY WILL on page 185 again pointed out that

> There was erroneous assumption by Chief Awolowo and others like him that he was the best and all others should see him and accept him as the best. But best in what and best for what? Best in political examination? Best in IQ? What are the criteria for judging the best politician except the verdict of the people at the polls and the proof of history?

This led to more critics and an uproar by Awolowo's followers. Alhaji Lateef Jakande, an Awolowo's disciple and former governor of Lagos State had described Obasanjo's treatise as unbecoming of a former Head of State. There are ways of saying things even unpleasant things, he declared. The book was a sell out. It was sold out in weeks and the publisher had to be asked to hastily do a reprint. Then in 1988 General Olusegun Obasanjo, acting as watchdog and voice of reason and defender of the masses declared that:

The Structural Adjustment Programme of the Babangida regime should be made to have a human face and milk of kindness running in its veins.

He had also extended it to the continued incarceration of his predecessor in office, Major General Muhammadu Buhari, and his number two man, Major General Tunde Idiagbon.

Then of course Babangida released them a few weeks later. Babangida had taken over the government of Nigeria when the price of oil fell to an all time low, exchanging for between seven and nine dollars a barrel which put the government in a difficult situation in dealing with its economic obligations. The foreign financial institutions like the IMF and World Bank adviced the government to devalue the currency, which had come through the Structural Adjustment Programme (SAP) and which eventually destroyed the middle class. As a result of the devaluation, finished products in Nigeria at the time and even till now are still predominantly imported. The exchange rate disparity where the Naira became devalued against foreign currencies in the west: the dollar, pound, Deutsche Mark etc. at the time had made goods and services and consumable products expensive. The salaries earned by the public and private citizens could not purchase the basic essentials and needs of workers. It was like their salaries had been reduced by 50%. This led to economic instability. This eventually led to a mass exodus of Nigerian professionals leaving the country in droves to anywhere they could get better opportunities like Saudi Arabia, America, Britain, France, Germany, Canada etc.

Many countries around the world grabbed these professionals like cookies, including South Africa who had just abandoned the apartheid policy and had released Mandela. Two decades later the policy would be blessing in disguise. It had brought in over 12 billion dollars annually through the western union transfers. Nigerians overseas had sent back money on daily basis to their families. This is what has saved Nigeria today from the situation of the Arab spring that took place in 2011 from imploding due to unemployment crisis despite the high rate of unemployment. Nigeria became insulated because of the Nigerians abroad who take care of family members through western union transfers and others.

Then on the 22nd of April, 1990, a bloody coup attempt was made against the regime of General Ibrahim Babangida by Major Gideon Orkar which was financed by Chief Ogboru. The coup was bloody and Babangida's ADC, UK Bello, got killed along with many other soldiers.

It was only then that General Babangida made a commitment to return Nigeria to democratic civilian rule. In a nationwide broadcast, he disqualified all registered political parties and associations and set up a two party system based on the American system of government. That is the Republican and Democrats. He formed two parties in Nigeria: National Republican Convention (NRC) and the Social Democratic Party (SDP). He said he was experimenting and so did he. The parties were funded by the government as their secretariats were built all over Nigeria in the local government areas.

The government organised local government elections nationwide on political party basis and this was conducted by the electoral body in December 1990.

Then on the 25th of August 1991, Babangida created nine additional states to the former twenty-one states to become thirty states in the federation.

The country was enjoying another oil windfall which was as a result of the Gulf War that had started in January 15, 1991. This was as a result of the invasion of Kuwait by Iraqi Army acting on the order of its President, Saddam Hussein.

The president at the time, General Babangida, had moved the federal capital to Abuja by December 1991 from Lagos. He discovered Abuja was a more difficult place to organise a coup and he also felt Lagos was already too choked up with both mechanical and human traffic.

The State Houses of Assembly and Governorship elections were held throughout the country. The National Assembly elections were conducted nationwide with the modified option A4 which was an open ballot system that brought transparency to the elections. During the regime of Babangida, Obasanjo had become an international statesman and was known worldwide as the only African military head of state to relinquish power willingly and hand over to democratic and civilian government.

CHAPTER FIFTEEN

Obasanjo And The Press

President Olusegun Obasanjo has had a hot romance with the press at both local and international levels. It had all started from the time he was appointed by the Head of State General Yakubu Gowon to take over from Benjamin Adekunle, the Black Scorpion, during the civil war in Nigeria.

He had replaced Adekunle at the war front and it was from then the press got introduced and interested in the Yoruba General. They had described him at the time as 'camera shy' and humble and by the time he brought the civil war to an end, along with his colleagues, he had become a point of reference.

It has always been challenging, interesting and engaging to interview General Olusegun Obasanjo especially as Head of State and President and also when he was out of office in his private life and capacity.

He did say in an interview that sometimes Nigeria can be quiet and you begin to worry that nothing is going on but then many times you say or write something and the whole environment comes alive and everybody is talking, commenting, criticizing or giving their views. He said it made Nigeria special.

Those who have interviewed the great man who is almost like an oracle with lots of wisdom often have to phrase their questions well and not be insistent on a particular view point.

Olusegun Obasanjo is human and his moods vary and he is calculating like a soldier he is trained to be, so sometimes the president has been known to blow hot air and if you take it personal then you might be embarrassed but a bold journalist would always endeavour to get their composure as the General astounds his audience and the press.

Obasanjo is the most cartooned president in Nigeria. He had never relied on people or press men to make the news. He has always been a headliner as his hard work, performance, dynamism and innovation automatically make the news. His actions have become news and this is how great leaders around the world get in the news.

However, there were times the press was mischievious as they once spread the rumor that Operation Feed the Nation had become Obasanjo Farms Nigeria (OFN). I guess it was just a way to criticize the president by some disgruntled Nigerians as no glaring evidence ever said Obasanjo was corrupt. He is a man who was able to invest his entitlements. All sources of his income are legal and legitimate.

It was only after Obasanjo had retired in 1979 that the Ota farm house had written on the gate at the entrance: *Dog, snakes and journalists not wanted*. The press at the time did not like it as they felt he compared them with animals.

However today, everybody wants to associate with Olusegun Obasanjo the father of the nation and the man who is fondly called *Baba* or *Baba Iyabo* (Iyabo's father).

Olusegun Obasanjo has become a role model in all Africa and Diaspora. Once you talk about politics and government around the world this name comes to the front burner of events

CHAPTER SIXTEEN

The June 12 Saga: Abiola Offered Premier

General Ibrahim Babangida had dropped the title of Head of State preferring to be called President. At some point, he also dropped his military uniform and made public appearances in civilian African traditional dress (agbada) for men. It was at this point he started talking about handing over to a democratically elected government. But many did not believe he was going to do so with this new title. They assumed from his actions and title change that he wanted to succeed himself and probably become a life president.

As General Babangida planned his exit as President he had set up a two party system. The NRC and SDP emerged. The process started in December 1991 where the two parties contested for elections. The NRC produced sixteen state governors while the SDP had fourteen governors. The SDP however got more seats in the legislatures around the states.[81]

Then in August 1992 when the two political parties held their primary elections to choose presidential

---
81 John LIiffe, Obasanjo Nigeria and the world Pg 113, Osaghae crippled giant Pg 207-23.

candidates, the elections were openly rigged and this made the process flawed. President Babangida intervened by ordering for a fresh election.

The NRC had produced two northern candidates, Adamu Ciroma who was a former governor of the central bank and Umaru Shinkafi, a former security chief. However, none of the two candidates met the requirement as they could not get one-third of the votes in two-thirds of the states that qualified them to run as presidential candidate. The SDP on the other hand produced Musa Yar'Adua, another northerner who emerged winner after the party primaries. He had a powerful political machinery which he had built and nurtured for about five years. He won twenty-three states forcing others to step down which made him the party flagbearer.

However, Babangida was not comfortable with Yar'Adua becoming president as he was once second in command to Obasanjo when he was Head of State and was his former boss. He knew Musa Yar'Adua was very influential up north and believed he would become too powerful. The problem, to him, was both party candidates were from the North, making the process dead on arrival.

In October 15, 1992 he consulted with his cabinet members who were also military officers. The outcome was the cancellation of the whole process. This led to postponement of the transition to civil rule and a division in the army and by one account, Abacha, had attempted unsuccessfully to oust Babangida on the grounds that people had lost confidence in his programme. It was a time it was believed Babangida asked that troops be withdrawn around the defence minister. The rumour was going around that Abacha was a soldier and minister without troops at the time.

Then in November 13, 1992 Babangida had a council of state meeting to endorse the decisions reached by government. Obasanjo got wind of his action and drafted a speech for the meeting and sent an advance copy to Babangida:

> The primary elections for the presidency it seems in retrospect were designed to fail.
>
> In the name of political engineering the country has been converted to a political laboratory for trying out all kinds of silly experiments and gimmicks, principle has been abandoned for expediency. All kinds of booby traps were instituted into the transitional process the result is the crisis we now face... prolongation of military rule cannot be the answer under the present circumstances the honor and integrity of the armed forces in whose name you have governed this country these past seven years are at great risk. The handing over of power to an elected civilian government on January 2 1993 must proceed apace. There lies the honour of the military which must not be destroyed. Nigeria needs peace and stability. It is too fragile to face another commotion. In God's good name drag it not into one. This is the time for you to have some honourable exit.

In his speech Obasanjo had suggested that each party should hold a convention to select a candidate so that the election could take place. When Babangida received this draft he cancelled the meeting and Obasanjo released the speech to the press.

A day after the publication Babangida announced that all the twenty-three candidates at the recent primaries were disqualified.[82] Yar'Adua declared in

---

82   *Guardian* 18 November 1992

anger he had a hidden agenda. However Obasanjo kept warning that Babangida would not go in 1993 and was not ready to step down yet or hand over. The governor of Niger State suggested recklessly that Obasanjo might have to be arrested. Obasanjo on the 9th of April 1993 denounced the regimes lack of integrity and revealed his increasing obsessive hostility to Babangida.

In another interview he described the administrative style of the government as one in deficit.

> Deficit financing, deficit trading, but more importantly we have an administration that is deficit in credibility, its deficit in honesty, deficit in honour, deficit in truth. The only thing it has in surplus is saying something and doing something else... All these have increased cynicism and skepticism about government and governance in Nigeria... It has now got to a state that when government says good morning people will look out four times to ascertain the time of the day.

Babangida, not knowing what to do and daring not to disrespect Obasanjo, decided to seize close to 70,000 copies of the interview from *Tell magazine*.[83]

He issued a sedition decree to check Obasanjo and others, threatening death penalty for spoken or written words that might disrupt the country's general fabric. Babangida then angrily said Obasanjo feels he is the only one that can conduct a political transition successfully.

Abiola and other politicians started discussions about joining the race. It was widely reported that Babangida had told Abiola that he (Babangida) could not handover to Abiola for reasons only known to them. Babangida it was also reported had offered Abiola the position of prime minister or premier which Abiola rejected.

---
83 John Lliffe, Obasanjo Nigeria and the world Pg 139

Abiola had said at the time "I won't play second fiddle to anybody." He continued: "why does the North feel a southerner cannot be president in Nigeria? Are their heads better than ours in the south?" Abiola also said he could not play the religious card as it was the Muslim northerners refusing their southern Muslim brother.

A few months later after this, tragedy struck the Abiola house, his first wife, Alhaja Simbiat Abiola, the pillar of the Abiola household died. During the burial ceremonies Babangida visited the Abiola home and made Abiola another offer of heading the transitional government but Abiola refused the offer again. It was like the premier job was dangled at him again. Abiola had rejected the offer to head the transitional government at the time, giving the excuse that his wife had just died and he was grieving. It was then the job was given to Sonekan.

The whole idea was at the time intended to groom Abiola for the presidency but he never understood fully, he did not think deep enough at the time. Babangida had told Abiola about his skepticism of how Abiola would address the nation or grant interview to the press due to the fact that Abiola was a stammerer. This made Abiola to improve on his eloquence throughout the period. It was the striking feature of his personality and nobody could change that. It made Abiola a unique personality.

The pressure to hand over led to the emergence of Baba Gana Kingibe who opted for the Social Democratic Party (SDP), where he declared his ambition and intention to contest for the presidency, after inviting media executives and the press.

Kingibe seemed the only formidable candidate with his fabulous posters and slogans and Nigerians were likely to have favoured his candidacy since all former members of the armed forces had been banned as they wanted pure civilians to contest the elections. Unfortunately many did not believe or buy the idea that Babangida was ready to leave Aso Rock, he actually wanted to stay till 1995 thereby making it ten years in office as had been allegedly predicted to him by one seer and maybe the ambition to beat the record of General Yakubu Jack Gowon, the former head of state, who led the country for nine years.

The believe at the time was that Babangida was leaving and politicians were encouraged to contest but many did not want to take the risk because not many could afford to loose their money on a transition programme that the military government can trauncate.

Then Abiola saw this as an opportunity, he then went to see Obasanjo at Ota farm house to intimate him about his intention to contest for the position of president of Nigeria. The response was negative. The former head of state warned Abiola seriously that there was no vacancy at Aso Rock for now. He then told Abiola: "God has blessed you even more than some presidents. You are a successful businessman, internationally recognized and wealthy." He had told MKO that he cannot have money and start seeking for power again. "The powers that be, the kingmakers, will not want that, you either have one of the two; not both."

Obasanjo finally advised him go and wait first, that after Babangida has left the place he can then declare his intention to contest the election. This angered Abiola so much, that all on appointment at his house to see him were asked to come another day.

He had two days later invited the press and media and eventually declared his intention to run for president. He said of Babangida at the time, "Babangida is my friend and he told me he is leaving Aso Rock Villa and has packed half of his belongings to Minna."

The reporters challenged him what evidence he had and that was Babangida really his friend? With all he had gone through with the military regimes with his newspaper house, the *Concord* Press shut down many times and with "the mad dog incident" with Nura Imam where they clashed with Abiola and air force men. They questioned if, Abiola really think the military will hand over power to him?

They observed he had served almost as de-facto vice president in the regime which angered many of the generals with the seating arrangement at public functions having him sitting next to the president, then the vice president and their wives and Abacha as number four on the extreme end.

He said he knew it had its odds, but that he would succeed. He then described the situation further that it was like riding on the back of a tiger and he would balance well and see he does not fall down or end up in its belly. Then Ebenezer Obey's daughter said if you win the election and they don't give you or if you loose what will you then do? He said: "I will go quietly to my house and do what I have been doing all my life." That is going back to my business. He also said if a man falls down he will get up again and that sealed the declaration.

Babangida was shocked at his declaration but never expected he could win. He invited him over several times but Chief Abiola refused to go. He had done his home work over the years and had used his wealth to help so many from every point of the compass, he was like the Aladdin genie from the Arabian tales always ready to listen and help others. Nigeria has not gotten his match till date as he opened his house to all even if he never knew you. He was always a helper and builder, fondly called MKO Naira by the immediate post Ooni of Ife or the "Father Christmas of Ogun state" by the former governor, Bisi Onabanjo of Ogun State.

The election primaries came and the Kingibe ticket was hijacked by Abiola. The convention had been very difficult in Jos. Kingibe was a force to be reckoned with. It took loads of money to get Abiola the SDP flagbearer ticket. Atiku had stepped down for Abiola and Kingibe was made his deputy because he started the campaign on SDP first and would probably have gotten the presidency if Abiola had opted out.

The election came and became the most successful in the history of Nigeria. Abiola had won the election but the military were not sure about his loyalty to them. They wanted to be sure he would not squeal on their past deeds in government and felt they would not be able to control him.

The election was won by Abiola but half way the results were delayed, Abiola had 58% of votes, 19 of the states and got support across regional and religious territories before the results were stopped. The (National Republican Convention) NRC party opponent in the election, Alhaji Tofa, had congratulated him already as the winner of the election.

When Nigeria and the world expected to hear the result and final outcome of the election, Babangida and the army generals in his cabinet prevailed on the

National Electoral Commission Chairman to stop the announcement of results. Then the National Defence and Security Council met on 22nd - 23rd June and decided to annul the election.

On the 24th Chief Abiola jets to Abuja with his first son, Kola. When they got to Babangida he said Kola should wait outside that they wanted to talk alone. They talked for about 45 minutes and Abiola came out with Babangida and both gave blank expression and refused to disclose the details of their discussion. A sealed secret Abiola refused to reveal as even Babangida also kept sealed lips. This was where Abiola consented to the annulment of the June 12 election.

The press, media and Nigerian public, especially from the southwest became disappointed. Abiola kept the secret till death. Two days later Babangida annulled the election and spoke on television, claiming the electoral process had been corrupt and divisive that both candidates had business relationship with the government and it was a conflict of interest. He promised to organise another election before August 27. Then on the 29th of June 1993 he told the governors that Abiola did not have the support and loyalty of the armed forces and could not have been able to command them. Then he said later he did not want Abiola dead because he realised the government would only last six months.

Obasanjo was in New York when he heard about the annulment. He warned Abiola by telephone not to announce the election results and declare himself president-elect, an advise Abiola ignored. There were about three factions who had different interests in the June

12 saga. Those who wanted Abiola's election validated, the Abuja group who were Babangida's people who wanted him or one of their own kitchen cabinet member to remain in power and the Lagos groups who wanted Sanni Abacha. The Abuja and Lagos group swore never to accept Abiola as their commander-in-chief. David Mark who was in the Abuja group had blown hot air, vowing to shoot Abiola. The days went by and there was an outbreak of riots all over Nigeria. The public declared they will confront the army which was getting divided as some were not in support of the annulment. The protest continued with nasty press releases. Obasanjo rushed back to Nigeria, consulted with Musa Yar'Adua, his one time second in command and deputy and negotiated with Babangida to uphold the election. When he refused they discussed the possibility of a broad-based government to which the SDP and NRC and military would each nominate one-third of the members. Obasanjo offered Abiola to accept the situation but would be accommodated in the new plan, but Abiola rejected the idea.

Abiola got wind of an assassination plot and travelled out on the 3rd of August to the United States of America and Britain. The international community was not in support of the mandate and will not force the military to give the mandate. They were not happy with him in diplomatic circles because he had gone around championing the delicate topic of Reparations which was the demand for foreign countries involved in slavery to pay compensation to African countries.

He was interviewed by the CNN on the problems in Nigeria. Here is the excerpts from the interview:

ABIOLA'S CNN INTERVIEWS THAT KILLED THE JUNE 12 ELECTION INTERNATIONALLY.

CNN: Chief Abiola why did you leave Nigeria?

Abiola: The water got too hot for the fish so I had to jump out.

CNN: You have been friends of the military government in Nigeria for a long time and General Babangida is your very good friend.

Abiola: Yes that is true.

CNN: You have also been a great supporter of the government over the years? Why are you now fighting the government?

Abiola: I won the election in Nigeria and I want my mandate because I want to make a change in the system.

CNN: Chief Abiola it is believed you are one of the beneficiaries of government contracts in Nigeria and you supplied bread called wonder loaf to ECOMOG soldiers, in Liberia.

Abiola: Yes I did.

CNN: For a man who wants to make a change in Nigeria why did you supply bread that is worth equivalent of 35 cents in the U.S.A at the rate of $5 dollars a loaf to ECOMOG soldiers, don't you think that is too exorbitant for a man that wants to change Nigeria?

He stammered and there was no good defense anymore. This was the interview that killed the June 12 election.

On August 17 1993, another interview took place where Chief Abiola pleaded with Babangida as a good Muslim to change his decision on the June 12 election and was good natured to wish him a happy birthday as it was Babangida's birthday. The CNN interview had killed June 12 internationally and Abiola knew the best was to come home and they negotiated and pleaded his return. Babangida had said that he and his colleagues were not only in government but also in power and that he will give Nigeria a President before he left. Babangida stepped aside with the nation burning and Sonekan was in place as interim President.

After Abiola returned, General Abacha sacked the Interim Government and took over and promised to correct all wrong doing. Abacha invited Abiola for talks. Abiola fell for the trick but at the meeting, Abacha told Abiola in confidence, "I want to be president too for sometime but will hand over to you after six months to one year."

He urged Abiola to move closer to him and close up the space between them on the three sitter sofa where they hugged, embraced and laughed. The public understood it to mean all was settled and everything eased off and the tension died down.

All presidents and heads of state all over the world work with a mind set of having a good successor. It has to do with loyalty and trust. Presidents, governors and others always have someone they groom to be their successors when election transitions go smoothly. It happened in Russia, France, and the USA with the Clinton and Bush family, etc.

However when a president is not very popular, he no longer holds on to the fact that his authority is final as was with the June 12 situation. Babangida had become a prisoner of his inner kitchen cabinet. All the tensions had made him make mistakes in the critical situation of the June 12 mandate. Abiola was a victim of "bad belle," Obasanjo had said. He was envied by all. He was not yet a president and had lived like one. They were further angered especially when Babangida under the privatisation exercise had given Summit Oil belonging to Abiola, one of the oil blocs to prospect for oil, making him one of the first Nigerians to get an oil bloc. The Volkswagen of Nigeria was acquired by him and the Berec Battery Company, Lagos. He unfortunately lost his guard when he went over the hill shouting about the oil bloc.

"Obe tun tun re o!!" Abiola exclaimed in a magazine that the oil bloc is new 'soup'! They had not started the business he had boasted that his children were the best and among the top five in their schools. He further boasted that his son had so much landed property and was widely travelled. All these complicated his chances after comparing his sons to eminent Nigerians of his own age group. This upset the army, Yoruba, the ruling elites and non Yoruba alike.

People now wondered, if Chief Abiola could behave like this because of one oil bloc, what will he do if he controls all the oil and he is in charge of Nigeria's oil wealth?

These issues among others reasons were the major reasons they felt he would not be able to govern Nigeria properly. Then some scandals came up from his personal relationships as he was accused of snatching the wife of a traditional ruler and a military colonel. These were some of the visible factors that brought about the annulment of his election. The army just did not trust him fully.

After the agreement that Abacha would hand over in six months and with a year gone by, he had not handed over. The military government of Abacha consolidated their position and had sacked all NRC and SDP governors giving way to a full military government. The former governors up North and the East accepted their fates as they were intelligent enough to know how the world works and how a military regime operated. They were not ready for any confrontation with the army as the army was back in government. There were some who pleaded with Abiola that since he was the one who settled the conflict between Maccido and Dasuki who both contested for the traditional throne of Sultan of Sokoto where the people wanted and chose Maccido but the powers in government at the time wanted Dasuki. They said he should use it as case study and accept his election annulment as an act of God.

They asked he should also accept June 12 as an act of God that if he would be president he could still get there at a later date.

The southwest continued the June 12 struggle but it was a difficult battle as there were no civilian governors anymore and a year had gone by with General Abacha in full control. General Sanni Abacha pleaded with the labour unions to stop their strike and resume their duties at work, promising to restore everything back to normal and to organise new elections within a short period. This diffused the tension. He promised to return all the money Chief Abiola spent for the election if he will be patient and abstain from causing problems.

Abacha had invited all the politicians from the election fall out, including Baba Gana Kingibe who was Abiola's running mate. Adamu Ciroma who had been disqualified among the twenty-three aspirants during the Babangida administration, Olu Onagoruwa and Lateef Jakande, former governor of Lagos State from the UPN and one of Awolowo's close associates were all invited to Abacha government. All had worked for Abacha for their various reasons some said for patriotic reasons, others said they wanted to be in government to put pressure on Abacha who promised to hand over to Abiola. Others said Abiola had given them the go-ahead to serve in the cabinet while others had gone for personal gain. Obasanjo refused to send any names for the Abacha government. Obasanjo declared at the time that Nigeria had to lead the black race in Africa by example and prove to the international community that Africa and the black race was not doomed.

The anniversary of June 12 election approached with NADECO putting pressure on the Head of State to step down and allow Abiola to form a national government but he had started to enjoy the job and had not fully settled down.

On the 11th of June Abiola declared himself president and went into hiding. He then addressed a rally of 5,000 people, drove a motorcade through the streets of Lagos and was eventually arrested on June 23 on treason charges. Obasanjo had advised Abacha not to arrest Abiola and on 18 July he led a powerful delegation of traditional rulers to a meeting with Abacha to initiate a dialogue between the military ruler and his prisoner. Abacha said Abiola could be free if only he was ready to renounce his mandate.

However Obasanjo asked for Abiola's release and a statement of Abacha's programme. Abiola refused to renounce and give up the mandate. This led to failed talks and Abiola remained in custody. Obasanjo took the brunt when riots broke out. Protesters got to Obasanjo's house at the Onikolobo area of the town of Abeokuta, smashing all the windows. After that they made to set the building ablaze, but the tenants prevailed on them.

His second house at Itoko was spared where two armed soldiers on guard had threatened to shoot if the protesters attempted to damage the house. Another office building, a four storey at quarry junction was not spared as the building was vandalized and three vehicles burnt. Obasanjo declared a loss of about 30,000 dollars[84] which was about 2 million naira at the time but he accepted the victimisation as a sacrifice he would not mind making towards peace and unity in Nigeria. All this persecution angered Obasanjo who saw it an unfair reward for his selfless service. He was being punished for refusing to be a tribal leader, after all he was not the one that cancelled the June 12 election, talk less of taking over the government and putting Abiola in prison. He further said:

> We do not need fighting in the streets, burning of properties, petrol bombing, paralyzing national strikes and a shut down of the economy. We need to return to democracy at the earliest possible time under an agreed leadership.

Then in May 1994 Obasanjo and Yar'Adua created the National Unity Promoters. An attempt was later made to expand the group into a National Unity Organization on Nigeria (NUON) at a meeting in Ota in June and this was obstructed by security agents sent by Abacha

---
84 TELL 1st August 1994 Pg 16

who felt it was an attempt to form a political party. They cordoned off the farm and arrested those seeking to enter the farmhouse venues. Despite the harassment with helicopters flying around, the organisation came to being and gained the backing of influential figures in the northern elder's forum.

It was later announced that the organisation had interim officers and members nationwide but could not do much until party politics officially resumed as when the government gave its approval. He had said the organisation would sponsor a presidential candidate and he would just oversee the activities of the party because he was not interested to be the presidential candidate.

In December 1994 Obasanjo organised the first of two meetings between Yoruba and Igbo politicians, but that did not attract either the Afenifere leaders who championed Abiola or representatives of the Igbo ethnic organisation, Ohaneze Ndigbo, who asked him to go and reconcile with his people first.

Then in February 1995 Obasanjo had made a speech calling for national unity, but the Yoruba leaders from Afenifere and NADECO asked him if there can be unity without justice? They reminded him that since he was not a tribal leader and preferred national unity above the Yoruba interest, they were not interested unless he also clarified his utterances about Abiola not being a messiah.[85] This ended in an uproar and Obasanjo lost his temper and turned to the north where he was received warmly. This alarmed Abacha. "What does this Obasanjo tell them and why do they trust and favour him so much." Then a plot was hatched to stop him.

---

85 *Daily Times* 4 June 1994
    Newswatch 13 March 1995 Pp 18-19

CHAPTER SEVENTEEN

Obasanjo Goes To Prison

General Olusegun Obasanjo became the most respected Nigerian leader because of his numerous selfless services to humanity. No former Nigerian leader, civilian or military, commands the respect and attention he routinely gets, within and outside the country. His Ota farm complex was a Mecca for various categories of people, including world leaders who are interested in the affairs of Nigeria and the rest of black Africa. So respected is the General that the regime of General Buhari, when faced with credibility problems, claimed that it was the offshoot of the Murtala/Obasanjo regime.

President Babangida also had occasion to leave the state house and travel to Ota to consult with Obasanjo. This visit generated a lot of controversies in the polity at the time. General Obasanjo was on many occasions the head of the federal government delegation to a countless number of countries in the days of apartheid. The federal government took advantage of his enormous clout and influence in the international community to make use of him as link between Nigeria and the black movement in South Africa.

General Abacha too had tried to woo him but Obasanjo refused on the grounds that Abacha should give an exit date and their relationship became frosty. Obasanjo also mobilized some leaders in the southern part of Nigeria to put pressure on Abacha. At one of these meetings held in Ibadan in mid January 1995 under the chairmanship of Chief Adisa Akinloye, it was resolved that Abacha be pressured to quit power by January 1, 1996. The date had been proposed by the constitutional conference set up by the regime which was then sitting in Abuja.

Major General Shehu Yar'Adua had single-handedly championed the date and ensured it was endorsed at the conference. This was his own sin– that was how he offended Abacha. General Obasanjo had asked Abacha to quit office as Head of State in a BBC programme in May, 1997. He said that if General Abacha refused to go, he should take responsibility for whatever he (Abacha) did and whatever became of him. He then described the administration as a government which took Nigerians for nothing and demanded it should either perform or get out. The good thing about Abacha was that he tried to woo all oppositions at the initial stage of his regime. It was when the oppositions refused to bow to his side and also continued their assault, that he bared his fangs.

For example in May 1994, General Abacha invited General Obasanjo to be part of his entourage to Nelson Mandela's inauguration as South Africa's first black president but Obasanjo declined the invitation, with the excuse that he had scheduled events to attend to in Europe.

Abacha had hoped Obasanjo's presence in his entourage would have boosted his administrations recognition to the international community because of the goodwill he enjoyed all over the world. This was not to be as Obasanjo now travelled to South Africa from London to witness the cold reception the Nigerian entourage got from world leaders present. This was a slap on General Abacha's face and one thing that worried him was that whenever Obasanjo became critical of any regime the government soon got toppled. General Abacha now got some African leaders to speak to Obasanjo, including President Nicephore Soglo of Benin republic who was his close friend. Obasanjo declared he had nothing against General Abacha as Head of State but he would only give his support when he had decided on an exit date that he would return the government to civilian rule.[86]

Obasanjo was difficult to silence as he had become an international statesman and an icon on the African continent. Ultimately the inner caucus and advisers of Abacha said the only way to catch him is to fake a coup. General Obasanjo was in Copenhagen in Denmark attending a United Nations conference on elimination of poverty from the world when he was told that some people had been arrested for a failed coup in Nigeria and his name was mentioned and that he escaped from the country through Seme border to forestall being arrested.

Walter Carrington, the American ambassador actually phoned the General advising him to put on hold his return to Nigeria for the events to unfold properly as the accusation for a coup plot was too

---

86 *Newswatch* 13 December 1993

serious to take chances. Probably if he had stayed back a few weeks then there would have been loopholes to puncture the accusations but he returned hastily to Nigeria believing he was senior in military rank to the Head of State. "What can Sanni do to me and how can I be involved in a coup when I handed over voluntarily and had never participated in one before?" It is on record that Obasanjo throughout his military career did not participate in any coup to overthrow a sitting head of state. How can he now plot a coup when in retirement against an officer far junior to him in rank? He saw the whole thing as a joke.

He returned to Nigeria on March 11, 1995. On arrival at the Murtala Muhammed International Airport, Lagos security men seized his international passport. They had broken military protocol and espirit de corp. It was the first time a sitting head of state would go after a retired head of state.

The following day he went for a meeting at the Ooni of Ife Oba Okunade Sijuade's residence in Ikeja, Lagos. Also in attendance was major General David Jemibewon retired. At the meeting Obasanjo's experience at the airport and his imminent arrest hung in the air. The meeting ended within two hours and Obasanjo returned to his farmhouse at Ota. The ordeal started within a few hours on the 13th of March 1995 about 6a.m. in the morning.

Obasanjo's deputy, Major General Shehu Musa Yar'Adua, who was until then a member of the Abacha constitutional conference and was at the time openly canvassing a January 1, 1996 terminal date for the Abacha government was arrested.[87] No statement

---
87 Newswatch 13 March 1995 Pg. 13-18

however was made on both General Obasanjo and Major General Shehu Yar'Adua. The army spokesman, Brigadier General Fred Chijuka, had tried to save the situation and embarrassment the nation and army was going through when he had used superior intelligence and completely denied the coup story in a press interview, claiming some officers were only arrested for questioning on issues capable of destabilising the nation and army. The public had heaved a sigh of relief and tongues were wagging all over the place commending the officer that he had saved the day as people believed the story was a misinformation.

Then not too long afterwards the Chief of Defense Staff Major General Abdulsalami Abubakar came up with another story altogether. In his words

> The nation was saved the irresponsible action of a group of overambitious and misguided officers and civilians by the vigilance of the loyal officers and soldiers in conjunction with the military intelligence operatives.

This almost destroyed his career and credibility save for the fact that military operatives later stated that Obasanjo's arrest had nothing to do with the coup story and that if it had indeed been a coup affair, then his arrest would have been effected by the military instead of the police who had carried out the arrest. The whole thing was becoming a ding dong affair.

After ten days of General Obasanjo's arrest, no formal declaration was made. Local and international pressures were then put on Abacha to tell the world why he was detaining Obasanjo. Then, Jimmy Carter, former president of the United States came calling. Mr. Carter and his wife, Rosalyn, arrived at Abuja on the 20th of March 1995. They met with the foreign minister Chief Tom Ikimi and informed him that the world was watching but that he or America had not come to interfere or meddle with Nigeria's domestic and internal problems but for concern of the arrest of Obasanjo and other political leaders. Mr. Carter met with General Abacha. The discussion was to free Obasanjo or preferably put him under house arrest. Abacha now told Carter that Obasanjo was involved in a coup plot.[88]

Then on the 22nd of March 1995 Abacha placed Obasanjo on house arrest at his farmhouse, and made sure that all electronic equipments were removed to deprive the house any phone connection to the outside world. Obasanjo was there for two months and he was denied visitors and access to the outside world and was guarded by about fourteen armed policemen.

World leaders who phoned Abacha were promised his quick release after interrogation. Also, Mandela and former Prime Minister Callaghan, together with the Commonwealth Secretary General were later told Obasanjo would be tried for conspiracy. Unfortunately the pressure was not enough.

The government after feeling the pressure of the international community decided to fabricate the evidence they would use for a trial. Colonel Bello Fadile, a military lawyer was the target used and forced to implicate Obasanjo on coup plotting. Bello Fadile was forced to sign a statement that he had gone to Ota farm to inform and involve Obasanjo in a coup. This made Obasanjo guilty of the capital offence of

---

88 *Newswatch* 3 April 1995 Pg 10-12
   TELL magazine 3 April 1995 P. 13

concealment of treason, under a decree he Obasanjo had himself made at the time of Dimka's coup when Murtala Muhammed was assassinated.

On 30th May, 1995 the Abacha government ordered that Obasanjo be moved from his farmhouse to the state security service interrogation centre at Ikoyi in Lagos where the interrogation began. They first asked him about his views on the June 12 crisis and its solutions. The next question came as a revelation from a witness which they claimed had visited Ota farm and told him of a coup. Obasanjo was still day dreaming about all the nonsense going on and he demanded to see the witness.

Colonel Bello Fadile was brought in chained. Fadile claimed to have informed Obasanjo of the plot and plan to set-up an interim government that would be headed by the General, in response he claimed, Obasanjo had wanted to know if the boys would accept that arrangement and Fadile claimed he replied in the affirmative. He then claimed that Obasanjo had informed him, Fadile, that he was about to travel out of the country and that Fadile should see him as soon as he got back.

This statement was tendered at the subsequent trial and used in evidence. However, when cross-examined by Obasanjo, Fadile claimed that the meeting took place in the General's farm office in Ota and that during the meeting he sat next to Obasanjo. Then Obasanjo had asked him the date and had punctured the false accusation that, the office had not been opened in two years and the office had a chair at the head of the table for him and two armless chairs opposite and so even if he used the office he would be facing any visitor and not sitting next to him. Then it is common knowledge if you go to Ota farm either to buy poultry, visit the hotel or Obasanjo's house, you had to sign the visitors book at the gate and Fadile's name was no where to be found. This brought about confusion and the investigating panel, having checked and confirmed Obasanjo's statement, recommended that he had no case to answer.

General Abacha, however set-up a trial before a military tribunal on the 19th of June, 1995. Obasanjo was refused his own counsel and was allocated a military lawyer whom he met only minutes before the trial. The judge dismissed his objection to a trial by a court headed by a junior officer to himself which did not conform with military practice. The trial was televised and Obasanjo, staring in disbelief at the Kangaroo way the government was turning the army into. It was the army ridiculing itself in reality and despite powerful men, both in the army and civil society, especially those from the North, the elites who were close to Abacha could not call him to order. Despite Obasanjo producing all evidences they sentenced him to twenty-five years imprisonment for concealment. Yar'Adua and fourteen others were sentenced to death. The sentence and trial divided the army but they did nothing which was too bad. It was the first time a former head of state in retirement was accused of coup plot by far more junior officers who had served under him.

It was President Clinton that saved the day when he warned Abacha about consequences of his actions which included an oil embargo if he executed anybody.[89] Then on the 1st of October, Abacha reduced Obasanjo's prison

---
89 TELL 20 May 1996. Ademiluyi, *From Prisoner to President* Pg 91-92.

term to fifteen years and changed the death sentence to imprisonment for Yar'Adua and others. Obasanjo spent three years in prison under the most harrowing experiences and he was transferred during the period to four different Nigerian prisons across the country.

He was kept in Ikoyi prison in a mosquito-infested room in isolation for almost four months where he slept on the floor. Then he was moved to the main Kirikiri maximum security Prison, Apapa. It was at Kirikiri that Bello Fadile apologised to Obasanjo that he was severely tortured to implicate him. Obasanjo with his large heart asked he put it in writing and signed by him. Bello Fadile did this. Obasanjo was satisfied by this action as it would clear his name and reputation. The letter was smuggled out of prison and forwarded to the press who published it.

This triggered Obasanjo's transfer to Jos prison. Again in Jos prison he took control of the situation he found himself. He was innocent so he did not feel bad and people around the world and in the prison all knew he was being victimized for speaking the truth. He began a religious worship and participated in the daily Christian fellowship and Sunday prayer meetings among the prisoners. Again word was sent to Abacha through his men that Obasanjo was breaking prison rules and he was then transferred to Yola prison.

Pandemonium broke out on his arrival at Yola prison as the prison was not designed and built for a special detainee or prisoner. The inmates lived in large wards that accommodated about a hundred prisoners per ward. Obasanjo lived among them until prison authorities were given permission to construct a special area for the former Head of State.

This was an ordeal for Obasanjo as the prison was overcrowded. The government of the day wanted to break his spirit as he was stopped from receiving visitors except those who had direct permission from the Internal Affairs Minister. Yola State was a different experience as the prison was depressingly dull and gloomy and the weather had its extremes. It was either too hot or too cold. Then it was dusty like the desert and had big nasty green flies.

Despite these tribulations he remained unbowed, the military training he had along with his upbringing had turned him into a steel. He was only allowed to read the Bible, and seriously, the word of God had strengthened him. Many countries around the globe kept pleading with General Abacha but he had become the prisoner of his supporters and inner caucus. They lied to him and he did not listen to other views.

International organisations sent emissaries to Abuja to convince, persuade and plead with him to release Obasanjo and other political detainees, including chief MKO Abiola, the man Nigerians elected as president on June 12 1993. The annulment of that election had led to unending crisis in Nigeria. Jimmy Carter was one of the first visitors to visit Abacha. Thabo Mbeki (South Africa's Vice President) and Arch Bishop Desmond Tutu of South Africa. Boutrous Ghali was sent from the United Nations but when he wanted to visit Obasanjo, Abacha refused him along with his team.

The Abacha government became paranoid and started targeting anybody who got too popular with the public, including people within the government. Then there were few bombings in Lagos targeted at the Governor of Lagos State, Col. Buba Marwa, who was getting too popular even amongst the Yoruba. But the government of the day accused NADECO the Yoruba and Southern Nigeria group that asked for the validation of the June 12 election of chief Abiola of being behind the bombings.

The shocking news of the death of Shehu Musa Yar'Adua was announced on Monday, December 8, 1997. It was suspected he was injected with poisonous substances. When Obasanjo heard the news he did not care anymore if he too did not make it as he cursed the government of Sanni Abacha and the General himself. During his time in prison, Danjuma and Major General Abubakar Abdulsalami who was the Chief of Defence Staff had visited him. He had been conditioned to speak less, eat less and sleep less and interact less with people.

Obasanjo had spent two years in prison and pressure continued to mount for his release. The Pope and many others added to the appeal for his release while they visited Nigeria. Obasanjo enjoyed the support of his wife, Stella, who stood by him through thick and thin and had travelled all over the world speaking to world leaders on the need to get him freed from prison. Obasanjo discovered Nigeria's prisons were one of the worst in the world and he wished his enemy never to experience it. Attempts were made to eliminate him in prison through poisonous injections but the help finally came on the 7th of June.

General Sanni Abacha had an unusual and unexpected visitor, Yasser Arafat, who was having no major business in Nigeria but just decided to stop over in Abuja to visit the head of state because he was within the continent. General Abacha had gone to the airport to see him off but there was an American or a man from the West in the entourage who shook Sanni Abacha. As Arafat bade him goodbye and once the plane had taken off Abacha returned into his car and felt a strange sensation but he was not sure what it was, so he still went about his routine and in the early hours of June 8 1998, Sanni Abacha suddenly died.[90] Though he had been sick from a terminal illness he had managed, but that was not the cause of his death. The whole country jubilated at his death. He was buried that very day according to Muslim rites.

The military commanders in the Arm Forces Ruling Council (AFRC) appointed General Abdulsalami Abubakar as new head of state and he was ready to restore civilian rule.

The news got to Obasanjo by about midday and he sent condolences to Mrs. Abacha and within a week the miracle happened, the prison gates opened and Obasanjo was released on Tuesday 16th June 1998. Ahmed Joda, a permanent secretary during the military regime of Obasanjo went to pick him up along with his personal effects. He was driven in a convoy amidst tight security. He left his prison abode into freedom to the Yola airport where he thanked everybody, and thanked his God for sparing his life as he boarded the presidential jet with registration 5N AGZ which took him to Lagos.

He returned to Ota farm. The next day he went to Abeokuta to a big reception and welcome from the Egba chiefs and people. His wife, Stella, had gone to the USA after she was attacked by robbers who came to rob the farmhouse and she sustained some injuries but

---

90 John LIiffe, *Obasanjo Nigeria and the world* Pg. 160
    Newswatch 22 June 1998

Obasanjo's children were home at Abeokuta to receive him. Those present were Iyabo, Segun jnr, Damilola, Bolanle and Gbenga, all children from Remi, his first wife, and there were others: Bisoye and Bunmi.

Despite the tribulation he faced in the hands of Abacha, Obasanjo forgave all, he took the whole incident as an act of God. There was a thanksgiving service at Owu Baptist Church on the 20th of June 1998 where praises and thanks were given to God for sparing his life.

Then Obasanjo embarked on a thank you tour in and outside Nigeria. The new regime headed by General Abdulsalami Abubakar was battling with how to tackle the country's political uncertainties. Then General Abdulsalami Abubakar who was the head of state sought help from two prominent men from the African continent. They were Kofi Annan from Ghana who was the Secretary General of the United Nations, and Emeka Anyaoku the Secretary General of the Commonwealth.

They both visited Abiola on 2nd July 1998 while in detention and he still insisted on his mandate. However, Anyaoku had warned him that after five years had passed the mandate was not valid and recognised internationally anymore.

On the 7th of July 1998 an American delegation led by Thomas Pickering visited him with two diplomats among whom was Susan Rice. Al Mustapha was sent on an errand as he was in charge of watching what Abiola was eating or drinking. They normally had a taster to taste anything before it was given him.

Abiola was convinced to drink a single cup of tea by the diplomats. Immediately he started sweating, coughing and rolling on the floor: he had just been poisoned. The man dropped dead before medical attention could arrive. Series of autopsy were conducted both locally and abroad, but they all came with report that Abiola died a natural death.[91]

The death of Abiola led to riots in the Southwest, and his death brought an end to the June 12 crisis. Somebody had wickedly sacrificed him to settle the nation or their interest. Al Mustapha on his return was in shock and knew he had been tricked or lured away for the deed to be done. He was very angry because he did not want the chief dead.

However, the new government invited the Yoruba leaders of Afenifere and after the meeting, Abraham Adesanya, the leader of the group came out and smiled a little and returned to southwest where they defused the tension and June 12 became history.

---

91 *New Nigerian* 12 July 1998. *Guardian* 9-10 July 1998

CHAPTER EIGHTEEN

Obasanjo Anointed By The Kingmakers

Immediately Obasanjo was released from prison, Babangida was one of the first august visitors to Ota farm on 27 June, 1998. He did fly in a helicopter from the airport to the farm to welcome home Obasanjo and probably to also inform him that he had been chosen by the elite ruling class and kingmakers as the next president. The new military government had prepared a transition to civilian rule. Though Abacha had planned a presidential election on 1st August 1998 at which he was to be the only candidate from all the five political parties where he had intended to succeed himself by transforming to civilian president. There had been campaign by different groups before his death such as Youths Earnestly Ask for Abacha and the 5 million Man March for Abacha amongst others.

With the unfolding events, Abdulsalami Abubakar wanted to leave the government within a short period and retire and Obasanjo had been tipped as the next president even though it was not disclosed publicly.

The NADECO and Alliance for Democracy AD had demanded for a National Conference and Abraham Adesanya also canvassed for a southern president and an immediate sovereign national conference to divide Nigeria into six zones declaring they were tired of the north dominating and taking the presidency at all times.

Chief Bola Ige, also a member of the Afenifere leaders had helped to form the PDP but when Abacha men joined the party he pulled out. The Afenifere also helped to establish the APP again but they withdrew from the party as other Abacha men and supporters joined and were admitted into the fold.

Then they decided to form their own party with a strong base in the Southwest. They got all the local governments during the election but nothing more. However, before the elections proper, the Afenifere and its caucus leaders had bypassed Chief Bola Ige as the presidential candidate and had opted for Olu Falae who was Babangida's finance minister at a point in time.[92] But the real reason Bola Ige was not given the presidential ticket was that the leaders believed that he was too difficult to handle.

They needed somebody that was with broad view like Falae, and not a train that had no breaks. Obasanjo in July 1998 travelled to South Africa, Britain and the USA to thank the world leaders, including Jimmy Carter, for all their efforts at getting him released from prison. In August 1998 he returned from the United States into the warm embrace of the PDP.

The PDM organisation which Atiku had taken effective control of promoted the candidature of Obasanjo, as the best material from the south west. They went about

---
92 TELL 13 July 1998 pg 17-18

campaigning and persuading the ruling class of the good qualities of Obasanjo, they trusted Obasanjo as he had proved it in 1979 when he gave power to the North.

Obasanjo was highly favoured and recommended by all as he was seen to have the wisdom of stabilising the nation.

He was the only Nigerian with an international recognition who was respected all over the world and his name opened doors worldwide. How he did it still remains a mystery to many. He was the man the Americans and their powerful leaders would visit in Nigeria. It was Sunday Afolabi that brought him the PDP membership application form and by the 28th of October 1998 Obasanjo joined the PDP as a full member.

Obasanjo became the choice of the elites and the populace even though throughout his life he had always been reluctant to rule but the baton always fell into his hands. He never showed eagerness even at the call of duty to be the leader of a mission. The mantle of leadership naturally just landed his way and he always did a good job at the end.

The north trusted him as he had dined with them using Chinese chop sticks rather than the English fork and knife. In using chop sticks it's like picking your food without much interest and you are calm but using the fork and knife it's like a lion tearing his meal and cutting through which shows eagerness and it could make a man look aggressive when he is famished.

Pressure mounted from all over Nigeria and outside despite a concerned opposition from his family concerning his personal safety, the majority carried the vote and swayed Obasanjo like the waves of the Atlantic Ocean to where the kingmakers wanted him to be.

It was the hand of God at work, his prison experiences and prayers had been answered and when the world saw what had been done to a war General and a former head of state who was almost destroyed by a friend and junior officer in the army all grudges and animosity disappeared from the minds of everyone when they saw how emancipated and frail looking Obasanjo had become. It was God's doing as not many people live long after that kind of an experience and it is only imagined how his children and wives felt about the events of the few years of his incarceration.

Obasanjo's safe return had opened a new chapter and people who had grudges in the past forgave him and he was given a second chance both by God and the people. The harrowing experience had taken his fame to international dimensions and recognition, everybody was waiting all over the world to see him in person. However, in the first week of November a crowd had gathered from all over Nigeria, about 2,000 people, in Ota to hear his speech and declaration to contest for the office of the president.

Obasanjo had said he was left with 20,000 naira and that his Ota farm and businesses were in ruins. He had canvassed for support if the people and party wanted him to contest as he knew it was an enormous task to contest for a presidential election.

But with this information coming from his lips the good deeds and goodwill of many years had not been forgotten. His friends of many years, the Danjumas, Babangidas, Atiku who also brought his friend Otunba Fasawe along, the Dangotes, Donald Duke and many more organised a fund raiser within the PDP which was national in outlook and had no ethnic or religious tilt and were able to raise a total of ₦356 million.

Obasanjo was given about 130 million personally but it was meant to help in his campaign and for logistics. The other candidates were no match and there was no contest really either financially or in the case of personality and general acceptability. Alex Ekwueme, a former vice president to Shehu Shagari could raise only 20 million and so also were candidates from other opposition parties.[93]

The party convention was held and Abubakar Rimi from the North announced his support for Obasanjo, Nwobodo and Ekwueme contested from the Eastern region.

The outcome of the PDP convention resulted in Obasanjo clinching the ticket to carry the party flag. Obasanjo had 1,658 votes against Alex Ekwueme who had 521. Nwobodo had 260 votes. The Northern delegates and southwest delegates had given their full support and votes to Obasanjo within the PDP. Obasanjo having won the PDP convention now had to pick a running mate as vice president. The party struck out Abubakar Rimi and then picked Atiku Abubakar who had made great contribution to the Obasanjo fund raiser and they felt he would be more loyal being a younger candidate and would not be a threat to Obasanjo's leadership.

However, Obasanjo wanted to be sure, he had asked Atiku, "Are you ready to take orders from me?" He was in the affirmative and he was asked to go and tell the party leaders. The presidential election took place on 27 February 1999 with international observers present consisting of a 23-member team called the Commonwealth Observer Group, the Jimmy Carter

---

93 John Lliffe, *Obasanjo Nigeria and the world* Pg 168.

Centre, in collaboration with the National Democratic Institute, National Institute for International Affairs (NIIA), human rights groups and other observer groups from Canada, Japan, Norway and some African countries. Obasanjo had a landslide win, Falae accepted the result even though they had initially tried to go to court, describing the election a farce, it was clear they had no case despite some irregularities observed, Obasanjo was the winner and preferred candidate. The election was declared free and fair.

Obasanjo lost all six states in southwest Yoruba states giving him about 62% to 28% of the votes but he got some votes from Ogun State. The reason was because he had said Chief Abiola was not the messiah for Nigeria at the height of the June 12 crisis and also because the Yorubas felt he did not give Chief Awolowo the presidency in 1979.

Also again they felt he was more supportive of Northern Nigeria but in reality Obasanjo is a detribalised and a statesman and had always favoured a united Nigeria from the time of the civil war and also when he became the head of state. He had understood the technicality of running the Nigerian state with all its different ethnic groups and had believed in fair play and equality throughout and across board. It was also the position Ladoke Akintola had adopted to work with other regions especially the North to harness the advantage of a United Nigeria.

However in March, after the victory in the elections, as the president-elect, Obasanjo began another tour again to thank world leaders for their support during his travail and for standing by him during the elections.

He visited eighteen countries meeting political and business leaders in Africa, Asia, Europe and the United States of America. He went to Togo, Cote d'Ivoire, Kenya, Tanzania, Benin, Niger Republic, Mozambique and South Africa. He discussed with African leaders the need to tackle the problem of poverty on the continent which had blown into a huge dimension and was becoming worrisome giving Africa a poor and bad image of being in need of foreign aid all the time. Then he also advocated the need for Africa to devise a mechanism that would promote trade among the OAU, now AU. Then he did speak of the continued civil wars in some African States asking African leaders that they had to work together to end the civil wars being experienced in some countries in Africa.

In the United States he met with President Clinton and in Europe, he visited Britain where he held discussions with Prime Minister Tony Blair and then moved on to France to discuss with President Jacques Chirac. He also went to India, China and Japan. All these countries were the strategic trading partners of Nigeria with their textiles, pharmaceutical, electronic and automobile industries present in Nigeria. Obasanjo had taken action immediately asking for foreign trade partners to invest more. He was president-elect but had started the job immediately even before he was officially sworn in. The balance of trade had tilted to favour foreign countries as Nigeria was importing everything including tooth pick and china was the biggest beneficiary.

He canvassed for more foreign investors to Nigeria and pushed for debt cancellation which had been given to other African countries. He also focused on economic reforms where African farmers could get their goods sold in Europe, America and Asia on a fair scale with better world prices.

Obasanjo finally discussed that foreign assistance be given where there were conflict in the countries like Rwanda, Burundi, Liberia etc where foreign powers had not intervened swiftly enough to stabilise the troubled countries. When it came to discussions about Nigeria, the American government declared the problem of Nigeria as having to do with good leadership which they knew Obasanjo could deliver, as president of Nigeria.

The American government had told him that when they saw enough efforts in tackling the corruption in Nigeria they would give a helping hand in reducing Nigeria's debts and other internal problems like electricity and developmental support through aid in medical areas, agriculture, education and the energy sector. He met with the Nigerians in Diaspora who were all eager to see him. It was a successful trip.

Then came the rumour of his death that Obasanjo had been killed. This immediately led to riots in southwest Lagos and Abeokuta in Ogun State, he had to make a quick appearance to refute the rumour. Then on the 29th of May 1999 Obasanjo was sworn in as the president of Nigeria, and the presidential oath was taken at the Eagle Square in Abuja in the presence of world leaders and dignitaries including Nelson Mandela.

CHAPTER NINETEEN

Obasanjo As Civilian President (1999-2007)

Olusegun Obasanjo, former military Head of State of Nigeria, was sworn in as civilian president on the 29th of May 1999 at the Eagle Square Abuja in the presence of dignitaries from all over the world. It was his second coming to the familiar terrain of leading Nigeria, the most populous black country in Africa. It was a special day as honour, dignity and prestige was bestowed on Obasanjo a second time as he had just returned from a harrowing prison experience for no offence committed. He was like Mandela who was also present at his inauguration but the difference was, Obasanjo was a former head of state before he went to prison and later emerged to become president a second time. Mandela was not a president before he was put in prison but a freedom fighter and politician in South Africa at the time.

Obasanjo had opened his inaugural address where he declared he had walked through the valley of the shadow of death. He however declared his mission and task before him stating that he would restore the

Nigerian state and economy to how it used to be many years ago when he handed over as head state to the civilian government of Alhaji Shehu Shagari.

Immediately he was sworn in he swung into action by retiring the service chiefs whom Abdulsalami had left in posts, replacing them with men from minority areas. Those chosen had not held political posts before.[94]

Two months later the retirement and purge continued. Over two hundred officers were asked to leave the service – many had political interests and were viewed as threats to the new government. The president did a lot of restructuring in the armed forces and brought about a proper and more balanced representation, especially in the army. The defence ministry was moved to Abuja from Lagos and he depoliticised the armed forces.[95]

As at 1999 the Nigerian society was badly divided and Obasanjo was faced with many varied problematic challenges that he had inherited from the Abacha and Abdulsalami government and people were traumatised by the authoritarian rule of General Sanni Abacha whose regime had introduce constant shortage of fuel in Nigeria. There were other socio-economic problems like electricity, poor infrastructures, shortage of water as everybody had to drill boreholes or wells in their homes, telecommunications were down and inefficient, there was poor (Gross domestic product) GDP rate, low purchasing power, high interest rates in the banking sector, high debt profile which was a burden, low foreign reserves and the middle class had disappeared with an unstable environment where clashes were breaking out too often over boundaries

---
94 *Newswatch* 14 June 1999 Pg 13
95 *Thisday* 11 June, 10 July 1999

and scarce resources. There was low investment as foreign investors refused to invest in Nigeria because they were not sure of the safety and stability of the Nigerian economy.

The country was also at the lowest point of international respectability. Obasanjo continued to work, making contacts and travelling around the world as nobody wanted to do business in Nigeria. Many Nigerians trying to do business transactions with foreigners when making enquires experienced problems as business men overseas were hanging up when they discovered the call was from Nigeria because the country was regarded of as corrupt and full of fraudsters.

Obasanjo worked very hard and continued to tackle the problems on ground. He would wake up at 5a.m. and spend 16-20 hours on official duty everyday. He never left any file unattended to once it got to his table. Decisions in Nigeria were made nocturnally and implemented during the day.[96]

Obasanjo had built a chapel in Aso Rock next to his residence for himself and the Christians who worked with him. He was very prayerful. The previous governments had only built a mosque. However, not long before he took office the society in Nigeria was engulfed in social conflict due to the transition which was going on where military style of governance was giving way to civilian and democratic rule.

There was violence during his first term in office. The North was on fire and over four hundred churches were burnt. There was a lot of violence and disorder as the leaders from the North were not satisfied with

96 *Newswatch* 11 December 2000 Pg 8-19.
   Guardian 15th April 2002

emerging events. They wanted to know where they belonged and stood, in the new government. They wanted assurances they would be treated fairly after the atrocities that they caused during the Abacha government because it was not the former head of state that did all the bad things, the people around him were also part of the problems.

The North of Nigeria had continued to make things difficult for Obasanjo promising to make Nigeria ungovernable for him. They asked for key positions but were not given; the petroleum ministry that was handled by the president himself was a wise decision to control and monitor the sector.

He however zoned several posts in the government to the North but made sure there was a balance in political appointments, both ministerial and those of advisers and many of the parastatals and boards. The government also lifted the embargo on employment which opened doors for many younger graduates who wanted jobs in the civil service, bringing in new vibrant youths who were computer literate and had skills in the new information technology revolution that was unfolding in Nigeria.

Olusegun Obasanjo had proved himself before in government as a military head of state when he governed Nigeria from 1976 to 1979. During the period he was innovative in many of the decisions he took concerning local government reforms, the land use decree and had been decisive in policy matters which was carried out in military tradition. He was known to always have insisted that all policies must be implemented with "immediate effect."[97] It was this

---
97   Olusegun Obasanjo The Presidential Legacy 1999-2007 Pg. 8

slogan that landed on the television hit series, the legendary *Village Headmaster* shown on the NTA where Chief Eleyinmi used the slogan that decisions at *Oja Village* must be taken and carried out with "immediate effect and automatic alacrity."

However, Obasanjo discovered things had been done differently over the years and so many things had changed - the aviation ministry, the maritime sector, and other sectors of the economy. The Nigeria Airways had lost most of the twenty-seven aircraft he left in its fleet in 1979 when he handed over power to a civilian government and was owing debts all over the world wherever it operated.[98]

The Nigerian National Shipping Line (NNSL) had lost most of its vessels and only had one left. This had been a vibrant shipping line which they had named the best National Shipping Line in the 1970s.

President Obasanjo was sober seeing that they had destroyed the "House Jack Built" i.e. the military era from 1966 to 1979 - it started with General Yakubu Jack Gowon, Murtala Muhammed and Obasanjo. The roads were bad, government hospitals had become mere consulting rooms as new equipment were not available and there were no drugs. The University teaching hospitals and the government run hospitals had been a place to go for the citizens of Nigeria in the 1970s. Once you see a doctor you are rest assured your problem was solved because immediately he prescribed the drugs they were readily available and given to you at the pharmacy of the hospitals. Even when they did not have they would source for it and ask you to come back to pick them up in 24 hours while

---
98 Ibid Pg. 9

they gave a temporary one that would give some relief; that was the good old days. The situation in 1999 had been the absence of experienced doctors most of whom had gone to Saudi Arabia, Britain and America.

Obasanjo realised he had to solve the problem by getting new equipments and upgrading facilities. Then he reviewed salaries and within the eight-year tenure people working in the civil service had gotten about six hundred percent increase in salaries. This triggered many developments and standard of living went up. The poor university lecturers started buying cars again and their standard of living became better.

Those on pension and in retirement got an upgrade, bringing comfort to them in retirement. The government also tackled the problem of corruption. There were many ghost workers in the civil service. This is a situation where the numbers of workers are inflated for a cartel of people to siphon money out of the government.

He also introduced new tax reforms. President Obasanjo was surprised at the level of corruption going on in Nigeria by 1999, people were now talking in billions and corruption was everywhere including the police force and judiciary. It became obvious that unless the menace being caused by corrupt practices was tackled there was no way the country could have peace, security or stability.

The first bill Obasanjo sent to the National Assembly was that of corruption and how to deal with it. Early in his tenure when civil servants got wind of it they all became cautious and careful. It was implemented two yeas after and deliberately delayed by the government legislators because they wanted the business as usual style, while he had insisted it would no longer be business as usual.

President Obasanjo had setup the Economic and Financial Crimes Commission (EFCC) and also the Independent Corrupt Practices Commission (ICPC). The EFCC was headed by a dynamic young man, Mr. Nuhu Ribadu, who was brought from the police force. The ICPC did not appear to have achieved much, maybe because it was headed by a very much older man – Retired Justice Akanbi Mustapha. The EFCC was very efficient and the politicians and press labelled it an attack dog of president Obasanjo and that it was sent after those who did not do what Mr. President wanted but that was not true. It did its work and was heard all over the world. Mr. Nuhu Ribadu was fearless and did his job very well, he got too tough and went after corrupt people irrespective of their status and influence.

The National Assembly trembled for fear of Ribadu and had tried to cut back and whittle down his power by amending the Act that established the EFCC to make it less dependent on the Presidency. However, the agency continued to do its work fearlessly and had recovered over 5 billion dollars.[99]

The first casualty of this new policy was the former Inspector General of Police, Mr Tafa Balogun, who was convicted of corruption. He had acquired so many properties, shares in blue chip companies and loads of cash. Money that was expected to be used for the development of the police force was converted to personal use.

---

99 Ibid Pg 51

The new police boss who took over, Mr. Sunday Ehindero, had to sack 10,000 policemen who were seen as the bad eggs in the force. He said the recruitment exercise done in the year 2000 had featured cases of inducement. Officers were given money in exchange for a placement in the police force - the statutory requirements like educational qualifications, age and height and background check were overlooked and ignored. The new Inspector General had declared that the police force did not have the requisite materials, equipment or facilities to train a modern police force. He described the situation as garbage in garbage out. He further stated that both policemen and women were poorly paid and could not refuse financial inducement coming from external sources. This led Chief Afe Babalola, the famous Ibadan-based lawyer who was also the president's personal lawyer to say sarcastically that the British government should come back and train the Nigerian police with the modern trends, training facilities and systems.

Obasanjo also had to confront the problem of the militants all through the country - those in the Niger Delta area, the East with Bakassi boys, the Fulani herdsmen and the Oodua Peoples'Congress popularly called the OPC which came into existence to promote and defend Yoruba interest. OPC arose as a reaction to the annulment of the June 12 elections. It was founded by Dr. Fredrick Fasehun. Following disagreements between its two chieftains the organisation lost its discipline and direction and began to engage in excesses. This led to the prosecution of its leaders for breaching the peace.[100]

---

[100] Thisday February 5 2002
John Lliffe *Obasanjo Nigeria and the world* Pg 188.

There were clashes between various communities over boundary demarcations that were ill defined and the problems that came from the indigene and settler communities which had resulted from internal migration over many years. The problems were seen in the Southwest with the Ife/Modakeke conflict . The Modakekes had come to Ife many years ago asking the Ooni of Ile Ife at the time for land they could settle in which he gave them. They were charged to be of good behaviour and pay their taxes and this gave them the settler title. The indigenous people were the original people found in the area who were the Yoruba from Ile Ife. The settlers were called Modakeke, meaning "I will stay peacefully and quietly within your domain."

Then two or three generations later they wanted to claim ownership of the land and installed their own traditional ruler.

It was Obasanjo's wisdom and treat of emergency, like he did in Odi, that settled the rift for over a decade and not a single crisis was heard again. The crisis that had erupted frequently and often led to death and destruction of property fizzled out.

There were other conflicts between farmers and the nomadic Fulani herdsmen. The Fulani allow their cattle to graze on farmlands and thereby destroys the farmers' hard work and crops. The Fulani would clash with the farmers over the damage, exchange hot words, the Fulani leave but later regroup and launch unexpected attacks killing the farm owners and burning their houses and raping their women. This has gone on in Nigeria for years with the Fulani getting away unpunished - now they feel they are untouchable.

The colonial authority under Her Majesty's government, as it was called at the time, had told the northerners through their leaders that for effective control of the frontiers of the North the Fulani who roam with their cattle should expand their frontiers by going further into territories that did not belong to them, especially up North in places like Jos and the Middle belt areas and look for unoccupied settlement within the frontiers of their distant neighbours and take control of the place by settling down in the deep forest, which also gave them allowance to graze their cattle.

The idea was that by the time population expansion got to the area they will surprise the inhabitants of those areas when they discover Fulani settlement is already within their frontiers. At times they were successfully apprehended and sent packing but many times they were left to stay because they had something to offer, because cattle dung fertilized the soil for planting. This was the genesis of having settlers springing up all over the North of Nigeria that were not the indigenous people of those areas and also outside the North to the southern territories till date.

After independence people began to move freely in different regions just like when the North and South were amalgamated in 1914 by Lord Lugard and Nigeria was formed as one union and people started trading freely between the regions that formed Nigeria.

During the military era with General Babangida as Head of State and president, he created a local government area in 1991 known as Jos North which was carved out from the Jos East and the Jos South Local Government Areas. It was designed to make the Hausa/Fulani settlers legitimate indigenes but since that event, the territory has known no peace. The Hausa/Fulani with this local government council felt it was now time to put this conquest to test by provoking crisis. A local government council of this nature legalised their stay as settlers, changing their status to indigenes. That is not possible since you cannot make a Yoruba man the Sultan of Sokoto because the Yorubas have lived for a century in Sokoto or then create a local government exclusively for them when they are merely settlers. It was same with Ife and Modakeke. Settlers cannot become the landlords over the indigenes of an area. What Babangida did was totally wrong and it should be corrected immediately.

The problem of Nigeria is enormous but national issues should be dealt with in a manner that requires courage, justice and equity. The original ethnic groups are the Berom, Afizere, Anaguta and Buji people. They are the indigenous people of Jos. The Hausa/Fulani are settlers in the town. The political space in Nigeria is controlled by hypocrisy and falsehood and the fear to stand on the right path when it's against the tide.

Then came the most troublesome topic in Nigeria, the introduction of Sharia Law in Zamfara State in Northern Nigeria by the All Peoples Party (APP) governor Ahmed Sanni Yerima. This was a man clean shaven like a cadet but immediately he got into office he grew his beard wild barbarian style and sang the new tune of Islamising his state. Northern Nigeria has always practiced Sharia Law but it was normally practised in civil cases under customary law and it depended on the agreement of both parties if they wanted to be tried under Sharia Law - the reason being that Nigeria's Constitution is supreme.

Technically speaking, trying to make Islamic law the governing law of the state meant you had created a sovereign state which was no more a part of Nigeria. It was like declaring an independent state outside of Nigeria. The Governor had tried to implement Sharia Law in both civil and criminal cases. Sharia Law had been restricted to civil cases at independence in Nigeria. The criminal code of the Constitution in Nigeria governed all states in Nigeria. Ahmed Sanni Yerima took advantage of the loosely drafted clause in the new Constitution that allowed a state to extend the jurisdiction of its Sharia courts. He urged Muslims to adopt the radical side of Islam which promoted Jihad and Sharia. He put a ban on alcohol, changed the dress code, and he said men and women could not go on the same bus or ride on a motorcycle together. He declared Sharia as the state law, nullifying the Constitution in his state. He declared an Islamic state and got away with it. He introduced the Sharia Code that negates the criminal code of Nigeria. Sharia legal code includes stoning for adultery, armed robbery and cutting of hands for theft. He did cut off a man's hand for stealing a goat to show his seriousness.[101]

The other Northern governors hailed him, without understanding the implication of this new radical idea. They supported him because all that had happened in Nigeria since independence had been North versus South and since the president was a Southerner they disdained him. They all went along with Sharia deliberately unmindful of the fact that it was causing tension in Nigeria and uproar around the world.

---

101 *Thisday* 6 October 1999
 Thisday 25 March 2000
 Thisday 2 February 2001
 Thisday 16 February 2000

Then crisis hit Kaduna State, the governor at the time, Alhaji Ahmed Makarfi, struggled to keep the peace. There was an anti-Sharia march in Kaduna on 21 February 2000 which led to a conflict, slaughter and death that spread to neighbouring towns and caused some 1,295 deaths before the army could restored order. The Igbos again suffered great casualty and when the bodies of Igbo victims returned to Abia and other southeastern towns, revenge mobs killed over 300 northerners.

Obasanjo summoned the Council of States meeting, an advisory body composed of former heads of state and Chief Justices together with incumbent governors. The Vice President Atiku Abubakar first held a meeting with the governors, he was from the North and a Muslim and they all agreed to suspend the implementation of Sharia and return to status quo.

Obasanjo announced that the council had approved this. Ahmed Sani denied he agreed to suspend Sharia. General Buhari denied that the council had considered Sharia and former president Shehu Shagari who did not attend concluded the council had no power or authority over the matter.[102]

The following months in Kaduna were those of division between the Muslims and Christians. It was at this point that the Vice President Atiku Abubakar started to offend and betray the trust President Obasanjo had for him. He could not do the right thing or stick his neck out and rather he followed the northern agenda of political Sharia. It was a slight on his person but I guess Atiku did not realize he was the

---

102 *Newswatch* 13 March 2000
   Thisday 1st, 3rd and 9th March 2000

one who got insulted having announced to the public on television broadcast only to be demeaned by his brothers up North that nothing of such decision was taken.

The Christians reacted with suspicion and felt the North wanted to Islamize Nigeria. The adoption and implementation of these laws was directed at destabilising the President because he was a southerner. They were a little cautions because Obasanjo had been a General in the army and during the civil war he had worked closely with the North in keeping Nigeria as one.

The Constitution of Nigeria states clearly that neither the federal nor any state government can adopt any religion as state religion. It states that Nigeria is a secular state. When the option of force was suggested to Obasanjo after all negotiations and suggestions about allowing the Supreme Court determine the matter had failed, he had opted not to do so. The reason being that it could cause some friction in the judiciary because both Christians and Muslims were equally represented in the apex court. So he described it as Sharia politics which he said would fizzle out and indeed it did after about three years. He had tried to dissuade Governor Yerima about the matter but had ignored him when the governor was adamant. He knew deep down that northern leaders had no intention to disrupt a federation from which their region received much needed revenue nor did they wish to alienate further the Christian areas in the middle belt from which Obasanjo's government got much of its support.

Ahmed Sanni Yerima had boasted that not even the Supreme Court could stop him. Lawyers debated the constitutionality of Sharia and wanted the government to take a stand. But Obasanjo had wisely said it would split the judiciary and it would become a no win situation.

Obasanjo was criticised by the southern part of Nigeria for not taking a stand. They had described Obasanjo's leadership style as an ostrich style of leadership. However, he was very careful in taking decisions that will heat up the polity and degenerate into serious unrest. It was the most controversial challenge as the attorney general had no clue to solving the problem. Chief Bola Ige defended himself by saying that after all it's their peoples hands they were cutting off. It was the time a man called Jangedi had his hand cut off for stealing a goat in Zamfara State on the orders of the governor when he wanted to prove a point he was serious. The same governor had later compensated the man who was pictured in the newspaper controlling activities in a busy warehouse. Many states in the north adopted Sharia after Zamfara State, but just as Obasanjo had predicted, it died a natural death

Then in September 2001, a minor incident had sparked of violence which lasted for about seven days. The news that the world trade centre in New York in America had collapsed intensified the conflict in Jos which claimed the lives of about five hundred people.

The carnage had taken place before the army regained control. President Obasanjo visited Jos where he was shocked at the level of destruction and loss of lives. He urged reconciliation but the violence did not abate as they felt Osama Bin Laden had conquered America and the violence spread with about one thousand people dead. The fighting had been between indigenes and settlers before the president declared a state of emergency in May 2004. Obasanjo suspended the state governor and brought in a military administrator for a six months period to restore order and peace to Jos.

However, failure to bring the perpetrators of violence in Nigeria to book or call them to order has increased and caused them to become bolder and more daring - worsening the situation.

Obasanjo had toned down his reactions after he was criticized late 1999 for the Odi crisis when the town was destroyed by the army. The problem had started with militant thugs called Asawana Boys that were employed as party thugs. They had terrorized the community and were causing problems in the peaceful town of Bayelsa. They took refuge in Odi and when police officers were sent to investigate the boys, they tortured, kidnapped and eventually killed the policemen.

Obasanjo had instructed the governor to apprehend those responsible. The governor reported back defiantly that he could not. Then Obasanjo handed the matter to the army where specific and unambiguous instructions were given. They were to dislodge perpetrators of violence, restore law and order and apprehend suspected murderers.

A force, reportedly numbered at between 300 and 1000 reached Odi on 20th November 1999 in armoured personnel carriers with heavy weapons as they did not know what to expect. The outcome was a disaster. The reports were disputed. The army chief of staff said they were ambushed at the entrance to the town and met serious resistance and another version said there was exchange of fire before the military cleared the town and spent several days destroying everything within except a church, bank and health centre. The official government figure of casualty said forty-three people died but a report by a local NGO put the civilian death at over 2,000 people. It is known that soldiers do not react that way without any provocation.

Obasanjo had visited the place four months after in March 2001 where he regretted the action, saying it was an avoidable incident. He said the soldiers had gone beyond their brief but the killing of people and officers in uniform by the militants was stopped.

Another incident had taken place at Zaki Biam, a village on the border between Benue and Taraba States. The region was disputed between the Tiv and Jukun people. This was Middle Belt of Nigeria where many military officers came from.

There was a conflict and serious unrest. Then in October 2001 nineteen soldiers had been sent to restore peace and order in the area. They were surrounded by Tiv militiamen who themselves were mainly ex-soldiers. The troops were taken to Zaki Biam believing they were Jukun militia men impersonating soldiers of the Nigerian army and they were brutally killed. This led to serious anger in the army. Obasanjo had declared that those who killed my soldiers must be fished out.[103]

He further spoke on television while being interviewed by local and international media and press: "You don't expect me fold my hands and do nothing because tomorrow neither soldiers nor policemen will go anywhere I send them." He also blew hot air when one British journalist came to interview him concerning

---

103 *TELL* 5 November 2001 Pg 35-43
   TELL 21 January 2002 Pg 33

Odi, Zaki Biam and about the Niger Delta unrest and was trying to challenge the president. Obasanjo roared angrily at the journalist, making the man trembled and embarrassed.

Obasanjo had asked him about what Margaret Thatcher did during the Falkland Island crisis where she used maximum force, sinking ships and declaring full war against Argentina. The president's spokesman said that Obasanjo had ordered minimum force. The army rounded up and killed about 200-300 people in about six villages.

Then Vice President Atiku Abubakar admitted that things went out of hand. Obasanjo again apologised on behalf of the army for their use of excessive force and loss of civilian lives. He had visited the area after a year. He said the military are only invited when all negotiations fail. Babangida had commended him and said it was only Obasanjo that could solve many of the problems springing up around Nigeria.

President Obasanjo had introduced the GSM Global Satellite Mobile that had revolutionised the telecommunication industry. It had initially been very expensive and only the rich could get one. But over the years the price came down drastically where every Nigerian family, no matter how poor got a phone to use in their homes. Today, Nigeria has more than four telephone network providers providing telephone service for the huge population and market. It helped the economy and business and people are grateful that Obasanjo did that.

Obasanjo had also tackled the problem of the HIV scourge and AIDs. There were no drugs in Nigeria when he became president in 1999 because only the very rich could get the drugs. He had gone to lobby the World Health Organization (WHO) and world leaders to assist Africa and Nigeria in getting the drugs at affordable and cheap prices. The world had gotten to the millennium years and Nigeria had to address her problems related to socio-economic reforms in a broad scale along with development goals that needed change.

The efforts of Obasanjo got the continent of Africa new opportunities for a rebirth where things were done differently with a new approach. This got Africa and Nigeria debt relief. The debt trap of Nigeria and other African countries had been like the dream of biblical pharaoh in which fat cows were grazing in the fields and suddenly some thin cows came out of the water and ate the fat cows but, despite eating the big cows, the thin cows were still very thin. That was the situation of Nigeria and her African neighbours. Obasanjo travelled all over the world fixing the image of Nigeria and had gone to about ninety-two countries around the world.

Obasanjo's diplomatic engagements around the world paid off as creditor nations realized that giving funds in form of aid to an indebted country did not help much but the outright cancellation of debts freed Africans from the financial albatross that seemed to be turning into a monster that seemed to increase on a gradual scale. Before the Obasanjo government came on board Nigeria's external debt stood at over 30 billion dollars owed to creditors.

As a result of this debt much of the revenue earned from oil exports was spent on debt servicing. The belief was that it was just the interest on the loans that was being paid and the original loans continued to accumulate and it became a mystery on how much debt was really owned to the creditor nations and their financial institutions.

President Obasanjo had gone into negotiations with the country's creditors and his team was often led by the finance minister Dr. (Mrs.) Ngozi Okonjo Iweala subsequent and payment of agreed amounts of about 12 billion upfront led to the cancellation of 18 billion which led to Nigeria's release from external debt trap early in 2007.[104]

That was the greatest thing any leader had achieved for Nigeria since independence and all hailed the president and thanked him for his tireless travels to all points of the compass. It was then the public press knew the value of the Owu General, it was like magic for those who understood the implication of what he had done. Nigeria was free to run her affairs as she pleased since she was not owing anybody a dime. She did what she wanted without external interference.

Also during his tenure he had introduced the prepaid meters for electricity users in the country. He said no more illegal disconnections as it was going to be like the GSM telephone system. You can now load your meter with the rechargeable card. The way you use your electricity consumption was going to be your business. It was aimed at saving the wastages of electricity. If you want light you put it on and if you want your card to read slowly you could turn it off especially if you travelled out of town.

---

104 Olusegun Obasanjo, *The Presidential Legacy* 1999-2007 Pg 113

This new innovation in the power sector did not go down well with corrupt officials because the old system allowed for corruption and overbloated billing, thereby swindly innocent Nigerians of their hard-earned money.

The power situation had been so bad that many companies and industries moved to Ghana like the tyre manufacturers -Michelin and Dunlop. They closed down along with many other companies citing the high cost of doing business in Nigeria as they were not making money or any profit. Immediately Obasanjo left they put fixed charged on the meters and started stealing and ripping Nigerians off in broad daylight and the situation became worse.

Then there was the privatisation of government parastatals and companies. From the time Nigeria became an independent country in 1960 the government had controlled the economy directly through its direct involvement in the production of goods and services which was controlled and managed by public enterprises.

This was to help industrialisation and economic development. It was government that had the finance to set up businesses at the time. However, over the years the public enterprise ended up in monumental failures as a result of mismanagement, corruption and unpatriotic managers who had poor skills, thereby bringing about technical failure. There were many commissions set-up to look into the reasons why the public enterprises were doing badly in output and performance. There was the Adebo Committees in 1969 among others. They had proffered solutions from various inquiries and investigations.

The factors that were identified as reasons for poor performance included bureaucratic bottlenecks and government interference in public enterprises. The operations had been politicised in reaching business decision, technical expertise and corruption by the managers of public enterprises who collaborated with officials of supervising ministries ending up in gross mismanagement.

The first process had started with nationalisation of British Petroleum and some other companies. Then in 1979 British Prime Minister introduced the system of privatisations, breaking the unions in Britain who were always going on strike. It was Margaret Thatcher who made the policy popular.

The first privatisation programme was done by General Ibrahim Babangida shortly after the British Prime Minister visited him in Lagos which was still the seat of power at the time.

Mrs. Thatcher had driven on the presidential route of Mobolaji Bank Anthony Way and Ikorodu Road and she exclaimed at the number of car dealerships along the route and the number of different luxury cars. She sarcastically asked: "Does your country manufacture vehicles?" It was then Babangida sent a signal to all car dealers to relocate from the route but the business elite persuaded him to ignore the comment and allow the car dealers to do their business.

Babangida embarked on the privatisation programme between 1989 and 1994. It was called the Technical Committee on Privatisation and Commercialisation (TCPC) established under Decree No 25 of 1988. When General Sanni Abacha took over and became the head of state, he continued with the programme but had cleverly opted for the best option of privatising government institutions. The military administration of General Sanni Abacha attempted to lease or contract out management but it did not take off because foreign investors and Nigerians were all living in fear. They were afraid of Abacha because of his high-handedness and because of the security situation at the time.

After Nigeria returned to civil rule in 1999 with Obasanjo in the saddle he revamped the privatisation programme because he discovered that all the public enterprises they had set-up in the 1970s had become moribund with the assets of most of them unaccounted for. The national shipping line had been destroyed and the aviation industry with Nigeria airways depleted on all fronts, the 27 jets had disappeared. The process was made public and transparent but only the affluent benefitted and some selected investors from outside.[105]

The government had accorded the programme with the kind of publicity and political support that gave confidence to the international community. Hotels were privatised, steel mills, some of the textile industries, the block making industries (red bricks) amongst others including the refineries. However, when Umar Yar'Adua became president in 2007 after Obasanjo had left, he reversed the sale of the refineries.

Then Obasanjo also set-up the Reconciliation panel which was headed by Justice Chukwudifu Oputa to look into all the grievances that had taken place in Nigeria from independence till his civilian administration in 1999. Obasanjo declared May 29 as democracy day as opposed to June 12 which the southwest states adopted. This annoyed the southwest

---
105 Ibid Pg 9.

and apostles of the June 12 1993 mandate. They were asking that Abiola be recognised as a president and the winner of the election.

The Oputa panel also looked into the extra judicial killings during the Abacha days. It was a successful reconciliatory commission. Obasanjo wanted people to pour out their hearts on the wrongs done to them by past governments including the time the Kuti family had a clash with the army where the legendary singer, Fela Anikulapo Kuti had his house burnt by rampaging soldiers who were displeased with his political songs "Zombie" and "yellow fever". There were other songs that criticized the government at the time but since Nigeria was under a military government and had not adopted civilian rule, fundamental human rights of citizens were violated.

The Oputa panel findings led to the arrest of the members and key officials in the Abacha government who were involved in extra judicial killings. President Obasanjo allowed the son of the head of state to see the other side of life as they had been pampered by Abacha. He had allowed Mohammed Abacha to have a taste of prison life.

Then there was the case of resource control during his tenure as president. The Niger Delta crisis had led the people of the southsouth called Niger Delta to ask for full control of the resources within their territory and region. They declared that the continental shelf belonged to them. The dispute came to a head when the federal government asked the Supreme Court in the case of *Attorney General of the federation v Attorney General of Abia State (2002)* which became a celebrated case to determine and interpret section 162(2) of the

1999 Constitution in the sharing of revenue derived from offshore resources. The Supreme Court was asked to determine the seaward boundary of a littoral state within the country for the purpose of calculating the amount of revenue accruing to the federation directly from any natural resources derived from the state. It was judged to be the low water mark of the land surface. The judgment was delivered on April 5, 2002 which was consequent on the suit instituted on February 6, 2001 by the late Chief Bola Ige.

In the hearing of October 29, 2001 Chief Bola Ige told the full court that with regard to land or waters over which Nigeria exercise sovereignty or over which it is authorised under the Constitution to exercise sovereign power, the federal government alone is the competent hand to exercise such sovereign powers. However I will go further to define offshore and onshore oil dichotomy.

Offshore oil means oil found in the water area and every body knows that offshore does not belong to any state but is owned and controlled by the federal government, because no state owns the sea of this country. The sea and oceans belong to the federal government. That is the law.

Onshore oil simply means oil found on the land. Dichotomy means division between the land mass and the sea. The territorial sea is that portion measured from the shore to the sea known as territorial waters. This is the belt of the sea under a state's territorial jurisdiction (formerly the range of a canon shot, or three miles, but now often controversial).

Territorial jurisdiction is the sovereign jurisdiction exercised by a state over all lands, waters, persons and properties within its boundaries. The high seas mean the unenclosed waters of the ocean, especially those beyond the territorial jurisdiction of any country or nation.

A littoral state is a state on the shore or a region lying along the shore. The 1982 convention on the law of the sea, as the constitutional lawyer, Professor Sagay said, is explicit in stating that territory that abuts the sea owns the continental shelf. That might be true to a point but it also applies where the territory is a sovereign state.

The continental shelf does not belong to the littoral state. This happens only if it is a sovereign state. He was wrong in asserting that in a federation the continental shelf belongs to the littoral states. However, Sagay was right when he said the continental shelf automatically becomes an underground part of the state which international law has accepted. But where the states are not sovereign the continental shelf becomes the right of the federal government as in the case of Nigeria.

If the littoral states gained the continental shelf, this would give them the license to secede as it would create another sovereign nation. Obasanjo had been very wise in handling the technicalities of the resource control problem.

What he eventually did for the Niger Delta State was to give them 13% extra from crude revenue and he had set-up the (NDDC) Niger Delta Development Commission to tackle the grievances and environmental problems of the area. It was also to bring the needed development to the area. However, natural resources located offshore within the territorial waters of Nigeria or within the exclusive economic zone and the continental shelf was therefore that of the federal government as it was within the territory of the federal and central government which was outside the ownership of the respective littoral states.

The loss of Bakassi deprived Cross River State of certain oil wells leading to a loss of revenue in later years. West Bakassi was ceded to Cameroon by the International Court of Justice at The Hague in 2002 and since two presidents who came after Obasanjo refused to appeal the judgment which was allowed within a twelve year period they take the blame because new evidence was discovered after the judgment. Professor Walter Ofonagoro brought out maps showing the British government had during colonial times accessed Calabar town through west Bakassi, meaning that it could not be Cameroon's territory.

The period between 1999 and 2007 and beyond had its fair share of violence and crisis and many state governors kept asking for state police, which was turned down by President Obasanjo. Successive Inspectors Generals of Police refused to agree that decentralising the police force would create a better security force and system.

Nigeria, with its peculiar composition as a nation, has continued to exist without disintegrating to a war as a result of the structure. The leaders from past and present governments had introduced it and have kept it that way. Many democratic countries operating federal structure normally have what you call a decentralized police system, that is, states have their own police within the state and the federal has what you call federal troopers or police. The balance is that the state police handle state matters, while the federal police deal with federal matters but are above the state.

This means that, when the case comes within federal jurisdiction the state police officers hands off. This can be seen in advanced countries like the United States of America and Canada.

The African countries that had tried the state police ended up in flames as a result of break down of law and order and misuse of power caused by tribal and ethnic sentiments. Nigeria refused to decentralize its police force after the experience from the 1959 elections and early 1960s experience when politicians used the police as private army to deal with their opponents.

The reality on the ground shows nothing has changed since 1950 from the actions, thinking and reasoning of politicians. The leaders are different but their ways are still the same. The leopard can not change its spots. State police is a danger for Nigeria. It is a system that would have enhanced security and worked for the country if it was a single nation but we are yet to throw away our tribal and ethnic sentiments. It is a mine field for even any region to contemplate having a state police. Those within the same region are not fully in harmony with one another. The Ijaws and Itsekiris and Urhobos are always quarrelling and are all from the southsouth, the Ijebus and Egbas of southwest, the Tivs and their neighbours the Jukun, Hausa Fulani etc. There are always conflicts within neighbouring towns and villages. It is evident the government will misuse it, as many are already power drunk.

The debate centres on those who claim that having state police in the country will help in reducing crime, especially in the face of the endemic insecurity being perpetrated even by the Islamic fundamentalist group and sect, Boko Haram, as well as other security challenges facing the nation. Those in the opposition are of the view that the nation would disintegrate if such is allowed. The truth of the matter is that Nigeria cannot afford to have governors controlling a state police. They will misuse it to fight their opponents and oppress the citizens of the state and anybody who dare criticize their government. They will even use it against the federal government. Take the example of Lagos when Governor Fashola used police and LASTMA to beat up Air force men and soldiers in uniform because they drove on the BRT Lane. LASTMA and KAI have on many occasions become terror agencies against the public. What will happen if Lagos has full control of the police? A governor who is a member of the Nigerian Bar Association does not obey court orders.

The case of Jos is unfortunate. Governor Jang as a God-fearing man said as Chief Security Officer of the state he cannot command the police or the army or even Boys Scouts in his state due to the way the Constitution has been structured. He further explained that during the crisis in Jos whenever he contacted the police commissioner, he would be told that they have not got directive from the Inspector General of Police from Abuja. That if he contacted the General Officer Commanding (GOC) the 3rd Amoured Division in Jos, he would be told that soldiers can only be called out to the streets if there was such an order from the defence headquarters or presidency and by the time directives would come many lives would have been lost.

At the height of a crisis people in charge of these security agencies had deliberately switched off their phones which should not have happened. That was during the Jonathan presidency in 2012 and many lives were lost. However when such a thing happens the president has to step in to investigate the matter and take proper action.

State police is also not workable in Nigeria, when the EFCC tried to arrest former governors for charges of corruption they used their personal militias to fight the EFCC off. This was done by some northern governors and two others in the Niger Delta. How do you fight or challenge the federal government by resisting arrest? If there was state police, what will they have done or how far would they go?

The northern governors are against state police because it could lead to a better balance of the security structure in Nigeria. The possibility that the south will use the opportunity to arm their states will arise. This gives governors from the south the power to acquire arms, use them and create storage of major military equipments including small arms and ammunition as well as sophisticated military equipment and weapons. Simply put, state police will entail individual states recruiting men for their police force, buying weapons and ammunition for them and being in control of when and how it is used. The northern governors have the fear that southern governors have higher purchasing power which is why they wanted to scrap the onshore/offshore dichotomy taking back the 13% Obasanjo had given the region during his tenure as president which was awarded to oil producing states.

They fear that a proper build up could challenge the federal might and military structure. Having a state police for Nigeria the way the country is structured with its mixed ethnic composition is not a good idea because today most Nigerians identify with their ethnic and tribal background before they declare they are Nigerians. Most people will say we are Hausa, Fulani, Yoruba or Igbo, etc before accepting to declare they are Nigerians.

Good governance and equiping and training of the police force are what we need. The police need good training, better equipment and the need to introduce the use of helicopters and not just keeping them as decoration in the police headquarters. We do not want a situation where greedy Inspector Generals of Police corner all the police funds for their own personal interest to create a personal paradise of luxury, buying houses, fleets of cars and shares. I think discipline and good management of police funds is a solution to the problem of insecurity in Nigeria.

If we however allow for state police, the regions will plan their exit from the strained relationship the core north has brought on other parts of Nigeria. It will lead to a confederation where regions will seek their independence and a break-up from the 1914 amalgamation of the north and south.

Controversy That Trailed Obasanjo's Second Term

As Obasanjo decided to go for a second term there were lots of people up north who cried foul, that he signed an agreement to stay in office for only one term of four years.

Then they heated up the polity and started media attacks. The then Governor of Sokoto State, Alhaji Attahiru Bafarawa, had said of Obasanjo: "We want our power back, you know the people in the North gave him, Obasanjo the mandate, we gave you people power, now we want it back."106

Then the vice president too was displeased and he struck a chord of disloyalty to Obasanjo. Vice President Atiku Abubakar threw caution to the winds – he had hoped to take over from Obasanjo after his first term but president Obasanjo had not finished his job as it was during his second term the debt cancellation deal came through. Vice president Atiku had forgotten his place and position in government.

A vice president is effective and active only if a president wants him to be, since he derives all his assignment from the president. It is only the president that determines what the vice president will do.

A moderate ego demonstrates wisdom. What specific roles a vice president will play depends not only upon his understanding of these rules but also upon the particular needs of the president and his administration. That a vice president will succeed the president after the expiration of his tenure is not automatic.

The framers of the Constitution felt a vice president was necessary in the event of the death or disability of the president. The loyalty of the vice president is a crucial and critical issue. Al Gore lost out in the elections in the United States of America as successor to Bill Clinton who was president on accusations of disloyalty on the Monica Lewinsky affair. Atiku Abubakar's politcal associates had misled him, they had told him

---

106 *TELL* 6 May 2002 Pg 28
   In Biafra Africa died
   The Diplomatic plot
   Emefiena Ezeani Pg. 207

to be confrontational and challenge Obasanjo but he never knew they were misleading him. I guess today when he reflects back in time he would have figured it out that certain friends who posed as his supporters had misled him.

Chapter Twenty

Obasanjo's Hot Romance With America

When Chief Olusegun Obasanjo emerged as military head of state in 1976 there were huge tasks before his government in Nigeria. The country was just picking up from the ashes of an earlier civil war which ended in 1970 but was still plagued by instability as a result of coups within the military at the time. The government also had a time table to hand over to a democratically elected government within a three-year period.

Despite the challenges, Olusegun Obasanjo was determined to leave a good legacy for his government and Nigeria. This became possible with his broad view, intelligence and experience which he got from the time he was a young cadet who had gone on various military assignment and training in Great Britain, India, the United States of America and within the African continent in countries like Ghana and Congo.

But America had brought him a totally different experience and he knew it was the future country of the world. The size, composition of different people living in America made him realize the need to keep Nigeria united as a nation.

He also discovered the economic and industrial power

of America and its military strength and felt Nigeria would need to partner with the United States to strengthen its economy and industrial capacity.

He then got his foreign affairs team together and a state visit was arranged. President Obasanjo visited the United States of America on October 11, 1977 as military Head of State of Nigeria while President Jimmy Carter was the sitting president. President Carter was one of the great presidents at the time around the world, who wanted and made every country inclusive and wanted world peace even though a few people felt he was too gentle and soft at the time. He gave respect to every race. He governed America with the rule of law, respect for human rights, and the right of others around other countries of the world. Nigeria was well received. Olusegun Obasanjo at the time had discussed the need for the western powers to ensure stability and rapid development of Africa which could come only through the quest for global peace and security.

He also talked about the apartheid situation in South Africa declaring it was a potentially dangerous situation that threatened international peace and security. Obasanjo further discussed efforts to foster cooperation and amity between the two countries noting the favourable tone of the Jimmy Carter government. Bilateral relations in technical and economic spheres got a boost between both countries. The state visit was successful and this led to the romance with the American government.

President Jimmy Carter was the first American president to come to Nigeria and it was the first state visit of an American president to sub-Saharan Africa. The visit was from the 31st of March to the 3rd of April, 1978. Franklin Roosevelt had been the first president to visit the continent of Africa in 1943 when he went to Liberia.

Jimmy Carter's visit to Nigeria led to a personal love for Africa and Nigeria and for the past two decades his love for Nigeria had never ceased to grow. Today, honourable Jimmy Carter and Rosalynn Carter continue to help in the eradication of schistosomiasis, a silent and destructive parasitic infection that leads to poor growth and impaired learning. They also helped with eradicating guineaworm. He urged that the medicine praziquantel be made more accessible to rural dwellers in impoverished communities. They also help local health workers to distribute drug treatments that prevent river blindness, disfigurement and organ damage. The Carter centre today in partnership with Nigerian health authorities has created a village-based health care delivery infrastructure to help treat multiple diseases. General Gowon had also worked hard and helped out in the eradication of guineaworm disease.

The following year on Tuesday 1st October, 1979, at a colourful celebration witnessed by many world leaders and dignitaries from around the world, General Olusegun Obasanjo stepped down as head of state of the federal military government of Nigeria and handed over power to a democratically elected president, Alhaji Aliyu Usman Shehu Shagari as the president and commander-in-chief of the armed forces of the federal republic of Nigeria.

The successive governments for the next two decades had been visiting the United States but none could repeat the feat of getting a sitting American president to visit Nigeria. General Babangida had tried to romance Chief MKO Abiola to accomplish the feat but it fell through.

Then in 1999 General Olusegun Obasanjo returned to power after twenty years and the magic started all over again. Everybody on the globe wanted to have a relationship with Nigeria. The leading men and women around the world courted Obasanjo and wanted to see him after the nasty experience he had gone through when General Sanni Abacha imprisoned him falsely on the trumped up charge of a coup where he declared that Obasanjo wanted to violently over throw his government. It was a miracle he survived like Daniel coming out of the Lion's Den.

Once he was installed as the president and sworn in on Saturday, 29th May, 1999, Madeleine Albright, America's Secretary of State declared Nigeria to be one of America's four democratic priorities. The other three at the time were Indonesia, Ukraine and Columbia. Within twelve months another sitting president came on a state visit to Nigeria. Nigeria was in the global news and back in business. The country got a new lease of life and the tattered image and hostility on Nigerians changed. It was a warm reception around the world for those who carried the green Nigerian passport. It was a period Nigerians were proud to be called Nigerians again.

President Bill Clinton arrived Nigeria on a state visit on the 26th-28th of August, 2000 in a colourful and glamorous state visit. The presidential dinner and ball party remains a memorable event today in Nigeria with King Sunny Ade who played Juju blues to which President Bill Clinton danced with Stella Obasanjo.

The visit had turned Nigeria's status from pariah

nation to a partner. Bill Clinton had said in his speech that;

"I am here because of your fight for democracy and human right." President Clinton told the joint legislative assembly: "For equity and economic growth, for peace and tolerance, your fight is America's fight and the worlds fight."

But the radical leaders up north got hundreds of Muslims, often the uneducated who were deprived of western education because of the old existence of feudal system and they made them protest the state visit, brainwashing the people that the presence of President Bill Clinton in Nigeria would deprive them of implementing strict Sharia law up North. The protest, though politically motivated, was peaceful with the mobilized youths chanting anti American slogans and burning of tires and the effigy of the American president.

This had been a time sharia was mischievously introduced in Zamfara state. This led to the death of about two thousand people throughout the country as a result of clashes between the Muslims and Christians. The agenda and talks on the Clinton visit included support for Nigeria's peacekeeping efforts in Sierra Leone.

The USA had committed millions of dollars in increased US aid to support education and the fight to bring awareness of the existence and reality of the HIV aids virus which many Nigerians were refusing to believe at the time existed.

President Bill Clinton at the time had supported President Obasanjo on the campaign for cheap drugs, the anti retroviral medicines to treat HIV and AIDS patients. There was no cure for the disease but the medicine slowed down the effects of the virus in the human body.

The drugs had initially been very expensive and developing African countries could not afford it. The people on the continent were dying in large numbers and a way out had to be found by the governments of African countries collaborating with foreign drug manufacturers who were mandated to find a way to make the drugs cheap and affordable.

President Bill Clinton and President Obasanjo worked together by creating awareness and they also worked for the problem that became associated with people living with HIV and AIDs, most especially the initial hostile stigmatization that came with the disease.

They solved the problem by getting the health and information ministries to spread the awareness of the dos and don'ts through television commercials, Bill boards, radio jingles and workshops and popularise the use of condoms. They got the drugs subsidised and available to save millions of African and Nigerian's.

At a visit to a women health centre, Mr. Clinton reiterated his call for more aggressive action throughout the continent to battle aids. He declared it was an embarrassing topic to discuss, declaring it was better to talk about it than watch a child die of AIDS. We have to break the silence about how the disease spreads and its preventions.

He had said it would rob a country of its future. And he sincerely hoped that we are not going to let that happen in Nigeria.

AIDS at the time had become the leading cause of

death in Africa. The United States government had promised to invest $9.4 million dollars for the AIDs and HIV prevention and $8.7 million dollars for polio eradication and $2 million dollars for the prevention of malaria.

Bill Clinton had also talked about the Peace Corps and its return to Nigeria. He also restored direct flights to the United States of America from Nigeria which had been cancelled during the June 12 crisis under Abacha government.

The American government also wanted Nigeria's assistance to increase the world oil production in order to stabilize price at home in the United States. On his part, Obasanjo told President Clinton that western nations had moral responsibility to ease Nigeria's debt profile and burden which stood at 32 billion dollars. He warned that the debts owed by Nigeria and other African countries prevented economic development.

While Clinton declined the invitation to cancel the $1 billion dollars United State's portion of Nigeria's foreign debts he did promise to intercede with the Paris Club of creditor nations to reschedule some of the payments. He said Nigeria shouldn't have to choose between paying interest on debts and meeting basic human needs, especially in education and health.

The state visit of President Clinton had been very successful that President Olusegun Obasanjo got excited and decided to give President Bill Clinton a name from each of the three major ethnic groups in Nigeria. President Obasanjo gave Mr. Clinton "Sodangi," a Hausa name meaning lover of the people, "Okoro" the Igbo name for a man of the people" and "Omo Wale," Yoruba for a "child that has returned home." Then within another three years another American president had emerged and was again on his way to Nigeria.

President George W. Bush came on a state visit between the 11th of July and 12th of July, 2003 to Abuja. President Obasanjo had visited him earlier in May, 2001. President Bush had emerged at a difficult and unusual time in America when terrorists attacked the United States. He had tackled the problem like a war hero making America safer and sending a signal around the world that America would not tolerate attacks on its people and on its soil. He had warned of weapons of mass destruction.

President George Bush had warned the world of this but nobody wanted to listen or believe him, today we all have felt the heat around the world and in Nigeria, Kenya, Sierra Leone and many more countries where terrorist continue to operate.

President Obasanjo and President Bush have similarities. President Obasanjo ended the civil war in 1970 taking the command and surrender of Biafra while George Bush rescued America from more terrorist attacks. If he had not taken drastic measures by invading Afghanistan and Iraq, the American people would have experienced more attacks. President Bush sending troops into hostile territories who were confrontational to the American government and people had done a great service to his nation. I once again commend his actions. He never moved against friendly neighbours but those who threatened the safe existence of America.

President George Bush on his visit to Africa showed

a lot of interest despite the American government's heavy commitment to rebuilding Iraq, brokering peace talks in the Middle East and facing down North Korea.

His tour had included Nigeria, South Africa, Senegal, Botswana and Uganda. The talks had focused on security, trade and aid. However, security had been the most important thing to Bush. This was further extended outside the shores of the United States into Africa. He wanted to protect and prevent terrorists attack on Americans in Africa. Al-Qaeda had little support south of the Sahara but they found it easy to operate in countries with lax security – hence its successes blowing up American embassies in Kenya and Tanzania in 1998 and the murder of Israelis in Kenya and the suicide bombings by an unknown Islamist group in Morocco in May 2003.

Mr. Bush had promised 100 million dollars to East African countries for security to be strengthened within their borders, airports, seaports and vulnerable places. He further stated that the American government would give aid towards well-governed countries with liberal economies which was to help in improving on health and education. This was to provoke the incentive to countries experiencing bad governance.

President Bush had just toppled the government of Saddam Hussein and the Taliban. He also wanted military bases in Africa under the Africom initiative. It was in response to the crisis that had taken place within the African continent where the problem of instability, wars and genocide had taken place in places like Liberia, Sierra Leone, Sudan which eventually split into two countries and the genocide in Congo, Rwanda and Burundi.

The people in various countries around the world

always felt the United States showed no interest in Africa but these countries were often two far away. The problem was that America needed military bases in order to fly into the region if they would have to mediate and bring stability to the region. This was necessary as the bases served as points to bring in their equipment and weapons and also a base to host the soldiers that would be involved in the peacekeeping. However, African leaders refused and former colonial masters did not want America meddling and interfering with their former colonies.

Today we can all see he had foresight as the man who saw tomorrow, the future and the need to curtail terrorism. He knew the world was in danger created by the activity of terrorists which had spread all over Egypt, Iraq, Syria, Nigeria, Kenya and many more territories.

At first, people around the world misunderstood his militaristic stance but today I guess we realize what his fears were fifteen years ago. Today Nigeria has been bogged down with activities of terrorists for almost a decade with the unimaginable happenings within Nigeria borders, suicide bombers and kidnapping by terrorist in the North East of Nigeria, including the popular case of the Chibok girls who are school children in northern Nigeria abducted by the Boko Haram sect.

The Bush administration continued with assisting Nigeria to get debt relief and cancellation from creditor nations. Besides defense package for Nigeria, there was also Memorandum of Understanding with Enron, General Electric and Siemens, a German engineering firm, Agip, an Italian oil group and Eskom, a South African company to help the power network.

President George Bush's visit was successful and

things changed for good in Nigeria. The country was debt-free and with the high oil prices the country built huge reserves to the tune of over 60 billion dollars by the time President Olusegun Obasanjo handed over power in 2007.

After the state visit, today more than twelve years has gone by, no American president has stepped on Nigerian soil. Olusegun Obasanjo has proved to be Nigeria's most successful ruler and God has always been kind to him as he has always been favoured with good economic climate well-managed by patriotic and selfless Nigerians.

CHAPTER TWENTY-ONE

Iyabo Obasanjo And Her Letter

Iyabo Obasanjo was born on the 27th of April, 1967. Her father, Olusegun Obasanjo, had named her Olusola, Iyabode, Ashabi Obasanjo. Iyabo became the prominent and her first name because of her striking resemblances with Obasanjo's late mother.

As she grew up, Iyabo displayed unusual wisdom for her age. From the moment she was born, her mother's status changed. Mrs. Oluremi Obasanjo was now called Mama Iyabo (Iyabo's mother) and her father, Olusegun Obasanjo, was called Baba Iyabo (Iyabo's father). Her name eventually became a household name in Nigeria because people referred to her father as Baba Iyabo.

Obasanjo is the only political figure in the country that once you say or mention the name of his daughter you know it is Obasanjo. He is the only one that has his daughter's name as one of his other names and it has remained so till date.

When Iyabo was born, Obasanjo, her father, it was reported, danced and sang to the admiration of nurses at the hospital. In African culture many men are known to walk away or show some form of disappointment when the first child is a girl or in other situations where the couple don't have a male child. He was full of joy displaying his dancing skills.

Despite loving his children over the years and showing a soft spot for Iyabo in particular, he did not spoil or pamper his children. He had allowed them to grow up like everyday kids despite the fact that they were born with silver spoons. Olusegun Obasanjo had given them gifts and things in moderation. It was tradition at the time and is still the best way to bring up children. It is the best kind of training that makes children level-headed and focused.

Iyabo grew up with her siblings and at age seven she was already showing special traits. She was at the time a student of the Corona School at Victoria Island.

The Obasanjos had become very influential and powerful when Murtala Muhammed became Head of State and Obasanjo became the second in command. Their lives changed never to be the same again. Then tragedy struck in Nigeria on February 13, 1976. Murtala Muhammed, Nigeria's head of state was assassinated and the likely successor was Obasanjo and his name started to take the stage. He was the deputy to the assassinated head of state but nobody was sure of the next development at the time. The army was full of surprises, although by seniority and hierarchy he was next in line.

Iyabo at this time was already nine years old and was the first child of the Obasanjos. Though she was so young at this time, she stood out as an intelligent person and had realised her father's destiny was about to change.

The army had been a risky place to be, anything could happen at anytime especially after the country had gone through a civil war. There was tension in the house and the atmosphere was charged, nobody knew what the future would hold. If Obasanjo was made Head of State, it was going to be a risky job, he could end up like Murtala Muhammed or otherwise. That day Iyabo had broken the tension, she had uttered and said:

"Daddy do not become Head of State" this startled the whole house and silence fell on the room like a grave yard. The drop of a pin could be heard. This was Africa and Nigeria, a country that had superstitious beliefs: some family members did believe it could be a warning from God that he should be careful and watchful or probably that he should not take the job.[107]

When Murtala was assassinated the pictures were in the newspapers and many children in Nigeria had gone through the papers. It was a horrific death, worse than the Hammer House of Horror series.

Murtala's body was riddled with bullets, blood everywhere - his eyes bulged out. Iyabo had seen the pictures and the horror and fear had never left her consciousness. It was from then she had developed a phobia for the seat of the Head of State and President.

Children at the time never forgot and when we did visit the museum few years later with the riddled Mercedes car on display it brought back the memories. I don't even think President Obasanjo understood the impact the event created at that time.

Iyabo had uttered what family members dared not say or could not discuss as it was a delicate and touching subject as it also had to do with Obasanjo's

---
107 Adinoyi Ojo Onukaba Olusegun Obasanjo, In the eyes of time Pg. 28

career. How could they? Who asked their opinion? After all they were not the ones that encouraged him to join the army.

That day Obasanjo's sister, Adunni, was grateful to Iyabo obviously because of its inherent risk. Adunni had never hidden her uneasiness over her brother's increasing prominence because it was a dangerous job. Then she became restless at times, thanking Olodumare, which means God in Yoruba, for the surprises he had done in their lives, as they were from poor background in Abeokuta but had become the corner stone in Nigeria and her brother was going to be the head of state and number one citizen. It was almost unbelievable and many times the speed at which things were happening to them was unimaginable.

Obasanjo had eased off the tension declaring to his little daughter Iyabo, "You have my word, Iyabo, I will resign at the end of the supreme military council meeting tomorrow and we will go to Abeokuta and live a quiet life," Obasanjo's declaration brought relief to all.

The promise meant a lot to Iyabo then. The little girl had hoped he would keep his promise. Obasanjo had thought he would but could not because of prevailing circumstances.

That day, as Obasanjo was about leaving he took his five children, one by one into his arms and kissed them, declaring the hug and the kiss as parting gifts to them in case he died and never returned. His wife, Oluremi, and Sister, Adunni, watched the ritual with misty eyes.

Major General Alani Akinrinade, the GOC 1st Division in Kaduna was at Lugard Avenue to pick him up for a meeting of senior officers who were in Lagos on that fateful Friday. The meeting had taken place at Dodan Barracks with Obasanjo presiding.

They scheduled another meeting for 10 a.m. the following day which was a Saturday. Obasanjo had told Danjuma and MD Yusuf he wanted to retire since the army was no longer dependable. They had told him that the army operates by hierarchy, and since Murtala was dead he would become the new Head of State. They had advised him not to retire prematurely.

He had asked Danjuma to take over as Head of State, but Danjuma declined. Both Danjuma and MD Yusuf had convinced Obasanjo to take the responsibility fate had thrown on him. Colonel Joseph N. Garba who was federal commissioner for external affairs also came to persuade him to take over. He had told him, "you are going to be the Head of State whether you like it or not." Garba promised to defend him if it meant giving up his life.

Garba had been offered the job by his admirers like Colonels Babangida, Mouktar Mohammed and Ibrahim Alfa of the Air force but he refused, noting that the position was for Obasanjo as he had become the most senior among them. He had told them it was an opportunity to demonstrate to the rest of the country that the North had no plan to monopolise the political leadership of the country.

Nobody knew how Babangida and his friends expected to install Garba as head of state. There were senior officers they would need to get rid of: Danjuma, Ibrahim Haruna, Mohammed Shuwa, James Oluleye, Emmanuel Abisoye and Olufemi Olutoye. Perhaps they were teasing Garba.[108]

---
108 Ibid Pg 30.

After seven days of mourning the Council of State announced that Obasanjo should take over. The reason was Obasanjo was a Yoruba man. The Yoruba were the only major ethnic group that had never produced either a Civilian President or Military Head of State. The Hausa/Fulani had Abubakar Tafawa Balewa, the first prime minister 1960-1966 and Murtala Muhammed (July 1975-february 13 1976). The Igbos had Nnamdi Azikiwe, the first indigenous President (1960-1966) and Major General Johnson Aguiyi Ironsi, the first military ruler (January1966-July 1966) and the Northern minorities had Yakubu Gowon, an Angas from Plateau State who ruled for nine years (1966-1975).

Destiny and fate had placed the crown on a Yoruba head and Obasanjo was expected to accept it without complaining. This was why Nigeria needed ethno-political balancing. Some other council members did not understand why Obasanjo was refusing to step into the shoes of Murtala and had to be persuaded which was the zenith and peak of a military career in Nigeria. However, some others said he was a coward and he did not want to be in an office that seemed to be eating up its occupants. Perhaps he was afraid of the northern hegemony. This was not possible for a man who fought a civil war and accepted rebel surrender.

It was Major General Emmanuel Abisoye that had saved the day when he sarcastically said if Obasanjo did not want the job, then, they should allow Dimka to take over. That was how Obasanjo accepted the job. The appointment of Obasanjo and that of Musa Yar'Adua were announced to the nation on the popular network news segment of the state radio.

Back at Obasanjo's house the family tuned the radio to the network news on the national radio where they heard the breaking news that Obasanjo had been appointed as the new Head of State and Commander in Chief of the Nigerian Armed Forces.

Iyabo the little girl who had sought and obtained her father's promise not to take the job burst into tears, she was afraid that her father would end up like Murtala. They knew the risk in the job. It was a risk that outweighed whatever priviledges and power that came with it. The flat was filled with gentle and muffled sobs of the Obasanjo family members. To the people, it was as if Obasanjo had signed his death warrant. After the ceremony he now came back to the family house to explain to members of his family why he accepted the job and had to bow to the wishes of his colleagues. His arrival in Ikoyi was with a difference and showed there was a transformation. There were armed guards, menacingly wielding guns, plain-clothed security officers sniffing the air for possible signs of sabotage. An army of outriders surrounded and escorted his car.

The security around the Head of State had changed with more equipment in defence of the new Number One citizen. The car of the Head of State became armoured. The house at No 7 Lawrence Road, Ikoyi took a different look as the serenity of the neigbourhood became a beehive of activity as security men surrounded the area.

While he was with his family it was Iyabo he had to beg for understanding because it was her that he had made a promise not to accept the job.

> I rejected it! I did everything but they said no. there was no way I could turn it down. It was unanimously decided that I should take over.

He explained carefully to Iyabo whom he was then cuddling. He explained to her that he had not deceived her. But somewhere in the little child's mind, he had lied to her. Obasanjo had spent about thirty minutes in the house before leaving. He went through pleasantries with his other children and descended the stairs into a waiting car. He had become a visitor to his own house and it dawned on the family members that Olusegun Obasanjo was no longer theirs alone but public property of Nigeria and its people, both within and outside the country. He had become the new leader of the people.[109]

Later that night Lieutenant General Olusegun Obasanjo made his maiden broadcast as Head of State and Commander-in-Chief of the Armed Forces.

He had gone and conquered as usual, he did a good job and handed over to a civilian government within three years in 1979. It was just as he did with the civil war when he took control and the war came to an end within a short period. While in retirement he acted as watchdog, observing the way the country was being governed and he sent his frank opinion both to the government and public through the press.

The Abacha government had accused him falsely of organising a coup for his failure to support and endorse the government. The Abacha government tried to humiliate him but they failed. His star and profile did rise all over the world instead. But the experience was nasty for his children and family.

Iyabo Obasanjo and her siblings were very hurt and did not like what General Abacha had done to their father. He attempted to kill him and had succeeded in

---
109 Ibid Pg 35.

humiliating them by putting their father in prison and the most annoying was that all the former leaders had failed to stop the persecution. There were powerful generals who seemed not to do enough.

God later intervened and the traumatic experience ended. Then Obasanjo became the beautiful bride of Nigeria and he was wooed to become president again. The fear returned again to Iyabo that they were putting her father again on the hot seat. She again remembered how Murtala had died and was disturbed also since General Abacha had just died under mysterious circumstances.

However, not knowing what to do again this time she blurted out and declared: "I know you want to die in office as a president but you know what," she continued "if you die I wont cry." This she knew would startle her father to make him think carefully before accepting the job. It did startle him but he took precaution and consulted widely asking whether he had the overwhelming support of the people. When this was confirmed he declared his intention to run for the office of president in 1999.

Iyabo has always been the most caring child of Obasanjo. She had no objection to his success but just wanted him to be safe. Olusegun Obasanjo became president in 1999 and did a two term of eight years, making Nigeria the hub of international interest. Then again he handed over to a civilian government in May 2007.

Iyabo Obasanjo got married in 1999 to Mr. Akeem Bello but retained the Obasanjo name as a compound name. She served as commissioner for health in Ogun State in 2003 through her effort in the Governor Gbenga

Daniel administration. During this period she had seen the many flaws in the way the country was governed and how the system worked. She had discovered the machinery of government had to function with inducement before anything could work many times in Nigeria.

Then there was an assassination attempt in the month of April 2003 on Iyabo Obasanjo Bello. It was the day of the general election when Obasanjo got a second term in office. His enemies had wanted to punish him for contesting and winning a second term election but they failed. Three adults and two children had been travelling in the convoy and were in Iyabo's car.

The assassins opened fire on the car at Ifo Road in Ogun State. The car had tinted windows so they did not see the occupants. Iyabo was not in the car but three adults and two children who were children of her friend, Adeife and Akinola Sodipo Akindeko were killed during the assassination attempt on Iyabo.

Iyabo was sitting with the mother of the kids that got killed in their own Mercedes car which was in front of the car riddled with bullets.

They watched in horror as the car was riddled with bullets and innocent lives were lost because of the selfish ambition of a group of people. It was such a sad story. The perpetrators were never found. Iyabo did not get over it as it became similar to the Murtala assassination in 1976. The memories came back again, only that this time she was the target. It was God Almighty that saved her that day. There had been five occupants in the car that was attacked but only one survived.

In 2007 President Obasanjo handed over power to a new civilian government and he retired to his farmhouse in Abeokuta, Ogun State. Iyabo during this dispensation became a Nigerian Senator representing Ogun Central Senatorial District of Ogun State in April 2007 during the Gbenga Daniel governorship tenure under the Peoples Democratic Party (PDP). She was chairman of the Senate Health Committee and also a member of the security, intelligence, land transport, and science and technology, education, national planning and inter-parliamentary committees. But where she became very popular was the awareness she brought up about child marriages in the north where the child brides were plagued with the VVF problem in the northern part of Nigeria. She made a case for the little girls who were married off too early and were having babies before they themselves were of mature age. The girls were married off as from the ages of seven. The crude belief was once the girls reached puberty, it was okay to have them as wives. Nigeria has the highest prevalence of the Vesico Vaginal Fistula (VVF) in the world with between 400,000 and 800,000 women living with the problem and about 20,000 new cases occurring annually while 90 percent are untreated. This implies that about 55 women are infected with VVF and 18,000 cases are untreated daily.

It is estimated that two million women suffer from obstetric fistula globally. In Nigeria the North alone has over 85 percent of these cases.

The issue however is often not discussed. To end VVF, the practice responsible for the primary cause of VVF must be stopped — child marriage.

Vesico Vaginal Fistula is a direct communication between the bladder and vagina resulting in leakage of urine into the vagina. This is a major gynecological problem in the country. It also occurs when blood supply to the tissues of the vagina and bladder is restricted during prolonged obstructed labour, the tissues die between these organs forming holes through which urine pass uncontrollably. Many women with VVF are regarded as social outcasts and marriages have been dissolved as a result of this.

Many girls between the ages of eleven and fifteen in the country become mothers either through early marriages or through unwanted pregnancy. They experience obstructed labour even as some unskilled birth attendants cut through the vagina to create a passage for the baby, this eventually results in VVF, which is the leakage of urine and faeces through the vagina. The situation is prevalent in Sokoto, Kebbi, Borno, Kano, Katsina and Plateau States, all in Northern Nigeria. Iyabo had brought this problem to the front burner but the conservatives in the north tried to suppress the laudable project.

In April 2008 Iyabo came under the spotlight of an investigation by the Economic and Financial Crimes Commission (EFCC). There was an investigation involving the former minister for health and her minister of state for health, for embezzlement of public funds. The ministry at the end of the financial year did not return all unspent funds to the government coffers. The amount was 300million naira which was allegedly distributed among the minister, her minister of state and top civil servants, Senate and House Health Committees which she chaired.

The minister and her deputy were forced to resign after returning their share of the money, they were later arrested and posted bail. Iyabo Obasanjo refused to return her portion of this money which was 10million naira. She claimed that the nine members of her committee lobbied for funds from the ministry they oversaw. She maintained the money was spent on a conference on capacity building some members of the health committee attended in Ghana. She refused to appear before the EFCC.

Although summoned along with the minister and other civil servants, she refused to appear in court. A week later a high drama ensued when she allegedly jumped over the fence of her home to evade arrest in Maitama District, Abuja as the EFCC tried to arrest her. In 2009 the case was thrown out of the High Court in Abuja as having no merit. She delcared she was being blackmailed. All these took place after Obasanjo had left office in 2007.

All the allegations seemed to be a witch-hunt because this money was already appropriated only that some government officials did not follow due process.

The public at the time speculated that they just wanted Iyabo to feel some heat as President Obasanjo had allowed the EFCC to grill Mohammed Babangida at a point. This period Iyabo had run to President Obasanjo alleging that she did nothing wrong. Obasanjo however dismissed her with a wave of his hands, not that he did not believe what she was saying but President Obasanjo felt that she should take responsibility for her action as a senator of the Federal Republic. She was an adult and a public figure who had served as a commissioner and was now a senator. The honourable senator did not understand her father's response since she expected to hear her father, retort, "Oh Iyabo my dear child I believe you." Definitely she did not understand the stand of her father but she felt her father did not believe her not knowing that such a stand was only to make her take responsibility for her actions.

After the demise of President Yar'Adua, lots of people were not pleased with Obasanjo when Jonathan emerged. There were very many uncharitable remarks from his close allies and friends both in the army and civilian circles. Some said the regime had been a bad dream and nightmare for Nigerians. Professor Wole Soyinka described President Obasanjo as a master of hypocrisy while others said he was a toxic leader. The the worst came from Theophilus Danjuma who said he should go back to jail. Iyabo had taken note of all these and knew her father had many enemies who many times had pretended to love him.

President Obasanjo at the peak of the presidential term of Goodluck Ebele Jonathan had written him a letter which became public, titled: "Before It Is Too Late". There was nothing really bad in the letter, mostly advise and some reminders concerning the re-election of the president who had promised he would stay in office for a single term tenure having almost spent the remaining term of the late president Umar Yar'Adua. President Jonathan had become prisoner of his supporters who had brandished and threatened there would be war in Nigeria if he Jonathan was not given a second term. Obasanjo's letter had other issues that he wanted the president to clarify e.g. the sale of crude oil which was stolen without any account given and the non-remittance of funds to the tune of 7 billion dollars. Other issues are based on accountability and the fear of a watch list of politicians and allegation of their secret training of snipers and other armed personnel and the clandestine acquisition of weapons for political purpose to eliminate opposing groups like in the Abacha era.

This had sparked off an uproar in the Jonathan camp. They added fuel and set everywhere on fire within the polity. There were those who supported what Obasanjo wrote and those who condemned it asking whether he would tolerate such a letter when he was president. Unfortunately, the letter was misunderstood, Obasanjo just wanted the president to clear the air and defend the issues raised but rather than a simple reply debunking the allegations, the sycophants and supporters of the president started a tongue-lash on Obasanjo with Chief E. K. Clark at the front where he should have been the peace-maker.

That was when Senator Iyabo Obasanjo wrote a strong letter to her father. People now call it the infamous letter. The ordinary Nigerian felt the letter was a sacrilege. Iyabo only used her wealth of wisdom and knowledge of the political landscape in Nigeria to cool down the tension that was already heating up the polity. It was done to actually redirect the attention of her father from the hot political circles. Iyabo actually panicked but forgot this was civil rule and President Jonathan would not hurt a fly. They just blew hot air.

She now wrote the letter which left many in shock and some confused.

But those who understand the scenerio knew that Iyabo was defending Baba and had used that letter to shield him from harm's way. President Jonathan and his supporters pulled the brakes on everything. Baba's letter just melted into thin air. But a few wise men discovered that what Iyabo had done saved the day. She had fired a missile which seemed to slow down the fast running train President Obasanjo was piloting and the missile also stopped the fighter jets from the Jonathan camp to change course.

The day was saved as traditional rulers intervened, giving Iyabo a soft landing. What a wonderful daughter. I guess if Chief MKO Abiola had gotten somebody to watch and check over him like Iyabo did, he would be alive today. The woman who did that, his first wife, Alhaja Simbiat, was that umbrella but had been folded up too early. I guess also that if the Saddam Hussein and Ghaddaffi's children or any of the disgraced leaders in some countries had children like Iyabo Obasanjo, their stories would be different today.

What Iyabo had done all her life was to look out for Obasanjo's safety. That is the kind of wife or daughter world leaders need - who can sometimes put a check on their parents or spouse if they tread dangerously. The letter was to protect Obasanjo from danger. She had declared Nigeria did not belong to her father so he should take it easy.

The letter had strong words and tones but most of it was taken from what her mother had already written in her famous and legendary book: *Bitter Sweet*, so many of the tales were already known.

This clearly shows it was a dramatic letter to appease the feuding side which was the government of the day and it worked. After a couple of months, both sides mended fences, compared notes and everything went back to normal. But the people of Nigeria wanted change and they got it in 2015 with the emergence of President Muhammadu Buhari through the APC.

CHAPTER TWENTY-TWO

Nigerias Most Successful Ruler

President Obasanjo has become the most successful ruler in Nigeria both as military head of state and civilian president.

This legendary achievements were possible after serving Nigeria in official and personal capacity where he displayed outstanding leadership qualities as the young soldier who brought the civil war to an end.

He became a legend having served Nigeria for five decades successfully with courage and humility and has continued to astound his admirers and enemies. He was destined for the top and conquering everything he put his hand on whether as a job or challenge.

From the moment he handed over power to a civilian president in 1979, Obasanjo's international image soared. He became identified as a personality that was not blinded or carried away by the glittering allure of power but a man whose word was his bond.

President Obasanjo has been the only Head of State and President, dead or alive, that has been able to bring three American Presidents to Nigeria on State Visits. Also during his second tenure as president he also repeated the feat and also crowned it with the commonwealth Heads of State meeting he hosted in Abuja Nigeria and the Queen of England stepped out and returned to Nigeria after over four decades.

He is an intelligent and charming personality and the G8 leaders see him as one of their own, only that his country Nigeria is not yet among the super power countries. This recognition also gave him a lot of respect in Nigeria and Africa. He became an international reliable statesman who stood for good governance, peace and democratic ideals.

He had become an African leader whom world leaders could identify with. He was the first African head of state to be honoured and invited to join the interactions which is the club of former leaders of democratic countries throughout the world. He developed official and personal relations with former presidents and heads of governments of countries like Britain, the United States of America, Germany, France, Japan, etc.

Jimmy Carter, Bill Clinton, George Bush, Lord Callaghan of Britain, Helmut Schmidt of Germany and Jacques Chirac of France are all his friends. He also formed Transparency International along with his group and international peers and is a member of the Commonwealth Eminent Persons Group that engineered the process and release of Nelson Mandela and the democratisation of the Republic of South Africa, bringing the end of apartheid.

Obasanjo has been endowed with wisdom. The God almighty always smiled his way whenever he was in power as the fortunes of the country always changed. In 1999 the price of oil was down to 9 dollars but as he got into office it began an upward climb into the hundreds of dollars a barrel and it remained constant for a while.

President Obasanjo did manage the resources meticulously giving Nigeria huge foreign reserves into over 40 billion dollar saving. This was achieved even after substantial amount had been paid to the creditor nations and their financial institutions like the IMF, World Bank and Paris Club to offset Nigeria's 30 billion dollar debt.

He is a man with the midas touch and is always ready to learn new things. He reads a lot. He also changed the fortunes of the Obasanjo farms as he learnt the methods of processing frozen chicken for international export.

These qualities are not achieved through paper certificates even though he recently enrolled into a PhD programme. It is hard work, inbuilt experience, wisdom, and the ability to always reinvent oneself. Obasanjo has become Nigeria's most successful ruler and he is the only Nigerian head of state or president who had full office terms and handed over successfully. The other head of state who handed over was only transiting as he spent only one year in office and that was Abdulsalami Abubakar who took over from the late Head of State Sanni Abacha. All others were either killed in office through coups or assassination or were forced and disgraced out of office. Obasanjo presidential legacy speaks volumes of his person.

As Obasanjo planned for his retirement from office as president, he had mixed feelings as a lot had happened in

Nigeria for the period of eight years. Those who had been participants were lucky to be a part of the history. They were almost like magical years for Nigeria.

The impact of the eight-year period were positive on the society. Nigeria returned to respectability in the comity of nations. The pluses recorded included the release of Nigeria from its albatross - the debt burden, strong foreign reserves, and the rapid development of the country. The country also enjoyed high oil prices improving the economy.

Then his beloved wife, Stella, had died in 2005. They had come in together in 1999 and by 2007 Obasanjo was retiring without her by his side. She had been the first lady and had stood by him during his troubled times. He had built a new house for his retirement in Abeokuta. A hill top mansion with lovely view of the town. He brought in another wife, Dame Bola Obasanjo, who also has children for him. He built a presidential library not far away from his new home. It was something positive that was taken from the American system.

Obasanjo had left a good legacy and earned his name and a place in the history of Nigeria, Africa and the western world. He had realised that as a leader, he would be assessed not on the basis of how long he stayed in office or how much economic resources he acquired and accumulated for himself and his business empire, family and friends, but on what the society could point to.

He had realised what happened to those who perpetuate themselves in power. It always ended in a disaster and he was not going to be disgraced like the Sadam Husseins of Iraq or Gaddafi of Libya etc. So there was never a third term agenda. It only came up because Obasanjo had not yet concluded on the arrangement of who would take over the state of affairs of Nigeria. But when this was done the rumour fizzled out. People had put the idea in the public domain and it burnt like fire in the harmattan season.

All presidents and heads of state all over the world always work to have a successor with loyalty, trust and continuity. President Obasanjo had structured his succession plan in a way that somebody from the Niger Delta will be vice president and possibly president after four years. He had done this so that Nigeria would not have fallen the way he structured it in 1979.

When the new President was chosen he had all they needed. President Umar Yar'Adua was a former governor from one of the states in the North. He was well educated and prudent when it came to managing funds. Obasanjo did not want a reckless spender that would liquidate Nigeria by squandering all the funds he had saved.

Obasanjo had hoped that when the new president, Umar Yar'Adua, finished his term in office, then Jonathan who was chosen as his vice president and who was from the Niger Delta might have the opportunity to be president.This was the first time a southsouth person from the Niger Delta region of Nigeria that produces Nigeria's oil became a vice president in Nigeria.

In fact, immediately it was announced that those were the contestants for the PDP presidential ticket and vice presidential ticket the crisis in the Niger Delta stopped immediately. They knew somebody from their area had been put forward to represent and fight for their needs, so the tension eased.

Yar'Adua and Jonathan ticket came to place. Obasanjo had sacrificed friendship to doing the right thing. His coup against his trusted friends up north was for peace and stability to return to the Niger Delta which came through his arrangement. It was not President Umar Yar'Adua that solved the problem of the Nigeri Delta but the foundation Baba Obasanjo built by making Goodluck Jonathan, one time governor of Bayelsa State, vice president, knowing full well that President Umar Yar'Adua had health issues that led to his short stay in office. This may be a bit blunt but it was the reality at the time.

Having a Niger Delta man as the vice president started the process of returning peace to the Delta and then President Umar Yar'Adua introduced the amnesty which put the icing on the cake. People of the region who were deprived of many possibilities were given scholarships and grants to study abroad and learn various different skills.

The beautiful bride from the Niger Delta was Jonathan who eventually became president when President Umar Yar'Adua died two years into his term in office. This was the foundation. Baba Obasanjo solved the problem and got himself more enemies from the North. But for national interest and peace he stuck out his neck and Nigerians were grateful.

The North had got wind of the plot and plan. Then came Boko Haram, a political tool of certain elite group up north to show their disaffection of the power shift to the south. President Jonathan recognises the amnesty given by President Umar Yar'Adua. But the Niger Delta militants did not kill Muslims or Christians. They only fought for the degradation of their towns by oil exploration activities and spillage caused by oil leakages from companies operating in the Niger Delta area which was a genuine cause and case recognised all over the world. Jonathan tried to appeal to the Boko Haram group to accept amnesty, they said they did not want it and that he should convert to Islam.

They said they were out to Islamize Northern Nigeria and later the whole of Nigeria. But apparently what I feel today is that certain people and groups want to take over the government as had happened in some other African countries. Coups were not easy for them to execute so they are going the guerrilla way to overrun the government of Nigeria. If the government does not deal with it swiftly as President Obasanjo had described the situation as a wound which if allowed to fester will be difficult to heal and courtail.

The government was not happy with this comment at the initial stage but later they knew Obasanjo spoke the truth and had not retired to a rocking chair but had continued to play an active role in the PDP as board of trustees chairman until he later resigned. Then he has kept close watch in retirement at the events happening in Nigeria.

He also recently enrolled for a PhD in the open University and had also taken a degree in theology as he wanted to remain prayerful and faithful to God for keeping him alive all these years and for giving him an eventful life. Almost like a fairly tale that had gone from one extreme end of poverty to super splendour, Obasanjo emerged as the crème de la crème and as Nigeria's must successful ruler and one of the legendary Generals in Nigeria and Africa.

He is a G8 president on the African continent. He was the most successful Head of State and President that has emerged till date and the most visible locally and internationally and the most focused on by the press. It is believed he is the most cartooned in the news media.

He continues to be relevant, solving many problems on the African continent and his advice in Europe, America and Asia are taken into careful consideration.

His five decades of serving Nigeria stands out in and out of office. He has travelled to every point of the compass and is still sort after to give lectures and speeches around the world. It is amazing where he gets the energy. He is Nigeria's most engaging president and all leaders continue to seek his advise, counsel and support. He is definitely the leader of the Yoruba people whether anybody accepts or not as his achievements are unmatched by any other person in the southwest of Nigeria, living or dead.

His exploits and biography when acted in film and documentary are guaranteed to be excellent box office.

It is time the people of Nigeria and the Yoruba open their eyes that this is a legend and man who we need to continue to showcase and shower with respect. Olusegun Obasanjo is a man to revere. A personality on the stage of life who has seen it all. The wisdom in him has made him Nigeria's most successful ruler from independence till date.

Index

Index

Aba 67, 72, 98
Abacha 119, 158, 170–71, 175, 180, 182–84, 188–92, 194–96, 198–99, 201–2, 231–32
Abacha government, 118, 183, 190, 193, 196, 212, 232, 247, 259
Abdullahi Mohammed 123–25
Abebe 113, 116
Abeokuta 1–3, 6–7, 9, 13, 52, 101–2, 104, 127, 133, 184, 198–99, 208, 255, 262, 273
Abiola 5, 142-3, 146, 155, 169, 171–85, 197, 199–200, 206, 231, 267
Abiola Farms 146
Abiola's election 178
Abubakar Rimi 205
Abuja 119, 158, 164, 177, 188, 191, 196–97, 210, 237, 248, 264
Aburi 55, 57
Aburi agreement 57
Aburi Report 49, 51, 53, 55, 57, 59
Action Congress of Nigeria (ACN) 149
Action Group (AG) 20, 22, 25
Adekunle, Benjamin 15–17, 68, 89, 91, 97, 114, 147, 149, 165
Adesanya, Abraham 200, 202
Adinoyi Ojo Olukaba 7, 24, 32, 39, 42, 47, 52, 58, 68, 70
Adinoyi Ojo Onukaba 115, 123, 125, 128, 133
Adunni 255
Afenifere 185, 202
Africa 21, 86, 139, 143, 167, 183, 207, 209, 242–43, 247, 249–50, 254, 271, 273, 277
African continent 189, 199, 241, 249, 277
African countries 81, 140, 146, 178, 206, 208, 227, 236, 246–47, 276
- developing 246
African Legacy Press 39, 42, 47, 52, 58
African military head of state 164
Africans 9
African States 9, 207
Agreement
- eight-point 94–95
Agriculture 136, 208

Aircrafts 79, 81, 95, 99, 213
Ajao 117
Akintola 22
Akisanya 104
Akure 62, 64
Alabi Isama 93, 132, 150
Alade 55, 62, 73, 77, 95
Aldershot 16–17
All Peoples Party (APP) 202, 219
America, 33, 62, 75, 78, 80, 137, 139, 163, 192, 208, 213, 241–45, 247–50, 277
American government 208, 242, 247–49
American president
- first, 242
- sitting 139, 243
Americans 2, 9, 12, 80, 83, 106, 139, 198, 203, 248–49
Ammunition 55, 77–78, 238
Amnesty 41, 275–76
Amos Obasanjo Bankole 17
Annulment 177–78, 182, 196, 216
Anti-Nigeria elements 64
Areas
- local government 163, 218
- riverine 67
Armed forces 12, 16, 23, 35, 58, 107, 109, 131, 171, 174, 177, 210, 243, 259
Arm Forces Ruling Council (AFRC) 198
Arms 38, 41, 55, 78, 80, 82, 84–85, 90, 97, 100, 130, 143, 238, 255
Army 12–14, 35–37, 42–43, 45–46, 49–50, 55–56, 103–4, 145, 149, 151–53, 159, 181–82, 194, 221–26, 253–56
Army officers 49
- hundred Igbo 49
Army officer's corps 18
Army School 32
Army Staff 89, 104
Army training depot 26
Arrest 39, 46, 191–92, 232, 237, 264
Ashabi, Bernice 1
Ashabi Obasanjo 252
Asia 207–8, 277
Aso Rock 119, 174, 211
Assassination 117, 261, 272
Association of Nigerian Authors 158

Index

Atiku Abubakar, 176, 202, 204-5. 221, 240
Auchi Northwest, 61
Awolowo 20–22, 54, 58–59, 109, 138, 140–42, 148–49, 153-4, 161, 183, 206

Baba Iyabo 167, 252
Babangida Ibrahim 133, 157–59, 162, 164, 170–78, 180–81, 201, 204, 219, 226, 230, 256
Babangida administration 158, 183
Babangida regime 162, 164
Bajowa 64, 131
Balewa 53, 58
Bakassi 235
Banjo, Victor 61, 64–65
Bankole 3–4
Baptist Boys High School (BBHS) 5, 7, 13, 104
Barracks 33, 43, 45, 51, 53
Battalion 18, 37, 45, 64, 72, 94
- fifth 24, 26–27
Bayelsa State , 275
Belgians, 23
Bello 46
Bello Fadile 192, 195
Benin 18, 38–39, 57, 61–63, 65–66, 207
Biafra 63, 67, 74, 76–81, 83–86, 91, 95–99, 102, 110, 141–42, 148, 248
Biafra Africa 49, 239
Biafran Army 62–63
Biafran army propaganda 73
Biafrans 62, 65, 73, 79, 81–84, 90, 92, 95–97, 142, 147–48
Biafran soldiers 64, 71
Biafran State 152
Biafran War, 85, 147–48
Biafra's army commander 148
Bisi Onabanjo 176
Black Scorpion 68, 72, 90, 147–48, 165
Blood 38, 44, 123, 254
Boko Haram 236, 250, 275–76
Bombings 196–97
Borders 62, 132, 152, 225, 249
Bridges 61, 63, 106
Brigadier 102–3, 124–25
Britain 4, 18, 20–21, 62, 75, 78, 86, 140, 163, 202, 207, 213, 230, 271

British 9, 12, 20–21, 23, 36, 75, 86
British colonial government 35
British government 21, 216, 235
British Prime Minister 230
Bruce, Murray 115
Buhari 152-53, 156–58
Bullets 9, 254, 261

Cadets 15–16, 36, 219
Calabar 67
Cameroons 19, 235
Candidates
- presidential 141, 170, 185, 202
Caritas International 78–79
Carter, Jimmy 139, 191-92, 196, 205, 242–43, 271
Cases, civil 219–20
Cattle 217–18
Central Bank of Nigeria 156
Child marriages 262–63
Children 1–3, 5, 68, 71–72, 78, 113, 117, 119, 199, 204, 253–55, 259, 261, 267, 273
China 207
Christians 19, 86, 211, 221–22, 245, 276
Civilian government 18, 54, 107, 134, 150, 164, 210, 213, 259–60
- elected 107, 171
- new 262
Civilian president 209, 211, 213, 215, 217, 219, 221, 223, 225, 227, 229, 231, 233, 235, 270
- new 143
Civilian rule 111, 140, 163, 189, 198, 201
Civil servants 112, 127, 214, 264
Civil war 79, 82, 99–100, 105, 107–8, 110, 134–35, 141–42, 147–48, 159, 165, 206–7, 254, 257, 259
Clinton, Bill 119, 180, 240, 245-47, 271
CNN, 179
Commander 33, 38, 51, 65, 89, 93, 114, 123, 133, 148, 258
- supreme 56–57
Commander-in-chief 22, 36, 52, 55–56, 100, 178, 243, 259
Commission, electoral 140–41

Commissioner
- federal 105, 108–9, 130, 256

Commonwealth Heads of State 111

Communities, international 75, 78, 147, 178, 183, 187, 189, 192, 231

Confederation 54, 56, 239

Conference, national 202

Congo 23–26, 241, 249

Congolese 24–25

Congolese army 24

Congolese soldiers 24–25

Congress for Progressive Change (CPC) 149

Constitution 56, 129, 139, 220, 232–33, 237, 240
  new 129, 220

Constitution of Nigeria states, 222

Corps 27, 33, 102, 190

Corruption 107–9, 126, 138, 161, 208, 214–15, 228–30, 237

Cotonu 83, 94–95

Council
- local government 218

Council of State 257

Countries
- advanced 235
- black 209
- bush 2
- democratic 235, 271
- fellow 132
- indebted 227
- independent 229
- industrial 137
- troubled 208
- well-governed 249

Coup 26, 33, 35, 37–39, 41, 43–47, 65–66, 109–10, 118, 123–25, 131–34, 163–64, 189–90, 192–93, 275–76
- counter 44–45, 109, 123
- first 23, 50, 159
- northern 47
- palace 46, 123, 153, 157

Coup plotters 38–39, 41–42, 44, 123–25, 131, 134

Criminal code 220

Crude oil 110–11

Currency 136, 154, 162

Dahomey 83–84, 94, 96

Danjuma 46, 109, 125, 129, 132–33, 204, 256

Dasuki 182

Debts 213, 227–28, 247

Delta State 113

Democratic 141, 163–64

Dimka 132–34, 257

Diplomats 199

Division
- first 72, 97–98
- second 63, 65–66, 149

Dodan Barracks 89, 158–59, 256

Dollars 81–82, 100, 138, 150, 154, 162–63, 179, 184, 215, 227, 245, 247, 251, 266, 272

Drugs 156, 213, 226, 246

Eastern Nigeria 36, 44, 49, 87, 141

Eastern region 23, 39, 41, 52, 54, 57, 59, 70, 78, 205

Eastern states 61

ECOMOG soldiers 179

Economic and Financial Crimes Commission (EFCC) 214–15, 237–38, 263–64

Edo State 18

Education
- western 1–2, 30, 36, 245

Effiong, Phillip 99–100

Eket 67

Ekwueme, Alex 148, 154, 157, 205

Elections
- primary 169, 171

Electricity 70, 208, 210, 228

Elites, northern 12, 159

England, 17, 29–30, 32, 50, 113, 271

Enterprises, public 229–31

Enugu 38–39, 57, 66, 68, 70–72, 75, 78, 90

Ethnicity 37–38

Europe 137, 146, 188, 207–8, 277

Europeans 2, 4, 9, 19, 62

Federal Electoral Commission (FEDECO) 140

Federal Executive Council (FEC) 57, 109, 130

Federal government 55–58, 61–62, 67, 74–75, 78–80, 83–86, 89, 91, 94–95, 107, 152, 154, 187, 232–34, 237–38

Index

Federal Republic of Nigeria 151, 153
Federal troops 62–64, 66–68, 71, 73–74, 84–85, 90–91, 98–99
Federation 164, 222, 232–34
Field commanders 90, 93
First lady 117–19, 121, 273
France 62, 75, 77, 163, 180, 207, 271
Fulani 50, 217–19, 238, 257

Garba, Joseph 125, 151, 256
General Certificate of Education (GCE), 11
Genocide 49, 51, 53–55, 57, 59, 73, 249
Girls 10, 253, 262–63
- commando 94
God
- act of 182, 199
Government
- broad-based 178
- conservative 26
- elected 169, 241
- interim 180, 193
- local 202, 219
- national 183
- rebel 72
- self 9
- transitional 173
Government contracts 179
Government hospitals 213
Government house 46
Government parastatals 229
Governor General 21–22
Governor Katsina 53
Governors
- northern 220, 238
Gowon 38, 47, 49, 52–54, 58–59, 64–65, 68, 70, 89–91, 104–5, 107–12, 123–24, 126–28, 140–41, 149–50
Grand Commander of the Federal Republic (GCFR) 151

Great Nigeria People's Party (GNPP) 140, 153
Groups
- elite 1, 27, 29, 275

Handover, 91, 172
Hausa, 20, 30, 50, 218–19, 238, 257

Head of State, 44, 46, 109–10, 117–18, 137, 139, 141, 143, 145, 169–70, 183, 188–90, 254, 256, 258
Headquarters
- brigade 31, 33, 153
Health 136, 246–47, 249, 261, 263
Hero 44, 90, 134, 147–48
Honouris Causa 151
House arrest 39, 154, 192
Humaitarian 77, 79, 81, 83, 85, 87

Ibadan 11–13, 35, 37, 45–46, 55, 64, 68–70, 83, 87, 93, 103, 113, 147, 188
Ibrahim Badamosi Babangida (IBB) 157
Idiagbon 156–57
Ife 113–14, 176, 217, 219
Igbo East 18, 20
Igbogun Olaogun 1–3
Igbo officers 37, 43, 45–46, 50, 54
Igbos 36, 42–43, 49–51, 53, 55, 57, 59, 67–68, 70–71, 73, 86, 99, 101, 109, 134
Ijebu Ode 62–63
Ikeja 38, 190
Ikeja cantonment 38, 123, 133
Ikenne 22, 142–43, 154
Ikot Ekpene 67
Ikoyi 131–33, 193, 258
Imo River, 98
Imprisonment 120, 194–95
Independence 12, 15, 18, 20, 23, 35–36, 76, 140, 142, 147, 220, 228, 231, 239, 277
Independent Corrupt Practices Commission (ICPC) 215
India 20, 32, 37, 207, 241
Inflation 111, 127, 136, 138
Insurance 113–14
International Committee of the Red Cross (ICRC) 78, 81, 83, 94–97
International Organisations, 75, 77, 79–81, 83–85, 87, 196
International Red Cross 79, 81, 84
Iran 137–38
Iranian Revolution 137, 139
Iraq 248, 250
Ironsi 36, 38–42, 45–46
Islamic state 220
Iyabo, 52, 87, 119, 199, 252–55, 258–67

Iyabo Obasanjo 52, 87, 119, 199, 252–55, 257-67
Iyabo Obasanjo Bello 261

Japan 206–7, 271
Jonathan 265–67, 274–76
Jos 50, 176, 218–19, 223, 237
Jos prison 195
Judiciary 160–61, 214, 222
Junior officers 33, 36, 131, 194, 204
Jurisdiction, territorial 233

Kaduna 16, 18, 31–33, 37–39, 41, 44–45, 50–52, 220–21, 255
Kano 32, 39–40, 51, 110, 133, 263
Kenya 207, 248–50
Killings 40, 50, 109, 119, 225
- extra judicial 232
Kingibe 173, 176
kingmakers 174, 201, 203, 205, 207

Lagos 31, 39–41, 52–54, 62–65, 68–72, 82–83, 89, 91–92, 95, 100–103, 106, 113–14, 127–28, 154, 237
- cabinet office 57
Lagos Executive Development Board (LEDB) 32
Lastma 237
Law 140, 156–57, 219–20, 222, 233–34, 236, 242
Law officers 56–57
Library 8
Littoral states 232, 234
- respective 234
London 29–33, 47, 49, 75, 96, 105, 113–16, 124, 189
Lord Lugard 218

Maccido 182
Maiduguri 44–45, 50–52, 151
Malnutrition 73
Mandela 192, 209
Marine Commando Division 66, 68, 89, 147
Marine commandos 66–67, 85, 89, 91, 98, 110

Marriage
- monogamous 104
Media 133, 175, 177
Middle Belt 225
Midwest 61, 63–66, 70
Military 33, 36, 106, 108, 131, 134, 151–52, 169, 171, 175–76, 178, 187, 191, 224, 226
Military administrator 64–65, 223
Military equipments, 86, 238
Military government
- federal 56, 77, 86, 97, 243
- regional 56
Military Head of State 257
Military headquarters 89
Military lawyer 192, 194
Military officers 170, 225
Military training 17, 58, 105, 196
Missile 267
Modakekes 217, 219
Money 3, 52, 73, 80–81, 85, 106, 116, 155, 163, 174, 176, 215, 229, 264
Mosques 155, 211
Mother tongue 4
Murtala assassination 134, 261
Murtala Muhammed 45–47, 65–66, 108–10, 117, 124, 126, 130–31, 133, 135, 140, 147, 151, 193, 253–54, 257
Muslims 21, 86, 155, 220–22, 245, 276
Mustapha 199–200

NADECO, 183, 185, 202
Naira 107–8, 150, 154, 162, 204, 263–64
Nation
- creditor 227–28, 247, 250, 272
National Assembly 214–15
National Council of Nigeria and the Cameroons (NCNC) 20, 22
National Council of State (NCS) 130
National Institute for International Affairs (NIIA) 206
National Party of Nigeria (NPN) 140, 143, 148, 152–53
National Republican Convention (NRC) 163, 169–70, 176, 178
National Unity Organization on Nigeria (NUON) 184

Newswatch 134, 146, 151, 160, 185, 189–90, 192, 198, 210–11, 221
Niger Delta 18, 49, 137, 216, 225, 232, 238, 274–76
Niger Delta Development Commission, 234
Niger Delta State 234
Nigeria 18–26, 35–47, 49–59, 116–20, 124–32, 136–43, 150–60, 162–66, 178–84, 206–14, 216–20, 222–32, 234–62, 269–74, 276–77
- change 42, 157, 179
- corporate 116
- denouncing 79
- history of 43, 53, 176, 273
- liquidate 274
- oil wealth 11
- southeastern 50
- southwestern 2, 12, 149
- western 7, 43, 62

Nigeria Advance Party (NAP), 153
Nigeria Airways 213, 231
Nigerian Armed Forces 258
Nigerian Army 12, 15–19, 21, 23, 25, 27, 35, 38, 53–55, 63, 72, 225
Nigerian Bar Association 237
Nigerian Biafran War 38
Nigerian Biafran War Letters 15
Nigerian Enterprise Promotion Decree 107
Nigerian National Petroleum Corporation (NNPC) 138
Nigerian National Shipping Line (NNSL) 213
Nigerian Peoples Party 153
Nigerian police 216
Nigerian prisons 195
Nigerian professionals 162
Nigerian railway, 29
Nigerian Revolution 148
Nigerians
- detribalised 35
- disgruntled 166
- eminent 181
- innocent 50, 228
- nationalist 20
- ordinary 266
- selfless 251

Nigerian Tribune 138, 145
Nigerian troops 24, 61

Nigerian Union 47, 58, 70
Nigeria People's Party (NPP) 140, 153
Nigeri Delta, 275
Niger Republic 207
Niger State 160, 172
Njoku 38, 44
Nnamdi Azikiwe, 18, 20, 22, 153, 257
North Atlantic Treaty Organisation (NATO) 105
Northerners 21, 36, 42–46, 53, 125, 135, 143, 154, 170, 217, 221
Northern Nigeria, 44, 52, 135, 206, 219, 250, 263
Northern Peoples Congress (NPC), 20
Nuhu Ribadu 215
Nwobodo 205
Nzeogwu 26, 32–33, 35, 37–38, 40–41, 43–45, 159

Obasanjo, Mathew Fajinmi Aremu Olusegun 1–2, 14-16, 18, 29-33, 35-36, 50–54, 64–65, 96–106, 114–19, 124–31, 133–41, 145–50, 183–85, 187–99, 201–17, 221–27, 237–45, 252–61, 270–77
Obasanjo, Stella 113, 115, 117–21, 244
Obasanjo Farms Nigeria (OFN) 166
Odi 217, 224–25
Office
- political 153–54

Officers
- commanding 37, 40
- northern 109, 123
- senior 31, 39, 104, 124, 151, 256

Offshore 233
Ofosu River 62
Oguchi 38–39
Ogun State 2, 64, 176, 206, 261–62
Oil bloc 181
Oil boom 107, 137, 139
Ojukwu 39–40, 42, 53–54, 57–59, 64, 66, 77, 79, 86, 96–97, 99, 142, 152
Okene 42, 63, 65
Olu Obasanjo, 99
Oluremi Akinlawon 10, 29–30
Oluremi Obasanjo 13, 30, 50, 52, 103, 252
OPC 216
Oputa panel 232

Ore 62, 64, 149
Organisation of African Unity (OAU) 84, 123, 207
Organisation of Petroleum Exporting Countries (OPEC) 111, 137
Osun State 148
Ota 2, 145, 184, 187, 190, 201, 204
Ota farm 117, 145, 187, 192–94, 198, 204
Owerri 72, 74, 85, 89, 92, 98–100
Owo 62–63
Oxfam 78–79
Oyo State 148

Party leaders 22, 141, 205
Peoples Democratic Party (PDP) 202–5, 262, 276
Peoples Redemption Party (PRP) 140, 153
Police 12, 16, 42, 64, 151, 191, 214–16, 235–38
Police funds 239
Political parties 19–20, 25, 107, 140, 153, 169, 185, 201
Politicians 25, 40, 58, 127, 150, 152, 154, 172, 174, 183, 209, 215, 236, 266
Port Harcourt 66–68, 90–91, 94, 100–101
Power 20–21, 56, 58, 135, 141–43, 174–75, 178, 180, 182, 213, 215, 238–39, 243–44, 270, 272–73
Premier Hotel 87
Premier of Northern Nigeria 37
President
- sitting 148, 242, 244
President Babangida 170, 187
President Bill Clinton 244–47
President George Bush 248–49, 251
Presidential election 140, 201, 204–5
Presidential Legacy 212, 228
President Jimmy Carter 242
President Jonathan 265, 267, 275
President Nixon 77, 84
President Olusegun Obasanjo 165, 247
President Shehu Shagari 143, 150–51
President Umar Yar'Adua 274–76
Prison 44–45, 58–59, 70, 184, 187, 189, 191, 193, 195–97, 199, 201–2, 209, 260
- Kirikiri maximum 154
Privatisation programme 230–31

Race, black 183
Racism 17
Radio Nigeria 70–71
- re-Christened 99
Rebel army 61
Rebel forces 64, 66
Rebels 62–65, 68, 72, 77, 82, 85–86
Red Cross 71, 78, 80, 83–85, 94–95, 97
Refineries 231
Reforms, local government 212
Refugees 67, 70–73
Relief flights 94–96
Relief materials 71, 78, 80, 82–84, 91, 95
Resources, natural 233–34
River Niger 66, 98–99
Rivers State 68, 95, 98, 101, 146
Rulers, traditional 182–83, 217, 267

Sagay 234
Samuel Akintobi Akinlawon 29–30
Sardauna 21, 31–32
Scandinavia 78, 80, 82
Secessionists 63, 77, 81, 97–98
Services
- civil 126, 212, 214
- postal 70–71
- selfless 184, 187
Sharia Law 219–201, 222
Shehu Shagari 149–50, 153, 157, 205
Shinkafi 159
Sierra Leone 248–49
Social Democratic Party (SDP) 163, 169–70, 173, 176, 178
Sokoto State 239
Soldiers 13, 16–18, 24–25, 31, 36, 45–46, 52, 54, 56, 61–63, 94, 102, 148–50, 225, 237
South Africa 139, 187–89, 196, 202, 209, 242, 249
Southerners 42, 46, 49–51, 53, 173, 220, 222
Southwest 61, 141, 177, 182, 200, 202, 217, 231, 236
Soyinka 64–65, 138
Spain 120
Starvation 78, 80–81, 97

State
- former head of 159, 174, 194, 204, 209, 212
- head of 44, 53, 70, 108–9, 124–25, 130, 135, 153, 197, 199, 206, 230, 232, 243, 255–56
- independent 20, 152, 219
- military head of 212, 241, 270
- minister of 263–64
- northern 44
- secular 222
- southeastern 67
- sovereign 79, 219, 234
- unitary 42
- western 149

State Executive Council 130
State Houses 187
State law 220
State of Emergency 59, 223
State police 235–39
State radio 258
State religion 222
State security 69
Statesman 143, 206
- international 164, 189
Structural Adjustment Programme (SAP) 162
Supreme Court 141, 222, 232
Supreme Military Council (SMC) 41–42, 55–56, 125, 130, 135, 141, 157–58
Surgery 120–21
- cosmetic 119–20

Technical Committee on Privatisation and Commercialisation (TCPC) 230
Terrorists 248, 250
Thisday 210, 216, 220–21
Training
- overseas 16, 18
Tribal leader 184–85
Troops 27, 39, 54, 62–63, 65, 98–99, 133, 149, 170–71, 225
- northern 54, 149
- rebel 61–62
- 63, 98

UAC 11, 115–16
Ukpabi Asika 70–71, 104
Uli 97, 99
Umuahi, 85, 97–98
United Insurance Company (UNIC), 114
United Nation 24, 86, 189, 196, 199
United States 82–84, 86, 138–39, 146, 191, 202, 207, 242–43, 247–50
United States of America 17, 207, 240–41, 247, 271
United States warship 95
Unity Party of Nigeria (UPN) 140, 153, 183
Universal Primary Education (UPE) 107
Uyo 67

Vasta 158–59
Vesico Vaginal Fistula (VVF) 262–63
Votes 140–41, 143, 148–49, 152, 170, 176, 203, 205–6

War 66, 68, 71, 73–74, 77–78, 81, 83–87, 89–91, 93, 96, 99, 101–2, 110, 141–42, 147–51
War Against Indiscipline (WAI) 154
Warri 61, 63, 113
Westerners 42, 53
Western region 18, 20, 22, 36, 53–54, 58, 65, 142, 161
Western union transfers 163
Wisdom 2, 53, 91, 134–35, 141, 166, 203, 240, 252, 266, 271–72, 277
World Council of Churches, 78–79, 81

Yakubu Gowon 38, 44, 59, 257
Yar'Adua 125, 170–71, 184, 194–95, 275
Yola prison 195
Yoruba 30, 35–36, 58, 65, 125, 134, 142–43, 181, 197, 217, 219, 248, 255, 257, 277
Yoruba West 18

Zaki Biam 225
Zamfara State 223, 245
Zik 20, 22

www.ingramcontent.com/pod-product-compliance
Lightning Source LLC
Chambersburg PA
CBHW050528300426
44113CB00012B/1996